GOSPEL PRINCIPLES
MANUAL
with side-by-side
COMMENTARY

KELLY MERRILL

CONTENTS

Forward

Mormonbasics.com is not affiliated with the Church of Jesus Christ of Latter-day Saints (LDS). Mormon Basics is a private website, and the comments and opinions expressed in these lessons are mine (Kelly P. Merrill), and are not from the LDS Church. The purpose of providing these lessons is to help give you ideas, and widen your scope and perspective as you review the lesson, either as a student or as a teacher.

Mormonbasics.com is pleased to bring you commentary based on the Gospel Principles manual published by The Church of Jesus Christ of Latter-day Saints. The original version of this commentary is printed in a two-column format. The original lesson, as presented in the manual published by the LDS Church, is in the left column. The comments on the right are provided by mormonbasics.com. If you are using the e-book version of the commentary on Amazon.com, the manual's original text is in black print followed by the commentary in blue text.

As you read each lesson I encourage you to prayerfully consider how what is being taught in the lesson fits with what is happening in your life currently. How does the prophetic counsel fit with what you understand, and what changes need to be made in your life to make your life fit with the prophet's counsel? You will find great blessings from these lessons if you approach them prayerfully, and humbly.

Kelly P. Merrill

Additional products from mormonbasics.com, and available on amazon.com, include:
Premortal Promises
Gospel Study Guides - Old Testament
Doctrinal Insights Vol. 1, Vol. 2
Merchandise in the Mormon Basics Store, such as Moroni phone cases in various colors (see the Moroni at the top of this page), mugs, shirts, etc.

Chapter 1

Our Father in Heaven

Gospel Principles, (2011), 4–7

There Is a God

• What are some things that testify to you that there is a God?

For teachers: Use questions at the beginning of a section to start a discussion and send class members or family members to the text to find more information. Use questions at the end of a section to help class members or family members ponder and discuss the meaning of what they have read and apply it in their lives.

Alma, a Book of Mormon prophet, wrote, "All things denote there is a God; yea, even the earth, and all things that are upon the face of it, yea, and its motion, yea, and also all the planets which move in their regular form do witness that there is a Supreme Creator" (Alma 30:44). We can look up at the sky at night and have an idea of what Alma meant. There are millions of stars and planets, all in perfect order. They did not get there by chance. We can see the work of God in the heavens and on the earth. The many beautiful plants, the many kinds of animals, the mountains, the rivers, the clouds that bring us rain and snow—all these testify to us that there is a God.

For some this question is easy and self evident. For others, this question will be difficult to answer because they have chosen to believe what the world has taught concerning the existence and creation of the human family.

It is important to understand the mind set of scientists. All truth is absolute, until new information changes what we know. That may seem a little silly, but that is how science works. Ask any scientist how something works and the answer will be in assured, positive, absolute terms that things are such and such because all our evidence supports this view. Then when something new is shown to upset their view, there is a period of time when they fight with each other about their opinions on the way things are or should be, but finally they change their mind and then a new truth is accepted, and anyone not accepting that new truth is ridiculed and cast out of their club.

A good example of this is the story of the shape of the world and its place in the universe. At first the world was flat, and if you got too close to the edge you would fall off. Then, when certain facts were introduced they couldn't argue with, the world was accepted as being round, but the sun revolved around the newly round earth. Eventually, the facts argued convincingly that the earth actually revolved around the sun, so they stopped burning people at the stake for claiming the earth revolved around the sun, and instead started to burn those who claimed our solar system revolved around the bigger galaxy.

This is the nature of science. Truth is a moving target to science. It is absolute in its certainty, but only until something else proves it wrong.

We believe there is a God, a perfect person who governs all creation and keeps it running from age to age. He organizes, creates, destroys, and manipulates according to His will. All that we know about has been created by this being we call God.

All the beauty of the earth, its seasons, its ability to repair itself, the balance between the plants and animals, the balance of the physical forces that govern the flow of water, air, and all other movement is set and determined by God to create a balanced and organized thing of beauty. This is our home we call earth. He has also set into motion and governs all that is and all that moves in the universe.

We choose to believe in this absolute ruler of all things. It is He to whom we look for answers, guidance, and give all honor and respect.

Understanding science is something that has to be done through textbooks and experiments in laboratories. Understanding God is something that is done by living the way He has taught us to live. We come to understand God by becoming more like Him by the way in which we live our lives. There is much more to it, but those principles will be discussed in other lessons.

The prophets have taught us that God is the Almighty Ruler of the universe. God dwells in heaven (see D&C 20:17). Through His Son, Jesus Christ, He created the heavens and the earth and all things that are in them (see 3 Nephi 9:15; Moses 2:1). He made the moon, the stars, and the sun. He organized this world and gave it form, motion, and life. He filled the air and the water with living things. He covered the hills and plains with all kinds of animal life. He gave us day and night, summer and winter, seedtime and harvest. He made man in His own image to be a ruler over His other creations (see Genesis 1:26–27).

Prophets are men, personally selected by God to give us His directions and teachings so we can be happy. His son, Jesus Christ, is His first born child. All that we know of in the universe was created by Jesus, under the direction of His Father. Everything that exists, Jesus made under His Father's direction. We call Christ the creator of heaven and earth because he literally made it all, under the direction of His Father.

Jesus even created the bodies of our first parents, Adam and Eve. They were created and given control, dominion, over all things, all His other creations on this planet.

God is the Supreme and Absolute Being in whom we believe and whom we worship. He is "the Great Parent of the universe," and He "looks upon the whole of the human family with a fatherly care and paternal regard" (Teachings of Presidents of the Church: Joseph Smith [2007], 39).

God is perfect in all ways. He has all knowledge, and all power. God lives a very orderly and organized life, filled with purpose and love, and all things good that generate joy. Everything about God generates goodness and happiness. All the laws by which He lives create harmony.

The Nature of God

• What are some of God's attributes?

Because we are made in His image (see Moses 2:26; 6:9), we know that our bodies are like His body. His eternal spirit is housed in a tangible body of flesh and bones (see D&C 130:22). God's body, however, is perfected and glorified, with a glory beyond all description.

Physically, God looks like us, because we were told by Him that we were made to look like Him. We were created in His image. So we know that He is a man that looks like any man would, with flesh and bone. But His body is perfect, and has been glorified beyond anything we can comprehend. Because He has a glorified and eternal body, He will never die. His body is permanent, whereas ours are temporary in nature.

God is perfect. He is a God of righteousness, with attributes such as love, mercy, charity, truth, power, faith, knowledge, and judgment. He has all power. He knows all things. He is full of goodness.

The scriptural definition of perfect is to be whole, complete, without anything missing or out of place. God is perfect. There is no divine attribute which he does not possess. He is completely good, completely kind, knows only the purest love, experiences the greatest joy from a life full of purpose and mercy. His knowledge is perfect, He lacks nothing.

All good things come from God. Everything that He does is to help His children become like Him. He has said,

This paragraph says three things:

"Behold, this is my work and my glory—to bring to pass the immortality and eternal life of man" (Moses 1:39).

1. All that we know about goodness and anything that is uplifting, comes from God. He is the source of all good things.

2. According to the prophet Moses, God said that He does what He does because He wants His children to have the same kind of immortality and eternal life He has.

3. We are His children. All that He has created, all that He does in the universe benefits in some way His children. His purpose is to offer to us what He has obtained. This is His source of happiness. This is what brings Him joy.

• Why is it important for us to understand the nature of God?

Think about the nature of God. He is a man, perfect in form and personality. His love for His family is perfect. His desire for His family to enjoy what He enjoys fills His life with purpose. If we can learn to become like our Father in Heaven, we can experience the same kind of joys and experiences He now enjoys.

Will that happen next week? Of course not. By claiming we are children of an eternal being, that makes us, by definition, eternal in nature as well. That means a lot of things, many of which will be discussed in future lessons. Becoming perfect takes time, and a lot of work. This is not something that will happen anytime soon. But understanding the nature of God helps us understand our own capabilities and our own nature. If God is our Father, in any sense of the word, then shouldn't we be able to become like Him? Isn't that one of the basic laws of nature, that a child can become like its parent?

Coming to Know God

• How can we come to know God?

As mentioned earlier, science can only be learned through books and labs. God, our Father, is learned about through experiences. He gives us a commandment. If we choose to live our lives according to the commandment He gives us, we learn wisdom and gain knowledge as to why God is the way He is. These are the same kinds of laws He lives by. These are the same kinds of laws that made Him who He is today. Commandments are transformative, they change the person who lives them. They teach us how to feel the way God feels, react the way God reacts, and to desire the things God desires. How else can we come to know God?

Knowing God is so important that the Savior said, "This is life eternal, that they might know thee the only true God, and Jesus Christ, whom thou hast sent" (John 17:3).

If we want to have the kind of life that Jesus and God enjoy, we need to come to know God and Jesus. They have given us commandments for this very purpose. Commandments change us for the better. They bring joy into our lives, they create compassion and mercy. They help us be forgiving and loving. They make us good, like God is good.

The first and greatest commandment is "Thou shalt love the Lord thy God with all thy heart" (Matthew 22:37).

There is no commandment greater than the commandment to love the Lord. Jesus said over and over again that if we loved Him we would keep His

The more we know God, the more we love Him and keep His commandments (see 1 John 2:3–5). By keeping His commandments we can become like Him.

commandments. So how do we show our love for God? Keep or live the commandments we have been given. There is no other way.

This paragraph repeats what I have already said. Commandments change us at a very basic level. They change the kind of people we are. They create goodness and kindness, and they give us understanding of the way God and Christ think and feel. We come to feel the same way. This increases our desire to continue to be obedient to the commandments, which increases our joy, which in turn increases our desire to be even more obedient. It is an upward spiral of goodness that is never ending.

We can know God if we will:
1. Believe that He exists and that He loves us (see Mosiah 4:9).
2. Study the scriptures (see 2 Timothy 3:14–17).
3. Pray to Him (see James 1:5).
4. Obey all His commandments as best we can (see John 14:21–23).
As we do these things, we will come to know God and eventually have eternal life.

1. Believing that God exists is not something that can be proven in a lab or in a book. This is something we simply have to choose to believe. If we are willing to even give Him the benefit of the doubt, and act on His commandments, He has promised that we will receive personal proofs that we have chosen well.

2. The scriptures are the teachings and revelations of God to His prophets. If we will study what He has told them we can learn many things about the nature of God, especially as we live what we learn.

3. Prayer is the method God has given to His children to communicate with Him. The more we talk to our Father, and the better we get at this form of communication, the more problems we will solve in life, and the happier we will be. We will study more about prayer in future lessons.

4. Notice that we are not told that we have to be perfect in our obedience of the commandments. We just need to obey them to the best of our abilities. Our abilities will increase with time and practice, just like anything that we do that needs practice. The important part is that we keep trying to live the commandments to the best of our abilities. This is what prepares us for eternal life, the kind of life Jesus enjoys with God, our Father.

• Ponder what you can do to draw nearer to God.

Additional Scriptures
• Acts 7:55–56 (Son at the right hand of the Father)
• D&C 88:41–44 (attributes of God)
• Psalm 24:1 (the earth is the Lord's)
• Moses 1:30–39 (Creation)
• Alma 7:20 (God cannot do wrong)
• Joseph Smith—History 1:17 (Father and Son are separate beings)
• Alma 5:40 (good comes from God)
• John 14:6–9 (Son and Father are alike)
• Mormon 9:15–20 (God of miracles)
• Amos 3:7 (God of revelation)

• John 3:16 (God of love)

Chapter 2

Our Heavenly Family
Gospel Principles, (2011), 8–12

We Are Children of Our Heavenly Father

• What do scriptures and latter-day prophets teach us about our relationship to God?

God is not only our Ruler and Creator; He is also our Heavenly Father. All men and women are literally the sons and daughters of God. "Man, as a spirit, was begotten and born of heavenly parents, and reared to maturity in the eternal mansions of the Father, prior to coming upon the earth in a temporal [physical] body" (Teachings of Presidents of the Church: Joseph F. Smith [1998], 335).

Every person who was ever born on earth is our spirit brother or sister. Because we are the spirit children of God, we have inherited the potential to develop His divine qualities. Through the Atonement of Jesus Christ, we can become like our Heavenly Father and receive a fulness of joy.

For teachers: You do not need to teach everything in each chapter. As you prayerfully prepare to teach, seek the Spirit's guidance to know which portions of the chapter you should cover and which questions you should ask.

• How does your knowledge that you are a child of God influence your thoughts, words, and actions?

We Developed Personalities and Talents While We Lived in Heaven

• Think about talents and gifts you have been blessed with.

The scriptures teach us that the prophets prepared themselves to become leaders on earth while they were still spirits in heaven (see Alma 13:1–3). Before they were born into mortal bodies, God foreordained (chose) them to be leaders on earth. Jesus, Adam, and Abraham were some of these leaders. (See Abraham 3:22–23.) Joseph Smith taught that "every man who has a calling to minister to the inhabitants of the world was [fore]ordained to that very purpose" (Teachings of Presidents of the Church:

Sometimes this teaching doesn't sink in. God is not our Father in a spiritual sense or a social sense, but is our actual father, like you are to your children. When we lived with Him before the earth was created, we lived with Him as part of His eternal family. He gave us our spirit bodies, the ones we brought with us to earth that enliven and gives life to our physical bodies. He actually is our Father, which makes all of us brothers and sisters in the literal sense of the word.

Just as a puppy grows into a dog and a kitten into a cat, so we have the potential to become like our heavenly parents. But our growth and progress to become like our Father in Heaven is more complicated than that of a mere animal. We must choose to be obedient to the laws and commandments of Jesus Christ, who prepared the way for us to return home to our Father. All of us, without exception, have the ability if we choose to pursue it, to return to God and become like Him, and share in His happiness.

Talents include any ability. We may be good listeners, patient, able to quickly forgive, a quick learner or great with our hands. It is easy to short ourselves when it come to recognizing our own talents. It might be easier to ask someone else this question and have them answer it for you. (Make sure you ask a friend.)

The Lord told Jeremiah, "Before I formed thee in the belly I knew thee; and before thou camest forth out of the womb I sanctified thee, and I ordained thee a prophet unto the nations" (Jeremiah 1:5). The Lord knew each of us, as any father would know His children. He chose from among us His most faithful men and gave them important assignments , like being a prophet, to help the rest of us make it back home.

Joseph Smith [2007], 511). However, everyone on earth is free to accept or reject any opportunity to serve.

We were not all alike in heaven. We know, for example, that we were sons and daughters of heavenly parents—males and females (see "The Family: A Proclamation to the World," Ensign, Nov. 1995, 102). We possessed different talents and abilities, and we were called to do different things on earth. We can learn more about our "eternal possibilities" when we receive our patriarchal blessings (see Thomas S. Monson, in Conference Report, Oct. 1986, 82; or Ensign, Nov. 1986, 66).

The proclamation on the family makes it clear that if we are female now, we have always been female. If we are male now, we have always been male. Our gender is an eternal part of who we are. Our Father in Heaven didn't just give callings to the prophets before we came to earth. We received special abilities and assignments as well. When we go to a patriarch we are privileged to receive a blessing from him that is meant only for us. No two blessings are alike. The Patriarch tells us what our spiritual heritage is, and gives us direction from our Father in Heaven to help us as we make our way through mortality.

A veil covers our memories of our premortal life, but our Father in Heaven knows who we are and what we did before we came here. He has chosen the time and place for each of us to be born so we can learn the lessons we personally need and do the most good with our individual talents and personalities.

In order for us to be free to make the choices that we need to make in mortality, we needed to forget about our heavenly home. We call it a veil of forgetfulness. Just because we have forgotten our life before coming here, it doesn't mean our Father in Heaven has forgotten us. He knows us just as well today as He ever has. He has placed us on earth at the time and place that will help us learn the best lessons we need to learn for our particular needs. Whether we learn those lessons is up to us.

• How have other people's talents blessed you? How can your talents and gifts bless others?

A talent is a key to blessings in our lives. If we use our talent not only are we blessed for having improved on our ability, but all talents strengthen, entertain, console, or bless in some way, other people. These talents are meant to bring joy to us and others. The Lord wants us to enlarge or practice our talents so we can accomplish the most good with them.

Our Heavenly Father Presented a Plan for Us to Become Like Him

• How does earth life help prepare us to become like our Heavenly Father?

This is a hard question to answer. Think about these things to see if they help you with your answer. There are some big differences between our personalities and God's personality. If we are going to become like Him we need to learn to think and act like Him. That means we need to learn more patience, better listening skills, learn to be more obedient, kind, generous, etc. We have so many ways we need to improve that we can't do it all in this lifetime. But we can get started. Remember that we are as eternal as our Father in Heaven is. We can't expect to become like our Father in just the few short years we are here. Becoming like God is a very lengthy process.

We haven't ever had physical bodies before. This is our first experience with a body. God has a body, and learned how to master it. We do too.

For teachers: Class members or family members are more likely to give a thoughtful answer to a question if they are given time to ponder their response. For example, after asking a question, you could say, "Please take a minute to

think about your response, and then I'll ask for answers."
Then give them time to ponder.

Our Heavenly Father knew we could not progress beyond a certain point unless we left Him for a time. He wanted us to develop the godlike qualities that He has. To do this, we needed to leave our premortal home to be tested and to gain experience. Our spirits needed to be clothed with physical bodies. We would need to leave our physical bodies at death and reunite with them in the Resurrection. Then we would receive immortal bodies like that of our Heavenly Father. If we passed our tests, we would receive the fulness of joy that our Heavenly Father has received. (See D&C 93:30–34.)

Our Heavenly Father called a Grand Council to present His plan for our progression (see Teachings of Presidents of the Church: Joseph Smith, 209, 511). We learned that if we followed His plan, we would become like Him. We would be resurrected; we would have all power in heaven and on earth; we would become heavenly parents and have spirit children just as He does (see D&C 132:19–20).

We learned that He would provide an earth for us where we would prove ourselves (see Abraham 3:24–26). A veil would cover our memories, and we would forget our heavenly home. This would be necessary so we could exercise our agency to choose good or evil without being influenced by the memory of living with our Heavenly Father. Thus we could obey Him because of our faith in Him, not because of our knowledge or memory of Him. He would help us recognize the truth when we heard it again on earth (see John 18:37).

At the Grand Council we also learned the purpose for our progression: to have a fulness of joy. However, we also learned that some would be deceived, choose other paths, and lose their way. We learned that all of us would have trials in our lives: sickness, disappointment, pain, sorrow, and death. But we understood that these would be given to us for our experience and our good (see D&C 122:7). If we allowed them to, these trials would purify us rather than defeat us. They would teach us to have endurance, patience, and charity (see Teachings of Presidents of the Church: Spencer W. Kimball [2006], 15–16).

Think about the growth teenagers go through when they leave home and have to start taking on the role of an adult. They change in some very material ways. They become more mature. They learn life lessons. They learn to be more flexible, and often learn to be more responsible, and so forth. Our needing to leave our Father in Heaven is the same thing. There were lessons we needed to learn that we couldn't learn in His presence. We needed to go away for a while to keep growing.

Our first body is a clunker, like the car our parents let us first learn to drive. Once we have passed our tests in mortality and we are resurrected, we will receive an immortal body, like God's. Only then will we be able to experience the joys He has to offer us. That is why it is so important that we learn to listen to Him while we are here, and work hard to learn all we can so we are able to get the kind of body He has at the resurrection.

We were not just tossed down to mortality with no information. A Grand Council was held for all of God's family. He explained everything to us. He told us all we needed to know in order to make wise choices. In the book of Job it says that all the sons of God shouted for joy (Job 38:7).

The veil that was to be placed over our minds is a very important part of this whole experience. We need to learn to trust God, not because He is God and is all powerful, but because we love Him. We needed to learn to love Him "from scratch" by learning to trust him and exercise faith in His instructions to us. He has left us clues and given us help in this process, but we still have to seek Him out. That responsibility is ours alone. Our eternal blessings depend on our willingness to seek out our Father and learn of Him and His ways.

There is no happier person than God. He wants to share that happiness with His children. But to do that we have to become like Him. And to do that we must be tested and tried to see if we will choose God in all things. So we come to earth and go through all kinds of trials, sufferings, temptations, and ultimately death. What we learn and how we grow from these experiences determines how much more like God we can become.

At this council we also learned that because of our weakness, all of us except little children would sin (see D&C 29:46–47). We learned that a Savior would be provided for us so we could overcome our sins and overcome death with resurrection. We learned that if we placed our faith in Him, obeying His word and following His example, we would be exalted and become like our Heavenly Father. We would receive a fulness of joy.

Because we all make mistakes, we needed someone to save us, a Savior. That was the role Christ filled. He reconciled our behavior with the laws of God so that God wouldn't have to lock us out from His presence forever for disobedience. If we place our faith in Christ and keep the commandments He gives us through His prophets, He can offer us mercy in the form of forgiveness for the violations of God's law we commit, our sins. As we are forgiven of our sins we become stronger in our faith, and He helps us become more like our Father in Heaven. He will forgive us as often as we choose to try again to obey God.

• List some of Heavenly Father's attributes. How does the plan of salvation help us develop these attributes?

Additional Scriptures
• Hebrews 12:9 (God is the Father of our spirits)
• Job 38:4–7 (premortal life implied)
• Abraham 3:22–28 (vision of premortal life)
• Jeremiah 1:5 (vision of premortal life)
• D&C 29:31–38 (vision of premortal life)
• Moses 3:4–7 (spiritual and temporal creations)
• 1 Corinthians 15:44 (spiritual and temporal creations)
• D&C 76:23–24 (begotten sons and daughters)
• D&C 132:11–26 (plan for progression)

Chapter 3

Jesus Christ, Our Chosen Leader and Savior

Gospel Principles, (2011), 13–16

The answer to these questions will be answered in the course of this lesson. Keep them in the back of your mind as you read the lesson and think about what is being taught.

A Savior and Leader Was Needed

• Why did we need to leave Heavenly Father's presence? Why do we need a Savior?

When the plan for our salvation was presented to us in the premortal spirit world, we were so happy that we shouted for joy (see Job 38:7).

We understood that we would have to leave our heavenly home for a time. We would not live in the presence of our Heavenly Father. While we were away from Him, all of us would sin and some of us would lose our way. Our Heavenly Father knew and loved each one of us. He knew we would need help, so He planned a way to help us.

It seems difficult to imagine that if we knew God personally that we would sin against Him and refuse to believe in Him. But He knew this is what would happen when we left home and came to earth without any memory of home. The point of this exercise in spiritual maturity we call mortality is that we learn to choose God over any other distraction or desire. Our Father in Heaven knew we would make mistakes and violate His laws. These violations would require us to be shut out from His presence forever.

He provided us with a Savior to enable us time and ability to change our minds and our behavior, and still be able to return to him. The process He established for this change is called repentance. Repentance was made possible by Jesus when He paid for all our sins through His atoning sacrifice in Gethsemane and on the cross.

We needed a Savior to pay for our sins and teach us how to return to our Heavenly Father. Our Father said, "Whom shall I send?" (Abraham 3:27). Jesus Christ, who was called Jehovah, said, "Here am I, send me" (Abraham 3:27; see also Moses 4:1–4).

The calling of Jesus was to be a perfect example of the kind of son or daughter we need to be in order to return home. Jesus followed His Father's will perfectly. He never disobeyed or put other interests before the will of God. The commandments Jesus has given us is what helps us learn to be like Him, and will one day enable us to return to God clean and happy.

The sacrifice Jesus made for us was great. He did it because He loves God, and He loves us. He was willing to do whatever it took to open the door so we could pass through and return home.

Jesus was willing to come to the earth, give His life for us, and take upon Himself our sins. He, like our Heavenly Father, wanted us to choose whether we would obey Heavenly Father's commandments. He knew we must be free to choose in order to prove ourselves worthy of exaltation. Jesus said, "Father, thy will be done, and the glory be thine forever" (Moses 4:2).

One of the great attributes of Christ is His humility. He wasn't interested in fame, money, or power. His concern was that He help get His Father's children back home again. He is completely selfless.

Satan, who was called Lucifer, also came, saying, "Behold, here am I, send me, I will be thy son, and I will redeem all mankind, that one soul shall not be lost, and surely I will do it; wherefore give me thine honor" (Moses 4:1). Satan wanted to force us all to do his will. Under his plan, we would not be allowed to choose. He would take away the freedom of choice that our Father had given us. Satan wanted to have all the honor for our salvation. Under his proposal, our purpose in coming to earth would have been frustrated (see Teachings of Presidents of the Church: David O. McKay [2003], 207).

The difference between Christ's desire to submit to His Father's will and Satan, is that Satan wanted all the glory and power for himself. He stepped up in the Grand Council and offered himself as the Savior. But his condition was that God step down from being God and give all the glory to Satan for doing for us what God could not.

At this time Jesus was still a spirit, just like us. God already had been through mortality and now had a glorified, resurrected body. He could not go back to mortality. Satan offered to save all of God's children, but the price for that act was to take away our agency, our ability to choose for ourselves, and to take away God's glory and take it for himself. Satan does not love us, he loves only himself.

The whole point of mortality was to help us learn how to become like God by making choices and having to live with the consequences. This is what repenting is. We need our agency in order to do this.

Jesus Christ Became Our Chosen Leader and Savior

• As you read this section, think about the feelings you have for the Savior.

The more you learn about what Jesus has done to bless your life, the more you will be able to feel gratitude for His sacrifices in your behalf. Consider the consequences if Satan had his way with us. We would not be able to make any moral choices, as he would have removed our right and ability to have that choice. All decisions for decisions of moral agency would have been his and his alone to make. We never would have learned to be wise and happy because we would not have been allowed to make our own choices.

After hearing both sons speak, Heavenly Father said, "I will send the first" (Abraham 3:27).

Jesus Christ was chosen and foreordained to be our Savior. Many scriptures tell about this (see, for example, 1 Peter 1:19–20; Moses 4:1–2). One scripture tells us that long before Jesus was born, He appeared to a Book of Mormon prophet known as the brother of Jared and said: "Behold, I am he who was prepared from the foundation of the world to redeem my people. Behold, I am Jesus Christ. … In me shall all mankind have life, and that eternally, even they who shall believe on my name" (Ether 3:14).

Through God's holy priesthood Jesus was made the Christ, the Redeemer, the Savior of all of God's children. God chose Jesus to be the example of the perfect, obedient son. Even before the world was created it became His responsibility to one day perform the atoning sacrifice to pay for all of our sins so we could return home to God, our Father. It is our responsibility to look to the Savior in all things and follow His example always.

When Jesus lived on earth, He taught: "I came down from heaven, not to do mine own will, but the will of him that sent me. … And this is the will of him that sent me, that every one which seeth the Son, and believeth on him, may have everlasting life: and I will raise him up at the last day" (John 6:38, 40).

The War in Heaven

We don't understand the full nature of the war in heaven, but we know that Satan was overcome in the end and cast out of heaven, along with all those who followed him and

Because our Heavenly Father chose Jesus Christ to be our Savior, Satan became angry and rebelled. There was war in heaven. Satan and his followers fought against Jesus Christ and His followers. The Savior's followers "overcame [Satan] by the blood of the Lamb, and by the word of their testimony" (Revelation 12:11).

In this great rebellion, Satan and all the spirits who followed him were sent away from the presence of God and cast down from heaven. A third part of the hosts of heaven were punished for following Satan (see D&C 29:36). They were denied the right to receive mortal bodies.

Because we are here on earth and have mortal bodies, we know that we chose to follow Jesus Christ and our Heavenly Father. Satan and his followers are also on the earth, but as spirits. They have not forgotten who we are, and they are around us daily, tempting us and enticing us to do things that are not pleasing to our Heavenly Father. In our premortal life, we chose to follow Jesus Christ and accept God's plan. We must continue to follow Jesus Christ here on earth. Only by following Him can we return to our heavenly home.

• In what ways does the War in Heaven continue today?

We Have the Savior's Teachings to Follow

• Think about how the Savior's teachings have influenced you.
From the beginning, Jesus Christ has revealed the gospel, which tells us what we must do to return to our Heavenly Father. At the appointed time He came to earth Himself. He taught the plan of salvation and exaltation by His word and by the way He lived. He established His Church and His priesthood on the earth. He took our sins upon Himself.

By following His teachings, we can inherit a place in the celestial kingdom. He did His part to help us return to our

supported him. The war in heaven was not a private argument, it included every daughter and son of God. We were all there and we all participated. Everyone had to choose a side and support their side.

The worst punishment the followers of Satan could receive was to be denied the chance to get a mortal body. Without a mortal body there is no hope of ever receiving a resurrected body like God's. This was the whole point of mortality, to become like God. A third part of all of God's children lost that opportunity because they supported Lucifer.

Satan's host were cast out of heaven and sent to earth. Here he and his servants seek to lead us away from God and the happiness He offers us. They want only our misery and will stop at nothing to see to it that we make as many poor choices as possible. They still remember who we are. They know our strengths and our weaknesses. They use our physical weaknesses and desires to try to get us to commit sin, to break the commandments. Satan hates us as much as Jesus loves us.

We really are in a neutral place with good encouraging us on one side and evil tempting us on the other. What we choose to do from hour to hour each day shows us and God where our true desires are. We can change at any time. The choice is ours.

Do you think Satan and his followers have forgotten what was "done to them" in the premortal world? Do you think they are the forgiving sort and will let us alone while we try to follow God's teachings? If the war is still raging today, is it a physical war, a war of ideas, or a war of popularity? What weapons are being used in this war?

The knowledge of God and His teachings have not been kept a secret. From the days of Adam onward Jesus has revealed God's will and commandments to men through prophets. He has told the prophets what would happen from one generation to another all the way down to the time of the final judgment and assigning to kingdoms of glory. Jesus has kept nothing secret.

He even told all the prophets that He would come and sacrifice Himself for us so we could return home again. He has shared His priesthood power with the prophets, and blesses our lives with more miracles and blessings than we can count. All this, in an effort to encourage us to be obedient to God's commandments so we can return home and be happy with Him in God's presence.

heavenly home. It is now up to each of us to do our part and become worthy of exaltation.

Additional Scriptures

• Moses 4:1–4; Abraham 3:22–28 (Savior chosen in premortality)
• D&C 76:25–29 (War in Heaven)
• Revelation 12:7–9, 11 (Savior's followers in the War in Heaven overcame Satan by the blood of the Lamb and by the word of their testimony)
• Isaiah 14:12–15 (why Lucifer was cast out)

For teachers: You could have class members or family members study the "Additional Scriptures" as individuals, in pairs, or as an entire group.

Chapter 4

Freedom to Choose
Gospel Principles, (2011), 17–21

Agency Is an Eternal Principle

• If someone asked you why it is important to have agency, what would you say?

"Thou mayest choose for thyself, for it is given unto thee" (Moses 3:17).

God has told us through His prophets that we are free to choose between good and evil. We may choose liberty and eternal life by following Jesus Christ. We are also free to choose captivity and death by following Satan. (See 2 Nephi 2:27.) The right to choose between good and evil and to act for ourselves is called agency.

In our premortal life we had moral agency. One purpose of earth life is to show what choices we will make (see 2 Nephi 2:15–16). If we were forced to choose the right, we would not be able to show what we would choose for ourselves. Also, we are happier doing things when we have made our own choices.

Agency was one of the principal issues to arise in the premortal Council in Heaven. It was one of the main causes of the conflict between the followers of Christ and the followers of Satan. Satan said, "Behold, here am I, send me, I will be thy son, and I will redeem all mankind, that one soul shall not be lost, and surely I will do it; wherefore give me thine honor" (Moses 4:1). In saying this, he "rebelled against [God] and sought to destroy the agency of man" (Moses 4:3). His offer was rejected, and he was cast out of heaven with his followers (see D&C 29:36–37).

Agency Is a Necessary Part of the Plan of Salvation

Agency makes our life on earth a period of testing. When planning the mortal creation of His children, God said, "We will prove [test] them herewith, to see if they will do all things whatsoever the Lord their God shall command them" (Abraham 3:25). Without the gift of agency, we would have been unable to show our Heavenly Father

Our agency in this life includes anything having to do with moral choices. In Doctrine and Covenants 101:78 the Lord refers to our "moral agency." That means that our agency includes any kind of moral choice or choices between right and wrong. Our agency does not include the right to choose to do wrong things without suffering consequences.

Please note that we have but two choices. We either choose liberty and eternal life (by following Jesus Christ) or we choose captivity and death (by following Satan). There are no other options. In this life we have but two choices. Which we choose is completely up to us, but we still only have two options.

The main difference between our Father in Heaven's plan for our happiness, and the plan put forth by Satan, was our right to choose for ourselves what we wanted. Our Father in Heaven knew we would be much happier (and He is all about our happiness) if we got to choose for ourselves, but Satan wanted to take that ability away from us and make it impossible for us to choose for ourselves. He wanted complete control over all our moral choices.

Jesus supports our Father in Heaven's plan to let us choose how we behave and what we do with our lives. That is why He was chosen to be our Savior. He was willing to pay whatever price needed to be paid to allow us to keep our agency so we could return to our Father in Heaven on our own steam, and by our own choice.

We could not make the choices we need to make in the presence of our Father in Heaven. We knew Him, knew His laws, and knew the punishment (banishment) for breaking even the smallest of laws. We needed to come to a place of neutral ground. By coming to earth and having a veil placed over our minds so we forgot about our previous life in the premortal world, we are free to be enticed by God's laws on the one hand and Satan's enticements on the other.

whether we would do all that He commanded us. Because we are able to choose, we are responsible for our actions (see Helaman 14:30–31).

When we choose to live according to God's plan for us, our agency is strengthened. Right choices increase our power to make more right choices.

Because we are free to choose whom we wish to follow, either God or Satan, we are held accountable for those choices.

This is an extremely important point about agency that we often don't consider. The nature of the choices we make either strengthens our agency or weakens it. When we choose to follow God then our agency is strengthened because we are then free to make additional choices. But choosing to break God's laws and follow Satan's enticements weakens our ability to make our own choices and gives him more power to force his choices on us.

Do you see the connection between the war in heaven and what we are going through here? This is exactly what we fought about in heaven. It is being played out here on earth. If Satan can get us to choose to ignore God's laws and do what we want then he gains the control over us he wanted in the premortal world. It is only through our choosing to obey God's laws here that God can strengthen our ability to make choices and follow through with the choices we make.

Our happiness is tied directly to our ability to make good choices. Once we start to give up our ability to choose, misery is always the end result.

As we obey each of our Father's commandments, we grow in wisdom and strength of character. Our faith increases. We find it easier to make right choices.

This is another good point. Our ability to make better choices, and more consistently make good choices, comes as a gift from God. When we make a good choice He rewards us in some way for our obedience. Making good choices to do what is right keeps us free of addictions and behaviors that would take away our ability to choose well. He actually strengthens our capacity for making good choices. But the initial choice is always up to us.

We began to make choices as spirit children in our Heavenly Father's presence. Our choices there made us worthy to come to earth. Our Heavenly Father wants us to grow in faith, power, knowledge, wisdom, and all other good things. If we keep His commandments and make right choices, we will learn and understand. We will become like Him. (See D&C 93:28.)

Just as Lucifer (Satan) and his followers were able to make their choices in the premortal world, so too were we able to choose to do good things and obey God. We learned and progressed according to our choices. The Lord has said that many became mighty and great ones in the spirit world. He chose them to be His prophets and leaders here in mortality because of their valiance in their choices.

• How does making right choices help us make more right choices?

Agency Requires That There Be a Choice

• Why is opposition necessary?
We cannot choose righteousness unless the opposites of good and evil are placed before us. Lehi, a great Book of Mormon prophet, told his son Jacob that in order to bring about the eternal purposes of God, there must be "an opposition in all things. If not so, … righteousness could

not be brought to pass, neither wickedness, neither holiness nor misery, neither good nor bad" (2 Nephi 2:11).

God allows Satan to oppose the good. God said of Satan:

"I caused that he should be cast down;

"And he became Satan, yea, even the devil, the father of all lies, to deceive and to blind men, and to lead them captive at his will, even as many as would not hearken unto my voice" (Moses 4:3–4).

Agency cannot be fully experienced unless you have the ability to truly go to either end of the spectrum. You cannot become fully happy unless you have experienced tremendous heartache. You cannot appreciate great health unless you have experienced great sickness. The greatest spiritual growth can only happen when we are placed on neutral ground between absolute good on one side and absolute evil on the other and have to choose which we want to experience. It is all part of our maturing process to become like our Heavenly Father.

In this verse in Moses it tells us that he who would have power over us can only do so if we "hearken" to his voice. Satan cannot control us and make us miserable unless we listen to him and obey his temptations. God cannot bless us and make us more like Him unless we listen to Him and obey His commandments. One of these two men will have the power to change our lives. Which one gets that power depends on the choices we make each day.

Satan does all he can to destroy God's work. He seeks "the misery of all mankind. … He seeketh that all men might be miserable like unto himself" (2 Nephi 2:18, 27). He does not love us. He does not want any good thing for us (see Moroni 7:17). He does not want us to be happy. He wants to make us his slaves. He uses many disguises to enslave us.

Since Satan must convince us that we would be happier without God in our lives, he spends a great deal of effort to keep us busy with things that distract us from obeying God's commandments. He uses media, popular people, and others to promote breaking the Sabbath, eating and living unhealthy lifestyles, immorality, and irresponsible behavior. He promotes anything that will divide us as brothers and sisters, and anything that causes people to be angry with one another. In short, he does everything he can to get us to violate God's decrees. He will use any lie, half truth, or misleading statement he can to achieve his goal.

When we follow the temptations of Satan, we limit our choices. The following example suggests how this works. Imagine seeing a sign on the seashore that reads: "Danger—whirlpool. No swimming allowed here." We might think that is a restriction. But is it? We still have many choices. We are free to swim somewhere else. We are free to walk along the beach and pick up seashells. We are free to watch the sunset. We are free to go home. We are also free to ignore the sign and swim in the dangerous place. But once the whirlpool has us in its grasp and we are pulled under, we have very few choices. We can try to escape, or we can call for help, but we may drown.

Just as obedience to truth sets us free, free to make more choices, disobedience to truth binds us, like the whirlpool. Disobedience limits our choices and traps us. With all sin it is easy to get into, but difficult to get out of. That is the nature of sin. We cannot change its nature just because we don't like it. The Lord encourages us to be obedient because He knows how hard it is to get out from under the bondage of sin, especially once a bad habit has been established. That weakness becomes a weakness in our armor of faith for a long time to come. Like they say, once an addict, always an addict. It takes great faith in God and hard work to overcome the dependency and become strong in that area where we allowed ourselves to become so weak.

For teachers: A simple picture can help learners focus their attention. If you discuss the analogy of a warning sign as it is presented in this chapter, you may want to draw a picture of such a sign on the board or on a large piece of paper.

Even though we are free to choose our course of action, we are not free to choose the consequences of our actions. The consequences, whether good or bad, follow as a natural result of any choice we make (see Galatians 6:7; Revelation 22:12).

Heavenly Father has told us how to escape the captivity of Satan. We must watch and pray always, asking God to help us withstand the temptations of Satan (see 3 Nephi 18:15). Our Heavenly Father will not allow us to be tempted beyond our power to resist (see 1 Corinthians 10:13; Alma 13:28).

Here are just a few of the rules of mortality.

1. God will never interfere with a person's agency, until we are held accountable in judgment at the last day. At that time we will have to account to Him for our use of the agency He gave us.

2. God will never force Himself on us in any way. We must choose to come to Him.

3. Satan cannot read our thoughts, that privilege is held by God.

4. Satan cannot tempt us beyond what we are able to bear. In other words, he cannot give us a temptation that is so strong we have no ability to successfully resist it. This restriction is placed on him by God to make things fair. The Lord tells us in the New Testament that He will always prepare a way for us to escape the Devil's temptations if we really want to get out from under them.

God's commandments direct us away from danger and toward eternal life. By choosing wisely, we will gain exaltation, progress eternally, and enjoy perfect happiness (see 2 Nephi 2:27–28).

The scriptural reference here stops at verse 28. I encourage you to read verse 29 as well. It finishes off the thought.

• What are some examples of actions that limit our choices? What are some examples of actions that give us more freedom?

Hint: Just as all truth sets us free in some way, all sin is either addictive or enslaving in some way.

Additional Scriptures

• Moses 7:32 (freedom of choice)
• Abraham 3:24–25 (earth life a test)
• Alma 41:3; Moroni 7:5–6 (works judged)
• 2 Nephi 2:11–16 (opposition is necessary)
• Moroni 7:12–17 (choosing good and evil)
• 2 Peter 2:19; John 8:34 (sin is bondage)
• 2 Nephi 2:28–29; Alma 40:12–13 (reward according to works)

Chapter 5

The Creation
Gospel Principles, (2011), 22–25

God's Plan for Us

• Why did we need to come to the earth?

When we lived as spirit children with our heavenly parents, our Heavenly Father told us about His plan for us to become more like Him. We shouted for joy when we heard His plan (see Job 38:7). We were eager for new experiences. In order for these things to happen, we needed to leave our Father's presence and receive mortal bodies. We needed another place to live where we could prepare to become like Him. Our new home was called earth.

• Why do you think we shouted for joy when we learned of the plan of salvation?
For teachers: Some class members or family members may not feel comfortable reading aloud. Before asking them to read aloud, you may want to ask, "Who would like to read?" Then call on individuals who have volunteered.

Jesus Created the Earth

Jesus Christ created this world and everything in it. He also created many other worlds. He did so through the power of the priesthood, under the direction of our Heavenly Father. God the Father said, "Worlds without number have I created; … and by the Son I created them, which is mine Only Begotten" (Moses 1:33). We have other testimonies of this truth. Joseph Smith and Sidney Rigdon saw Jesus Christ in a vision. They testified "that by him, and through him, and of him, the worlds are and were created, and the inhabitants thereof are begotten sons and daughters unto God" (D&C 76:24).

Carrying Out the Creation

• What are the purposes of the Creation?
The earth and everything on it were created spiritually before they were created physically (see Moses 3:5). In planning to create the physical earth, Christ said to those who were with Him, "We will go down, for there is space there, … and we will make an earth whereon these [the spirit children of our Father in Heaven] may dwell" (Abraham 3:24).

Under the direction of the Father, Christ formed and organized the earth. He divided light from darkness to make day and night. He formed the sun, moon, and stars. He divided the waters from the dry land to make seas,

The doctrine, the beliefs of the LDS church are unlike any other Christian faith. They believe we come into existence when we enter mortality. We are created to serve God and to give Him glory. We are nothing in the universe and nothing to God. We were created as a means to His ends to give himself more glory.

We believe that we are His children. He loves us with all the perfection only God can possess. He wants us to be happy as He is happy. He wants us to grow and progress and eventually become like Him. Isn't that what all parents expect, that their children will grow up to become like them?

Since we needed a place to come to continue our growth and development God create this world as a place for us to come and prove ourselves in all things. This earth was made to house the children of God. As such it was created with all the care and love a parent could pour into it.

We know that Jesus created everything in the universe. In the New Testament in John 1:3 it says that all things were made by Christ. As the Father's first born, and Savior of all His children, Jesus was given the assignment to create all things. He was directed in His work by our Father in Heaven. Jesus made this earth on which we live. So even though Jesus is the Son of God, He is also the father of heaven and earth, because he created all the planets and objects in the universe. By definition, a father is one who creates or organizes something. Jesus fits that definition.

All things were created spiritually before they were created physically. Just as we existed before we received our physical bodies, so even the planets, plants, and animals were created spiritually before they received their physical form. This earth was made specifically for us to live here and receive our mortal experience. That is the whole reason earth is here. Who else, but God would build an entire planet as a place for His children to live?

The creation of the earth was done in a very organized and systematic way. It was not created by accident, but was organized and assembled from pre-existing materials.

rivers, and lakes. He made the earth beautiful and productive. He made grass, trees, flowers, and other plants of all kinds. These plants contained seeds from which new plants could grow. Then He created the animals—fish, cattle, insects, and birds of all kinds. These animals had the ability to reproduce their own kind.

Now the earth was ready for the greatest creation of all—mankind. Our spirits would be given bodies of flesh and blood so they could live on earth. "And I, God, said unto mine Only Begotten, which was with me from the beginning: Let us make man in our image, after our likeness; and it was so" (Moses 2:26). And so the first man, Adam, and the first woman, Eve, were formed and given bodies that resembled those of our heavenly parents. "In the image of God created he him; male and female created he them" (Genesis 1:27). When the Lord finished His creations, He was pleased and knew that His work was good, and He rested for a time.

God's power is shown through His speech. He speaks and the universe obeys His voice. In this case, it was His Son who was obeying. He created Adam and Eve. They had bodies that looked just like God's, i.e. two arms, two legs, head, etc. We were created in His image.

God's Creations Show His Love

• How do God's creations show that He loves us?
We are now living in this beautiful world. Think of the sun, which gives us warmth and light. Think of the rain, which makes plants grow and makes the world feel clean and fresh. Think of how good it is to hear a bird singing or a friend laughing. Think of how wonderful our bodies are—how we can work and play and rest. When we consider all of these creations, we begin to understand what wise, powerful, and loving beings Jesus Christ and our Heavenly Father are. They have shown great love for us by providing for all of our needs.

This question is one we don't ask ourselves often enough. The scriptures tell us that all things testify there is a God. The whole order of the universe, and all the little details testify of a loving God. This earth was made with all the care of a loving Father. It is self repairing, and self sustaining. It is full of rich things like ore and oil, water and gas. All things we need to make life comfortable here are available in rich supply.

We are surrounded by unbelievable beauty from rainbows to glaciers, baking deserts to lush rain forests, from magnificent waves of turbulent seas to the gentle lapping of a lake shore at dusk. There is beauty all around us. And the beauty is not just for our eyes. There are wonderful smells that bring pleasure to the soul, and tastes that excite our senses. He thought of everything.

Plant life and animal life were also made to give us joy. The Lord said, "Yea, all things which come of the earth, in the season thereof, are made for the benefit and the use of man, both to please the eye and to gladden the heart; yea, for food and for raiment, for taste and for smell, to strengthen the body and to enliven the soul" (D&C 59:18–19). Even though God's creations are many, He knows and loves them all. He said, "All things are numbered unto me, for they are mine and I know them" (Moses 1:35).

The Lord could have been merely practical and just given us pigs, cows, and chickens for meat, but instead He gave us thousands of varieties of birds, mammals, fish, and so forth. We are still discovering new creatures we didn't know even existed. Who, but a loving God would give us animals we can use to comfort us in our loneliness, like dogs or cats? His children are so varied that we were given many kinds of choices of sights, sounds, smells, tastes, and companions to please us. These are all evidences of God's love for us.

• What are some things you appreciate about God's creations?

Additional Scriptures

• Genesis 1; 2:1–7; Abraham 3:22–23; 4–5; Moses 1:27–42; 2–3 (accounts of the Creation)

• Hebrews 1:1–3; Colossians 1:12–17; D&C 38:1–3 (Jesus the Creator)
• D&C 59:18–20; Moses 2:26–31; D&C 104:13–17; Matthew 6:25–26 (Creation shows God's love)

Chapter 6

The Fall of Adam and Eve
Gospel Principles, (2011), 26–30

Adam and Eve Were the First to Come to Earth

• What evidence helps us know that Adam and Eve were valiant spirits?

God prepared this earth as a home for His children. Adam and Eve were chosen to be the first people to live on the earth (see Moses 1:34; 4:26). Their part in our Father's plan was to bring mortality into the world. They were to be the first parents. (See D&C 107:54–56.)

For teachers: Use questions at the beginning of a section to start a discussion and send class members or family members to the text to find more information. Use questions at the end of a section to help class members or family members ponder and discuss the meaning of what they have read and apply it in their lives.

Adam and Eve were among our Father's noblest children. In the spirit world Adam was called Michael the archangel (see D&C 27:11; Jude 1:9). He was chosen by our Heavenly Father to lead the righteous in the battle against Satan (see Revelation 12:7–9). Adam and Eve were foreordained to become our first parents. The Lord promised Adam great blessings: "I have set thee to be at the head; a multitude of nations shall come of thee, and thou art a prince over them forever" (D&C 107:55).

Eve was "the mother of all living" (Moses 4:26). God brought Adam and Eve together in marriage because "it was not good that the man should be alone" (Moses 3:18; see also 1 Corinthians 11:11). She shared Adam's responsibility and will also share his eternal blessings.

• What can we learn from the examples of Adam and Eve?

The Garden of Eden

• Under what conditions did Adam and Eve live in the Garden of Eden?

When Adam and Eve were placed in the Garden of Eden, they were not yet mortal. In this state, "they would have had no children" (2 Nephi 2:23). There was no death. They had physical life because their spirits were housed in physical bodies made from the dust of the earth (see Moses 6:59; Abraham 5:7). They had spiritual life because they were in the presence of God. They had not yet made a choice between good and evil.

This is an interesting question. The wording of the question, of course, assumes that Adam and Eve WERE, in fact, valiant spirits. If you were God, the Father, would you send down to earth as the very first humans a lazy pair of good-for-nothings or someone who would represent you well to all the children of earth as your prophet? Which would you choose as your first representative on earth? That should give you some idea as to the quality and caliber of this couple. It also gives us a clue as to how much respect God had for them as people.

Okay, so this paragraph spills the beans and tells you exactly what kind of people Adam and Eve were. Adam was Michael, the archangel. This is the man God chose to lead his armies against Satan's revolt in heaven. He was set at the head of the whole human race. He is still our first father in mortality, and is still fulfilling his responsibilities as the head of the human family. The Lord says that his title of prince of all the nations of the earth would never be taken from him.

Our Father in Heaven is a big believer in being equally yoked. Eve is Adam's equal in all ways. She is an elect lady, valiant and courageous, righteous and honorable. As the mother of all living, she had difficult choices to make in the garden of Eden. More about that later.

Not only were Adam and Eve not yet mortal, but they were innocent as a little child. They had adult bodies, but knew no sin, no pain, no death, no deception, just the peaceful life they had been given by the Lord in the garden of Eden. Their physical bodies would have lived forever in their premortal state. They were allowed to eat as much of the fruit from the tree of Life as they wanted. The only tree they were forbidden to even touch was the tree of the knowledge of good and evil.

God commanded them to have children. He said, "Be fruitful, and multiply, and replenish the earth, and subdue it, and have dominion over … every living thing that moveth upon the earth" (Moses 2:28). God told them they could freely eat of every tree in the garden except one, the tree of knowledge of good and evil. Of that tree God said, "In the day thou eatest thereof thou shalt surely die" (Moses 3:17).

Satan, not knowing the mind of God but seeking to destroy God's plan, came to Eve in the Garden of Eden. He tempted her to eat of the fruit of the tree of knowledge of good and evil. He assured her that she and Adam would not die, but that they would "be as gods, knowing good and evil" (Moses 4:11). Eve yielded to the temptation and ate the fruit. When Adam learned what had happened, he chose to partake also. The changes that came upon Adam and Eve because they ate the fruit are called the Fall.

Adam and Eve's Separation from God

• What physical and spiritual changes occurred in Adam and Eve as a result of their transgression?
Because Adam and Eve had eaten the fruit of the tree of knowledge of good and evil, the Lord sent them out of the Garden of Eden into the world. Their physical condition changed as a result of their eating the forbidden fruit. As God had promised, they became mortal. They and their

Eternal life is to live forever in the presence of God, with physical bodies. They had lived with God as spirits, but now they lived with Him with physical bodies.

The word "replenish" is an interesting choice. In current English it means to fill again, but Adam and Eve were the first people. But replenish also means to continually keep full. At the time the Bible was translated into English (KJV) replenish meant "to fill completely."

Satan's temptation was one third lie and two thirds truth. It was true that they would be like God, knowing good from evil, but it was also true that they would die. There is a difference between a rotation of the earth - one day - and one day in God's reckoning. The New Testament says that a day to God is a thousand years to us. So it was true that they would not die in the next rotation of the earth, but it was not true that they would live beyond a day in God's time. This sort of "splitting of hairs" or playing with definitions is just what Satan loves to do to convince us to break the commandments or accept his lies.

Eve was not stupid when she ate the fruit. She knew that in order for them to obey the commandment to have children they would have to leave the garden. She made the conscious choice to pursue this greater commandment at the expense of the lesser commandment. This was a brave and scary thing for her to do. Fortunately, Adam also saw the wisdom in her decision and ate the fruit as well.

But the consequence of choosing one good thing over another good thing, because making that choice violated a commandment of God, meant they had to leave God's presence. God cannot tolerate sin or violations of His law in the least degree or He would cease to be a ruler of order, and hence would cease to be God. He had no choice but to expel them from the garden. This "permanent" separation from the presence of God is what we call the first death, or the Fall. I put quotes around permanent because the separation would have been forever if it hadn't been for the atonement of Christ that gave us a way to get back to God through repentance.

By eating the fruit, Adam and Eve were no longer immortal. Their bodies were changed to a mortal state. Now they could, and would die. But the change was not just to their bodies. They had now violated a commandment and were shut out from the presence of God, never to be able to return to be with Him again, unless a payment for their transgression was made. This was paid for by Christ with His atonement.

children would experience sickness, pain, and physical death.

Because of their transgression, Adam and Eve also suffered spiritual death. This meant they and their children could not walk and talk face to face with God. Adam and Eve and their children were separated from God both physically and spiritually.

When they became mortal they also became susceptible to all the physical conditions of mortality, like sickness and death. Interestingly enough, they were told that it was for their sakes that they would suffer in mortality. It is through what we suffer that we learn the lessons of what it means to be like God. We learn patience, tolerance, forgiveness, etc.

There are two kinds of death talked about in the scriptures. The first death was Adam and Eve's separation from God, being cut off from His presence. The second death would be their physical death when their spirits would leave their physical bodies. In the other references in the scriptures the "second death" normally refers to the final judgment when those who would not accept Christ's atonement are permanently cut off from the presence of God forever.

Great Blessings Resulted from the Transgression

• How does the Fall provide opportunities for us to become like our Heavenly Father?
Some people believe Adam and Eve committed a serious sin when they ate of the tree of knowledge of good and evil. However, latter-day scriptures help us understand that their Fall was a necessary step in the plan of life and a great blessing to all of us. Because of the Fall, we are blessed with physical bodies, the right to choose between good and evil, and the opportunity to gain eternal life. None of these privileges would have been ours had Adam and Eve remained in the garden.

Some have taught that Adam and Eve committed sexual sin, and that is what is what is referred to as the forbidden fruit. But modern revelation tells us that God married them in the garden, so it wasn't a sexual sin, but the actual eating of a fruit that was the cause of their being expelled from the garden. They did not commit a major sin to kicked out of the garden. What they did is even referred to in the scriptures as a transgression, a very minor breaking of a law. And remember they were innocent at the time they made the choice. But innocent or not, a law had been violated, so they had to go.

What Adam and Eve did was built into the plan for our salvation. Before we came to earth the Lord had made a Savior ready for us to save us from our sins. But God cannot force us to sin. He had to place Adam and Eve in a situation where they had the choice to remain pure and innocent or choose to sin, otherwise His judgments would not be just, for He cannot force any of us to be disobedient then punish us for doing what He made us do. The choice to disobey had to be Adam and Eve's decision and no one else's.

Though it is lamentable, sad, that they had to leave the garden, it is such a blessing to us. Because of their choice to enter mortality we have the opportunity to repent and become like God. That opportunity would not be ours if they had chosen to remain in the garden. We should be eternally grateful for their choice in the garden to open the door of opportunity for us to come to earth and receive our bodies, learn from our experiences, and accept Christ's atonement through repentance so we can become like our Father in Heaven. This is the plan for our salvation, the Great Plan of Happiness referred to in the scriptures.

Page 23

After the Fall, Eve said, "Were it not for our transgression we never should have had seed [children], and never should have known good and evil, and the joy of our redemption, and the eternal life which God giveth unto all the obedient" (Moses 5:11).

The prophet Lehi explained:

"And now, behold, if Adam had not transgressed he would not have fallen [been cut off from the presence of God], but he would have remained in the Garden of Eden. And all things which were created must have remained in the same state in which they were after they were created. …

"And they would have had no children; wherefore they would have remained in a state of innocence, having no joy, for they knew no misery; doing no good, for they knew no sin.

"But behold, all things have been done in the wisdom of him who knoweth all things.

"Adam fell that men might be; and men are, that they might have joy" (2 Nephi 2:22–25).

• Why do you think it is important to know about the Fall and how it influences us?

After they fell from God's grace in the garden, Adam and Eve learned that they had made a wonderful choice. They were very grateful they had chosen as they did. This verse is the only statement in all of the scriptures where Eve talks about her choice to eat the fruit and break the commandment.

This last verse is important to remember. Mankind is not made with the purpose to be miserable. The Lord wants us to experience joy. That is the purpose of mortality, so we can become more like Him and experience the kind of happiness He experiences. Yes, we have trials in this life that cause us suffering and sorrow, but those are to teach us lessons. Those trials are not the sole purpose of this life. Joy is the final purpose of mortality.

Knowing what you now know, was the Fall a good or a bad thing? Is mortality a punishment or a blessing? Does knowing about the Fall change how you see the purpose of your life?

Additional Scriptures

• 1 Nephi 5:11; 2 Nephi 2:20 (Adam and Eve first parents, family)
• 2 Nephi 2:14–21 (opposition and the Fall; life a probation)
• 2 Nephi 2:22–26 (Fall part of the plan of salvation)

Chapter 7

The Holy Ghost
Gospel Principles, (2011), 31–33

The Holy Ghost Came to Adam and Eve

• Why did Adam and Eve need the guidance of the Holy Ghost?

After Adam and Eve left the Garden of Eden, they began to till the earth and work at other tasks for their living. They had many children, and their sons and daughters also married and had children (see Moses 5:1–3). Thus, spirit children of our Heavenly Father began leaving His presence to come to the earth as they had been promised (see Abraham 3:24–25). As they came to earth, the memory of their heavenly home was taken from them. But our Father did not shut them away from His influence. He sent the Holy Ghost to comfort and help and guide all of His spirit children.

For teachers: When you call class members by their names, they know they are important to you and that you care about them. Learn their names, and call them by name during each lesson. Help them learn each other's names.

Adam and Eve called upon Heavenly Father in prayer. He spoke to them and gave them commandments, which they obeyed. An angel of the Lord came and taught Adam and Eve the plan of salvation. The Lord sent the Holy Ghost to testify of the Father and of the Son and to teach Adam and Eve the gospel. (See Moses 5:4–9.)

Through the power of the Holy Ghost, Adam "began to prophesy concerning all the families of the earth, saying: Blessed be the name of God, for because of my transgression my eyes are opened, and in this life I shall have joy, and again in the flesh I shall see God" (Moses 5:10). Because of the witness of the Holy Ghost to Eve, she said, "Were it not for our transgression we never should have had seed, and never should have known good and evil, and the joy of our redemption, and the eternal life which God giveth unto all the obedient" (Moses 5:11).

• How is our need for guidance from the Holy Ghost similar to that of Adam and Eve?

This is a profound question. If we need the Holy Ghost to come to know God, didn't Adam and Eve already know Him? God Himself taught Adam and Eve. What did they need the Holy Ghost to teach them? These are just a couple of questions you should be able to answer by the end of this lesson.

This paragraph's last sentence tells us that the Holy Ghost is not just about giving us information, but is also here to give us comfort and peace to our souls. He teaches us how to follow God's teachings so those teachings become part of who we are. We begin to think like God and act like God, because we only do good in all things. The Holy Ghost helps us learn to find joy in being good like Christ and God are good.

Adam and Eve set a good example for us. When we are given a commandment and we obey that commandment, sooner or later we will receive more information from the Lord. Once He knows we value what He gives us we will be given more. This is a universal pattern for all of God's children. The Holy Ghost testifies of the reality of God and Christ so we will believe and obey. In obedience we find happiness.

Who are these "families of the earth?" Adam had many children, and their descendants became the families of the earth, so he was prophesying about his own posterity.

The Holy Ghost helped Adam and Eve to understand the teachings of the Lord after they left the garden of Eden. He helped them to understand the big picture of the plan of salvation and how they fit into it. Through their obedience to the commandments they received from the Lord they were able to find joy in their redemption through the sacrifices made by Christ who should come.

Just as we live in the last days and have to learn to believe in what has happened between God and His people in the past from Adam down to our day, so Adam and his family had to have faith in all the dealings God would have with His children in the future of the earth, including the coming of the Messiah in the meridian or middle of time. So we all have to have faith in the Lord's plan of salvation, whether we were born in Adam's day or born in our day. The Holy Ghost teaches us the truth and testifies of God's love for us so we will believe and obey.

Attributes of the Holy Ghost

• How does the Holy Ghost differ from the Father and the Son? Why is that difference important to us?

The Holy Ghost is a member of the Godhead (see 1 John 5:7; D&C 20:28). He is a "personage of Spirit" (D&C 130:22). He can be in only one place at a time, but His influence can be everywhere at the same time.

Heavenly Father, Jesus Christ, and the Holy Ghost are called the Godhead. They are unified in purpose. Each has an important assignment in the plan of salvation. Our Heavenly Father is our Father and ruler. Jesus Christ is our Savior. The Holy Ghost is the revealer and testifier of all truth.

The Holy Ghost is our Heavenly Father's messenger and is a special gift to us (see chapter 21 in this book).

Here is another way to look at the roles of those in the Godhead. The Father is the law giver. He upholds all the laws of the universe, and requires and gives us justice in all things. Jesus is the Christ or Messiah (Savior) and having satisfied God's laws of justice can turn around and offer us mercy by giving us the opportunity to repent and be better today than we were yesterday. The Holy Ghost is a God whose purpose is to witness of the reality of God and Christ and teach us all that we need to know and do in order to return home and live with them someday. He is our personal tutor in all things spiritual. Next to giving us Jesus as our Savior, God, our Father could not have given us a greater gift than to give us another God as a personal instructor to teach us how to return home.

The Mission of the Holy Ghost

• What are some of the truths that the Holy Ghost reveals to us?

The mission of the Holy Ghost is to bear witness of the Father and the Son and of the truth of all things.

The Holy Ghost will witness to us that Jesus is our Savior and Redeemer (see 3 Nephi 28:11; D&C 20:27). He will reveal to us that our Heavenly Father is the Father of our spirits. He will help us understand that we can become exalted like our Heavenly Father. (See Romans 8:16–17.) The prophets of the Lord have promised, "By the power of the Holy Ghost ye may know the truth of all things" (Moroni 10:5).

Without the Holy Ghost, we could not know that Jesus is the Christ. The Apostle Paul wrote, "No man can say that Jesus is the Lord, but by the Holy Ghost" (1 Corinthians 12:3). The Savior Himself said, "And this is life eternal, that they might know thee the only true God, and Jesus Christ, whom thou hast sent" (John 17:3). It is by the power of the Holy Ghost that we are led to understand and live the gospel of Jesus Christ.

The things listed in these two paragraphs are essential to our understanding of the nature and personality of God. We need this knowledge to exercise strong faith in them. Once we know that we can become like our Father in Heaven, we can be far better people than we could have been without that knowledge. The gift of the Holy Ghost helps us set our sites higher than we could have imagined possible. How could we come to know the truth of all things, like God, if we couldn't ever become like God? The Holy Ghost helps us understand that there is no limit to the possibilities of our advancement in the eternities.

Anyone can read about Jesus and believe that such a man lived, and that He did marvelous things. But to exercise the faith required to change our lives and to become obedient to all the commandments it takes a witness, a knowledge of God that goes beyond belief alone. The Holy Ghost bears witness to our very spirit, which changes us in a way that earthly knowledge cannot do. Knowledge from the Holy Ghost makes us better people, and strengthens our desire to be obedient to God.

The convincing power of the Holy Ghost is so great that there can be no doubt that what He reveals to us is true. President Joseph Fielding Smith said:

"When a man has the manifestation from the Holy Ghost, it leaves an indelible impression on his soul, one that is not easily erased. It is Spirit speaking to spirit, and it comes with convincing force. A manifestation of an angel, or even of the Son of God himself, would impress the eye and mind, and eventually become dimmed, but the impressions of the Holy Ghost sink deeper into the soul and are more difficult to erase" (Answers to Gospel Questions, comp. Joseph Fielding Smith Jr., 5 vols. [1957–66], 2:151).

President Smith also said, "Through the Holy Ghost the truth is woven into the very fibre and sinews of the body so that it cannot be forgotten" (Doctrines of Salvation, comp. Bruce R. McConkie, 3 vols. [1954–56], 1:48).

As members of The Church of Jesus Christ of Latter-day Saints, we should make ourselves worthy to receive this special messenger and witness of our Heavenly Father and Jesus Christ.

Someone who has had a witness of a truth from the Holy Ghost may not live up to what they know, but it is almost impossible for them to deny that they knew at one time the truthfulness of what the Holy Ghost had witnessed to them. The "indelible impression" the Holy Ghost leaves on our soul is like permanent ink. The truthfulness of what we learned may fade through disobedience, but it always stays a part of us. Only obedience will make it become bright in our soul again.

The gift of the Holy Ghost is only found in Christ's church, The Church of Jesus Christ of Latter-day Saints. We receive this gift through the laying on of hands at baptism by those who hold God's priesthood authority to give this special gift.

This gift is worth any sacrifice we have to make to receive and keep it. The Holy Ghost is our link, our guide back to our eternal home.

• Think about times when the Holy Ghost has helped you grow in your testimony. As appropriate, share some of these experiences with class members or family members.

Additional Scriptures
• Moses 5 (story of Adam's family)
• D&C 130:22 (Holy Ghost identified)
• John 14:26; 15:26; 16:13; Luke 12:12; 2 Nephi 31:18; 32:5, 8; 33:1; Alma 14:11; 3 Nephi 27:20; 4 Nephi 1:48; Moroni 10:6–7; D&C 8:2–3; 11:12–13; 20:26 (roles of the Holy Ghost)

Chapter 8
Praying to Our Heavenly Father

Gospel Principles, (2011), 34–38

What Is Prayer?

For teachers: This chapter is organized under five section headings. Each heading is a question about prayer. You could use these questions as a guide for your lesson. If the classroom setting allows for small group discussion, consider dividing class members into groups of two to four. Assign each group one of the sections in the chapter. Have each group read and discuss their assigned section and share personal experiences that relate to it. Then discuss the five sections as a class, focusing on the questions that are of most interest to class members.

Jesus taught, "Ye must always pray unto the Father in my name" (3 Nephi 18:19).

Prayer is one of the greatest blessings we have while we are here on earth. Through prayer we can communicate with our Heavenly Father and seek His guidance daily.

Prayer is a sincere, heartfelt talk with our Heavenly Father. We should pray to God and to no one else. We do not pray to any other being or to anything made by man or God (see Exodus 20:3–5).

We are sent to earth without any memory of our Father in Heaven. Our task while on earth is to show our Father in Heaven that we will follow all our impulses to do good, to obey Him in all things so we can become like Him once we leave mortality. There is just one problem, we need help doing what we were sent here to accomplish. We can't do it all by ourselves.

God gave us the ability to talk to Him through prayer. We don't have to know exactly how it works, just that it does work. He has promised us that if we will focus our minds and our hearts on Him, and talk to Him, He will hear us and help us. We cannot talk to anyone else in the universe in this way, only our Father in Heaven. Whether we send feelings or thoughts or spoken words to Him, He hears and receives them all.

Why Do We Pray?

Prayer has been an important part of the gospel from the beginning of the world. An angel of the Lord commanded Adam and Eve to repent and call upon God in the name of the Son (see Moses 5:8). This commandment has never been taken away. Prayer will help us draw closer to God. All of our thoughts, our words, and our actions are influenced by our prayers.

We should pray for strength to resist the temptations of Satan and his followers (see 3 Nephi 18:15; D&C 10:5). We should pray to confess our sins to God and ask Him to forgive us (see Alma 38:14).

We should pray for the Lord's guidance and help in our daily lives. We need to pray for our families and friends, our neighbors, our crops and our animals, our daily work, and our other activities. We should pray for protection from our enemies. (See Alma 34:17–27.)

Our Father in Heaven wants to help us through our time in mortality, but as part of our test we have to ask for His help. He cannot be the one to start the conversation or it would hurt our ability to exercise faith in Him. This partnership is up to us. The more we pray and work to listen and feel for answers to our prayers, the closer we become to God.

There are no limits on what we can pray about and pray for, but wisdom tells us that we should not pray over trivial or small things over which we have complete control, like which breakfast cereal to eat today. But the Lord is anxious to help us with things even as small as remembering to read our scriptures or remembering to be nice to someone. There is nothing too big or too small to take to Him in prayer.

We should pray to express love to our Heavenly Father and to feel closer to Him. We should pray to our Father to thank Him for our welfare and comfort and for all things He gives us each day (see 1 Thessalonians 5:18). We need to pray to ask our Heavenly Father for strength to live the gospel.

Just as we should express gratitude to our parents and our spouse (and others), we should also express gratitude to God. Occasionally expressing just thanks in our prayers, rather than always just asking for things, is a good habit to get into. God appreciates a little show of appreciation just as much as anyone. And expressing our thankfulness for what we have received shows Him that we are aware of how much He is doing for us. Expressing gratitude regularly in our prayers helps us not fall into an attitude of entitlement where we just expect the Lord to cater to our every desire.

We should pray so we can keep on the strait and narrow path that leads to eternal life. We must pray to God, the author of all righteousness, so we may be righteous in our thoughts, words, and actions.

• How has prayer helped you draw nearer to Heavenly Father?

When Should We Pray?

We can pray whenever we feel the need to communicate with our Heavenly Father, whether silently or vocally. Sometimes we need to be alone where we can pour out our souls to Him (see Matthew 6:6). In addition, we can pray during our daily activities. We can pray while we are in a Church meeting, at home, walking down a path or street, working, preparing a meal, or wherever we may be and whatever we may be doing. We can pray any time of the day or night. We can pray when we are alone or when we are with other people. We can keep our Heavenly Father in our thoughts at all times (see Alma 34:27). We can "pray always" (D&C 10:5).

Thinking a prayer is relatively easy, but praying out loud requires that we formalize our words and put them into full sentences. This can be much more intimidating. But it is also good for us, as it requires that we commit ourselves to say the words out loud.

Praying silently can be done anywhere, and at any time. Praying out loud requires privacy in order for us to be properly reverent when we pray. Of course there are prayers where we act as the voice for a whole family, class, or congregation, but personal prayers should be said in private.

In His effort to encourage us to talk to Him, the Lord has told us we should pray morning, noon, and night. In other words, all the time, and as often as we want to. He is anxious to hear from us and listen to our struggles so He can help.

At times we may not feel like praying. We may be angry or discouraged or upset. At these times we should make a special effort to pray (see 2 Nephi 32:8–9).

A great way to overcome anger and many other negative emotions, is to pray and ask for help overcoming them. Pray until you feel better. It works!

We should each pray privately at least every night and every morning. The scriptures speak of praying morning, midday, and evening (see Alma 34:21).

We are commanded to have family prayers so that our families may be blessed (see 3 Nephi 18:21). Our Church leaders have counseled us to pray as families each morning and night.

Not only is personal prayer a powerful tool for good, but praying with others and for others is also very helpful. When many of God's children pray for the same thing, whether in a group or individually, their combined faith and prayers generate spiritual power that is generally stronger than just a single prayer can create.

We also have the privilege of praying to give thanks and ask a blessing on the food before each meal.

We open and close all of our Church meetings with prayer. We thank the Lord for His blessings and ask for His help so we may worship in a manner that pleases Him.

How Should We Pray?

No matter where we are, whether we stand or kneel, whether we pray vocally or silently, whether we pray privately or in behalf of a group, we should always pray in faith, "with a sincere heart, with real intent" (Moroni 10:4).

As we pray to our Heavenly Father, we should tell Him what we really feel in our hearts, confide in Him, ask Him for forgiveness, plead with Him, thank Him, express our love for Him. We should not repeat meaningless words and phrases (see Matthew 6:7–8). We should always ask that His will be done, remembering that what we desire may not be best for us (see 3 Nephi 18:20). At the end of our prayer, we close in the name of Jesus Christ (see 3 Nephi 18:19).

"With real intent" means that we expect something to happen because of our prayer. That expectation is how we exercise our faith. We believe that God will answer that prayer; that belief is the expectation that God is listening and will respond.

A sincere prayer is not something that is just a series of repeated phrases that we always say. Sincere conversation is genuine, unique, and said for that occasion only. Sometimes we have to spend some time thinking and feeling to find the words we really want to say. Spending time thinking about what we want to say or how we want to say it in a personal prayer is okay. The Lord has all day. He is patient, and He wants us to learn to express ourselves to Him so we learn to talk to Him in productive ways. Prayer is a way to practice how to talk to God. He loves it when we take the time to learn how to communicate with Him.

How Are Prayers Answered?

• Why do you think answers to prayers are not always readily apparent? Why do you think answers to prayers do not always come when we want or in the way we want?

Our sincere prayers are always answered. Sometimes the answer may be no, because what we have asked for would not be best for us. Sometimes the answer is yes, and we have a warm, comfortable feeling about what we should do (see D&C 9:8–9). Sometimes the answer is "wait a while." Our prayers are always answered at a time and in a way that the Lord knows will help us the most.

It is important to remember that we often need to grow and change before we are ready for the answer we are asking for. So when the Lord doesn't answer us right away, don't stop asking for what you want, keep at it. As you change and grow in spiritual things the answers you seek will begin to come to you. Like the lesson says, the Lord will ALWAYS answer your question, but often we have to wait for that answer so that when it comes we are ready to receive it in faith, understand it, and act on it appropriately.

Sometimes the Lord answers our prayers through other people. A good friend, a husband or wife, a parent or other family member, a Church leader, a missionary—any of these individuals may be inspired to perform acts that will answer our prayers. An example of this is the experience of a young mother whose baby was injured in an accident at home. She had no way to get the baby to a doctor. She was new in the neighborhood and did not know her neighbors. The young mother prayed for help. In a few minutes, a neighbor came to the door, saying, "I had a feeling I should come and see if you needed any help." The neighbor helped the young mother get the baby to a doctor.

One of the great blessings of prayer is to ask the Lord to be an instrument in His hands for doing good for other people. The Lord often blesses us through those around us. When we become one of those people He can use to do good for others, not only are their lives blessed, but we change and become better people and happier in the process.

Often God gives us the power to help answer our own prayers. As we pray for help, we should do all we can to bring about the things we desire.

This is an example of one of those prayers where the Lord doesn't give us an answer right away. If we can answer the question ourselves, with just a little growing up or changing then the Lord will usually opt for the "personal growth" option instead of just telling us the answer. After all, we are here in mortality to grow and mature in spiritual things. This is why we need to be studying the scriptures all the time. We often receive answers to prayers through the scriptures, which we could not receive if we weren't reading them.

As we live the gospel of Jesus Christ and pray always, we will have joy and happiness. "Be thou humble; and the Lord thy God shall lead thee by the hand, and give thee answer to thy prayers" (D&C 112:10).

This is one of the best verses in all the scriptures, in my opinion. Just as a parent leads a child by the hand when the child doesn't know the right way to go, so the Lord can gently lead us along the right path if we will let Him. We do that by praying and keeping the commandments, and learning to listen and feel for the answers that will come from the prayers we utter.

• In what ways has Heavenly Father answered your prayers?

Additional Scriptures and Other Sources
• James 1:5 (what to pray for)
• 1 Thessalonians 5:17; Psalm 55:17; 2 Nephi 32:9 (when to pray)
• Alma 34:26 (where to pray)
• 3 Nephi 19:6, 24 (how to pray)
• D&C 88:63–65 (how prayers are answered)
• Moroni 10:3–5; Alma 37:37 (promises for prayer)
• James 5:16 (the power of a prayer from a righteous person)
• Bible Dictionary, "Prayer," 753

Chapter 9

Prophets of God
Gospel Principles, (2011), 39–43

Prophets Are God's Representatives on the Earth

• What powers and gifts does a prophet have?

"Surely the Lord God will do nothing, but he revealeth his secret unto his servants the prophets" (Amos 3:7).

Many people live in darkness, unsure of God's will. They believe that the heavens are closed and that people must face the world's perils alone. How fortunate are the Latter-day Saints! We know that God communicates to the Church through His prophet. With grateful hearts, Saints the world over sing the hymn, "We thank thee, O God, for a prophet to guide us in these latter days" (Hymns, no. 19).

A prophet is a man called by God to be His representative on earth. When a prophet speaks for God, it is as if God were speaking (see D&C 1:38). A prophet is also a special witness for Christ, testifying of His divinity and teaching His gospel. A prophet teaches truth and interprets the word of God. He calls the unrighteous to repentance. He receives revelations and directions from the Lord for our benefit. He may see into the future and foretell coming events so that the world may be warned.

A prophet may come from various stations in life. He may be young or old, highly educated or unschooled. He may be a farmer, a lawyer, or a teacher. Ancient prophets wore tunics and carried staffs. Modern prophets wear suits and carry briefcases. What, then, identifies a true prophet? A true prophet is always chosen by God and called through proper priesthood authority (see Articles of Faith 1:5).

Latter-day Saints sustain the First Presidency and the Twelve Apostles as prophets. However, when we speak of "the prophet of the Church," we mean the President of the Church, who is President of the high priesthood.

Through the Ages God Has Called Prophets to Lead Mankind

• In what ways have prophets guided God's children in the past?

There have been prophets on the earth since the days of Adam. Experiences of these great men excite and inspire us. Moses, an Old Testament prophet, led thousands of his people out of Egypt and slavery to the promised land. He wrote the first five books of the Old Testament and recorded the Ten Commandments. Nephi, a Book of Mormon prophet, journeyed from Jerusalem to the

Amos 3:7 talks about God revealing his secret to his prophets. When God knows something that we don't we refer to it as a mystery. Once God reveals it to us it is no longer a mystery. Until the Lord called prophets again in this last dispensation of time, the whole world was in the dark as to what the Lord's will was. Everything was a mystery. As long as the people are willing to accept and follow His prophets, the Lord will continue to call them and reveal His will to them so we can know what the Lord will do among the children of men.

We can each receive personal direction from the Lord for our own life, but only one man at a time can act as the Lord's official spokesman, and that is the prophet. When the Lord wants to tell the world what is going to happen or what His children need to be doing today in order to prepare for the trials of tomorrow, those words come only through His ordained prophet. What a blessing to have someone in regular communication with God to tell us what we need to know on a regular basis.

The calling of the prophet is one based on faithfulness and devotedness to the Lord. He is ordained through the regular channels of the priesthood as a prophet, seer, and revelator.

The prophet is the head of the whole church. Even though all of the apostles also are prophets, seers, and revelators, only one is allowed to act in that capacity for the whole church, and that is the president of the church.

Whether we know of some great and spectacular thing a particular prophet did or whether he lived a quiet and reasonably uneventful life makes no difference. What makes any prophet special is that he is God's mouthpiece to all of God's children on earth. It is through the living prophet that we learn the Lord's will for us today, just as the children of Israel learned the Lord's will for them

Americas 600 years before the birth of Christ. This great leader and colonizer gave us many important writings in the Book of Mormon. John the Baptist was chosen to prepare the world for the coming of the Lord Jesus Christ. Through Joseph Smith, a latter-day prophet, the Lord restored the Church. Joseph Smith also translated the Book of Mormon while a young man.

• What have you learned from the lives and teachings of prophets?

We Have a Living Prophet on the Earth Today

• Why do we need a living prophet today?

We have a prophet living on the earth today. This prophet is the President of The Church of Jesus Christ of Latter-day Saints. He has the right to revelation for the entire Church. He holds "the keys of the kingdom," meaning that he has the authority to direct the entire Church and kingdom of God on earth, including the administration of priesthood ordinances (see Matthew 16:19). No person except the chosen prophet and President can receive God's will for the entire membership of the Church. The Lord said, "There is never but one on the earth at a time on whom this power and the keys of this priesthood are conferred" (D&C 132:7). The President of the Church is assisted by his counselors in the First Presidency and the members of the Quorum of the Twelve, who are also prophets, seers, and revelators.

We should do those things the prophets tell us to do. President Wilford Woodruff said that a prophet will never be allowed to lead the Church astray:

"The Lord will never permit me or any other man who stands as President of this Church to lead you astray. It is not in the programme. It is not in the mind of God. If I were to attempt that, the Lord would remove me out of my place" (Teachings of Presidents of the Church: Wilford Woodruff [2004], 199).

• In what ways has the living prophet influenced the Church?

through prophets like Moses, Joshua, and Elijah. Every prophet is special in his own day and in his own way. Our lives are better because we have been blessed with living prophets.

The reason we are so blessed to have a living prophet is that no matter how valuable the words of Adam, or Moses, or Abraham may be, their words will not direct us to do all those things that today's society requires of us. By having a living prophet among us we are able to receive the Lord's will for us today. Living faithfully by the counsel of the living prophets helps us gain a greater testimony of the teachings and lives of the dead prophets.

The living prophet is the only one of the apostles who is able to exercise or use all of the keys or rights of administration of the priesthood. He directs, and is ultimately responsible for every aspect of God's earthly kingdom. He is, in a sense, God's chief steward over His earthly kingdom, and the prophet answers directly to God for how he guides and directs that kingdom.

The Lord has set up a system for choosing His prophet in these last days. Once a man is made an apostle he remains an apostle for life. The Lord controls who becomes the next prophet through the death of those ahead of that prophet. This means that the senior apostle always becomes the next prophet. If the prophet were to try to go against God's will and get the Church to do something they shouldn't do, God would take his life. That is what President Woodruff means when he says that "the Lord would remove me out of my place."

If you study the lives of the living prophets you will see a pattern. Each prophet, no matter how short their time in the office of president of the Church, performs something special that no other prophet has done for the kingdom. They all have a calling from the Lord, a task to perform during their time as prophet.

One prophet consolidated and coordinated all the instruction for the Church. Another prophet set up the welfare program, others are known for being temple builders or great missionary promoters. Every prophet has his own mission to perform. President Monson, for example will be known for changing the age missionaries can serve. The men went from age 19 to 18, and the women from age 21 to 19. That made a huge difference in the missionary efforts of the Church.

When Moses was leading the Israelites in a war with a great tribe, as long as his arms were raised above his head they won the war. If his arms dropped then the enemy began to beat them. His brethren sustained him by holding his arms up for him when he was too tired to hold them himself.

We Should Sustain the Lord's Prophet

• What can we do to follow and sustain the prophet?

Many people find it easy to believe in the prophets of the past. But it is much greater to believe in and follow the living prophet. We raise our hands to sustain the President of the Church as prophet, seer, and revelator.

Prophets have a great burden to bear for the Lord. He is responsible for the Lord's message to the whole earth. He is personally responsible to the Lord for the spiritual welfare of millions and millions of members of the Lord's kingdom. He can use all the help we can give him.

How can we sustain the prophet? We should pray for him. His burdens are heavy, and he needs to be strengthened by the prayers of the Saints.

There is power in a person's prayers. There is even greater power in the prayers of many people. We should all be praying for our prophet and his counselors. They need our prayerful support.

We should study his words. We can listen to his conference addresses. We can also subscribe to the Ensign or Liahona so we can read his conference addresses and other messages he gives.

It does us no good to have a living prophet if we ignore what he says. We should be listening to his talks, looking for letters and announcements from the Brethren, and reading their monthly messages that come through the magazines and publications of the Church.

We should follow his inspired teachings completely. We should not choose to follow part of his inspired counsel and discard that which is unpleasant or difficult. The Lord commanded us to follow the inspired teachings of His prophet:

Once we learn what the Lord wants us to know and do through the words of His prophet, we need to support the prophet by following his counsel. If he tells us to be more careful in our observance of the Sabbath day, or if we need to make sure we are paying a generous fast offering, whatever it is, we need to do what we are told to do. If we want the Lord to bless us we need to make sure we are obeying His words as delivered to us through His authorized servants, the prophets.

"Thou shalt give heed unto all his [the prophet's] words and commandments which he shall give unto you as he receiveth them, walking in all holiness before me;

"For his word ye shall receive, as if from mine own mouth, in all patience and faith" (D&C 21:4–5).

The Lord will never allow the President of the Church to lead us astray.

• What has the President of the Church taught or emphasized recently?

Great Blessings Follow Obedience to the Prophet

If we obey, the Lord promises, "The gates of hell shall not prevail against you; yea, and the Lord God will disperse the powers of darkness from before you, and cause the heavens to shake for your good, and his name's glory" (D&C 21:6). When we do as our prophet directs, blessings pour down from heaven.

In the Old Testament the people were punished by the Lord all the time for not listening to and doing what His prophets had told them to do. When they did listen and obey, the Lord worked miracles for them. The pattern has never changed. When we listen to the prophet and obey his counsel the Lord pours blessings upon our heads. It never fails.

In order to stand, the true Church must be "built upon the foundation of the apostles and prophets, Jesus Christ himself being the chief corner stone" (Ephesians 2:20). We are blessed in this insecure world to have a prophet through whom the Lord reveals His will.

The Church of Jesus Christ of Latter-day Saints offers a mix of blessings the world has not seen in many centuries. We look at the Old Testament and the people followed prophets. We look at the New Testament and the people followed Jesus, then later they followed the apostles. For almost two thousand years there were no prophets, apostles, nor was Christ to be found. We are saying, come and follow Christ, whose church this is by listening to His prophet and apostles. Base your faith in Christ by following the inspired direction given by the prophet and apostles Christ has called to lead us.

• What experiences have you had when you have obeyed the counsel of the prophet?

For teachers: Sharing experiences and bearing testimony invite the Spirit. As you conclude this lesson, consider sharing an experience you have had when you have followed the counsel of the President of the Church. Share your testimony of the living prophet.

Additional Scriptures
• Numbers 12:6 (God speaks through prophets)
• 1 Samuel 9:9 (prophet called a seer)
• Amos 3:7 (God reveals His secrets to the prophets)
• Mosiah 8:16–18 (a seer can know of things past and things to come)
• Luke 1:70 (God speaks through prophets)
• D&C 45:10, 15 (God speaks today as in days of old)
• 1 Nephi 22:2 (by the Spirit things are made known to prophets)
• D&C 68:3–5 (when the Lord's servants speak as moved by the Holy Ghost, it is the mind, will, and voice of the Lord)
• D&C 107:65–67, 91–92 (duties of the President of the Church)
• D&C 43:1–7 (only the prophet is authorized to receive revelations for the Church)

Chapter 10

Scriptures

Gospel Principles, (2011), 44–49

The Scriptures Are Available to Us Today

• What are some of the blessings that we enjoy today because the scriptures are so accessible?

When the Lord's servants speak or write under the influence of the Holy Ghost, their words become scripture (see D&C 68:4). From the beginning, the Lord has commanded His prophets to keep a record of His revelations and His dealings with His children. He said: "I command all men, both in the east and in the west, and in the north, and in the south, and in the islands of the sea, that they shall write the words which I speak unto them; for out of the books which shall be written I will judge the world, every man according to their works, according to that which is written" (2 Nephi 29:11).

The Church of Jesus Christ of Latter-day Saints accepts four books as scripture: the Bible, the Book of Mormon, the Doctrine and Covenants, and the Pearl of Great Price. These books are called the standard works of the Church. The inspired words of our living prophets are also accepted as scripture.

For teachers: To encourage discussion about the four standard works, you could assign each class member or family member a number between 1 and 4. Ask those with number 1 to read what this chapter teaches about the Bible, those with number 2 to read what this chapter teaches about the Book of Mormon, those with number 3 to read what this chapter teaches about the Doctrine and Covenants, and those with number 4 to read what this chapter teaches about the Pearl of Great Price. Then ask them to share what they have learned.

The Bible

The Bible is a collection of sacred writings containing God's revelations to man. These writings cover many centuries, from the time of Adam through the time when the Apostles of Jesus Christ lived. They were written by many prophets who lived at various times in the history of the world.

The Bible is divided into two sections: the Old Testament and the New Testament. Many prophecies in the Old Testament foretell the coming of a Savior and Redeemer. The New Testament tells of the life of that Savior and Redeemer, who is Jesus Christ. It also tells of the establishing of His Church in that day. "We believe the

We have many blessings people in past centuries didn't dare dream about. For almost two thousand years most people only heard of Christ and stories about God's dealings with His children. They never actually read them or possibly even ever saw a copy of the scriptures. Scriptures were very difficult to come by. They had to be hand copied by a monk and took many years to make one copy. Often times only the clergy were even allowed to own a copy of the Bible.

Today we can all read, and the Bible is readily available online and in print almost anywhere. Anyone can read it, and there are thousands of commentaries and books that talk about what is contained within its pages. What blessings would be missing in your life if you didn't have any of these advantages?

We have more scriptures today available to every person than has almost ever been had in the history of the world. The standard works of the Church are just the beginning. They are the canonized scriptures, but we also consider the written and spoken words of our living prophets to be scripture, which means we receive more scripture all the time.

The Bible was created by scholars several hundred years after Christ's resurrection. Many of the prophets who lived and taught God's word have not been included in the Bible, mainly because we don't have their writings. Those we do have, we don't have any way to verify that the prophet actually wrote the text, so we are missing a massive amount of scripture because we can't verify where the texts came from.

A testament is a covenant. The Old Testament is the old covenant that God set up with Moses. It was prophesied that when Christ came God would give a new covenant to His people. Jesus gave them new commandments, so we refer to what He and the apostles taught as the New Testament. We understand that we don't have the

Bible to be the word of God as far as it is translated correctly" (Articles of Faith 1:8).

original documents that made up the New Testament, so based on what we have we say, "We believe the Bible to be the word of God as far as it is translated correctly" (Articles of Faith 1:8).

Through the Prophet Joseph Smith, the Lord has expanded our understanding of some passages in the Bible. The Lord inspired the Prophet Joseph to restore truths to the Bible text that had been lost or changed since the original words were written. These inspired corrections are called the Joseph Smith Translation of the Bible. In the Latter-day Saint edition of the King James Version of the Bible, selected passages from the Joseph Smith Translation are found on pages 797–813 and in many footnotes.

One of the blessings of having prophets is their ability, when commanded by the Lord, to translate documents. Joseph Smith restored many passages and phrases to the Bible that had been either lost or changed over the centuries. These passages really clarify many parts of the Bible that are otherwise difficult to understand.

The Book of Mormon

The Book of Mormon is a sacred record of some of the people who lived on the American continents between about 2000 B.C. and A.D. 400. It contains the fulness of the gospel of Jesus Christ (see D&C 20:9; 42:12; 135:3). The Book of Mormon tells of the visit Jesus Christ made to the people in the Americas soon after His Resurrection.

Joseph Smith translated the Book of Mormon into English through the gift and power of God. He said that it is "the most correct of any book on earth, and the keystone of our religion, and a man would get nearer to God by abiding by its precepts, than by any other book" (introduction to the Book of Mormon).

A precept is a teaching.

President Ezra Taft Benson helped us understand how the Book of Mormon is the keystone of our religion. He said:

"There are three ways in which the Book of Mormon is the keystone of our religion. It is the keystone in our witness of Christ. It is the keystone of our doctrine. It is the keystone of testimony.

"The Book of Mormon is the keystone in our witness of Jesus Christ, who is Himself the cornerstone of everything we do. It bears witness of His reality with power and clarity. …

"[It] broadens our understandings of the doctrines of salvation. … The Book of Mormon … was written for our day. … In [it] we find a pattern for preparing for the Second Coming. …

"… The Book of Mormon teaches us truth [and] bears testimony of Christ. … But there is something more. There is a power in the book which will begin to flow into your lives the moment you begin a serious study of the book. You will find greater power to resist temptation. You will find the power to avoid deception. You will find the power to stay on the strait and narrow path. The scriptures are called 'the words of life,' and nowhere is that more true

This quote from President Benson is absolutely true. I can't explain how it works, but when you study the Book of Mormon consistently each day things start to change in your life. You see things differently. You recognize truth more quickly than before. You understand truth more easily. There are many blessings that come from a consistent study of the Book of Mormon.

than it is of the Book of Mormon. ... 'Every Latter-day Saint should make the study of this book a lifetime pursuit'" (in Conference Report, Oct. 1986, 4–7; or Ensign, Nov. 1986, 5–7; quoting Marion G. Romney, in Conference Report, Apr. 1980, 90; or Ensign, May 1980, 67).

The Doctrine and Covenants

The Doctrine and Covenants is a collection of modern revelations. In section 1 of the Doctrine and Covenants, the Lord reveals that the book is published to the inhabitants of the earth to prepare them for His coming:

"Wherefore the voice of the Lord is unto the ends of the earth, that all that will hear may hear:

"Prepare ye, prepare ye for that which is to come, for the Lord is nigh" (D&C 1:11–12).

This book contains the revelations regarding the Church of Jesus Christ as it has been restored in these last days. Several sections of the book explain the organization of the Church and define the offices of the priesthood and their functions. Other sections, such as sections 76 and 88, contain glorious truths that were lost to the world for hundreds of years. Still others, such as sections 29 and 93, shed light on teachings in the Bible. In addition, some sections, such as section 133, contain prophecies of events to come. God has commanded us to study His revelations in this book: "Search these commandments, for they are true and faithful, and the prophecies and promises which are in them shall all be fulfilled" (D&C 1:37).

The Old and New Testaments and the Book of Mormon tell stories. The Doctrine and Covenants does not. The Doctrine and Covenants is a compilation of revelations given to mainly the prophet Joseph Smith. Each revelation came for a different reason. Some came because he was asking specific questions of the Lord. Others came because the Lord had directions He needed to give to either Joseph or the Church. When reading the Doctrine and Covenants for the first time, you really should read the preface at the top of each section to learn why this particular revelation was given.

The Pearl of Great Price

The Pearl of Great Price contains the book of Moses, the book of Abraham, and some inspired writings of Joseph Smith. The book of Moses contains an account of some of the visions and writings of Moses, revealed to the Prophet Joseph Smith. It clarifies doctrines and teachings that were lost from the Bible and gives added information concerning the Creation of the earth.

The book of Abraham was translated by the Prophet Joseph Smith from a papyrus scroll taken from the Egyptian catacombs. This book contains valuable information about the Creation, the gospel, the nature of God, and the priesthood.

The writings of Joseph Smith include part of Joseph Smith's inspired translation of the Bible, selections from his History of the Church, and the Articles of Faith.

• What are some stories from the scriptures that have inspired you? What are some teachings from these books of scripture that have helped you?

Some of the clearest and most informative writings on the pre-earth life and about Adam and Eve are found in the Pearl of Great Price. There are truths found in this book found in no other book of scripture. It may be small, but it is a powerful addition to our available scriptures.

Words of Our Living Prophets

In addition to these four books of scripture, the inspired words of our living prophets become scripture to us. Their words come to us through conferences, the Liahona or Ensign magazine, and instructions to local priesthood leaders. "We believe all that God has revealed, all that He does now reveal, and we believe that He will yet reveal many great and important things pertaining to the Kingdom of God" (Articles of Faith 1:9).

• Where can we find the words of our living prophets?

Studying the Scriptures

• What blessings can we receive when we study the scriptures?

We should each study the scriptures every day. We should share these truths with our children. We should read the standard works with our children so they will learn to love them and use them for the truths they contain.

If we desire to avoid the evils of this world, we must feed our minds with the truth and righteousness found in the scriptures. We will grow closer to God and to each other as we read and ponder the scriptures together.

As we read, ponder, and pray about the scriptures and ask God for understanding, the Holy Ghost will bear witness to us of the truth of these things. We will each know for ourselves that these things are true. We will not be deceived (see Joseph Smith—Matthew 1:37). We can receive the same feelings Nephi expressed when he said, "My soul delighteth in the things of the Lord; and my heart pondereth continually upon the things which I have seen and heard" (2 Nephi 4:16).

• How can we keep the commitment to study the scriptures each day? Consider planning a time and a place to study the scriptures each day.

Additional Scriptures
• 1 Nephi 14:20–26 (prophets commanded to write)
• 1 Nephi 19:1–3, 6–7; Alma 37:1–8 (great worth of scriptures)
• 2 Nephi 33:10 (scriptures testify of Christ)
• Alma 29:8 (Lord speaks to all nations through scriptures)
• Alma 31:5; Helaman 3:29–30 (the word of God is powerful)
• Helaman 15:7–8 (scriptures lead us to be firm and steadfast in the faith)
• 2 Timothy 3:16–17; 1 Nephi 19:21–24 (why and how scriptures are given)
• 2 Peter 1:20; Alma 13:20; D&C 10:62 (scriptures bring to light true points of doctrine)

One of the greatest blessings of being alive in the last days is the amount of scripture the Lord is giving us to live by. We are constantly being taught by the prophets through General Conference talks, articles that appear in the Liahona and Ensign magazines, and through special meetings where the members of the Church are taught the Lord's will for today.

Because we worship a living Christ, we should expect to have a continual flow of information coming from our God, and we do.

• D&C 128:18; Articles of Faith 1:9; 1 Nephi 14:25–26 (scriptures yet to come)
• 2 Nephi 29:3–10 (scriptures to Jews and to Gentiles)

Chapter 11

The Life of Christ
Gospel Principles, (2011), 50–58

The Life of Christ Was Predicted Long before His Birth

Every person who comes to earth depends on Jesus Christ to fulfill the promise He made in heaven to be our Savior. Without Him, the plan of salvation would have failed. Because His mission was necessary, all of the prophets from Adam to Christ testified that He would come (see Acts 10:43). All of the prophets since Christ have testified that He did come. All of us need to study the life of the Savior and follow Him faithfully throughout our lives.

For teachers: This chapter probably has more material than you will be able to cover in class. As you study it in preparation to teach, seek the Spirit's guidance in determining which portions will be most helpful for those you teach.

Adam learned that the Savior's name would be Jesus Christ (see Moses 6:51–52). Enoch saw that Jesus would die upon the cross and be resurrected (see Moses 7:55–56). Noah and Moses also testified of Him (see Moses 1:11; 8:23–24). About 800 years before the Savior was born on the earth, Isaiah foresaw His life. When Isaiah saw the grief and sorrow that the Savior would suffer to pay the price for our sins, he exclaimed:

"He is despised and rejected of men; a man of sorrows, and acquainted with grief. …

"… Surely he hath borne our griefs, and carried our sorrows. …

"He was wounded for our transgressions, he was bruised for our iniquities. …

"He was oppressed, and he was afflicted, yet he opened not his mouth: he is brought as a lamb to the slaughter" (Isaiah 53:3–5, 7).

Nephi also saw a vision of the Savior's future birth and mission. He saw a beautiful virgin, and an angel explained, "Behold, the virgin whom thou seest is the mother of the Son of God, after the manner of the flesh" (1 Nephi 11:18). Then Nephi saw the virgin holding a child in her arms. The angel declared, "Behold the Lamb of God, yea, even the Son of the Eternal Father!" (1 Nephi 11:21).

About 124 years before Jesus was born, King Benjamin, another Nephite prophet, also foresaw the Savior's life:

We don't have all the writings of all the prophets, but Acts 10:43 tells us that all the ancient prophets prophesied of the coming Messiah and the sacrifice He would make to save His people. That is amazing when you think that every prophet from Adam down to Malachi, the last Old Testament prophet, testified of the coming Savior and the importance of His mission. Every prophet since the Savior's day has also testified that He came and fulfilled His promise to work out the conditions of our salvation. This makes Him and His life central to all we believe in.

The name Jesus went by before He was born was Jehovah. They are one and the same person. Jesus was His mortal name. Jesus is a form of the name Joshua, which means "God is salvation." Jehovah means "Lord," "Eternal," or "the self existent one." In the Old Testament sometimes God would identify Himself as I AM or I AM That I AM, meaning "the self existent one."

As you read through this list of prophecies about Jesus, mentally tick them off the list of things that actually happened to Jesus. And most of these prophecies were many hundreds of years before Jesus's birth.

Note that raising the dead is not the same thing as resurrection. A person raised from the dead will die again

"For behold, the time cometh, and is not far distant, that with power, the Lord Omnipotent who reigneth, who was, and is from all eternity to all eternity, shall come down from heaven among the children of men, and shall dwell in a tabernacle of clay, and shall go forth amongst men, working mighty miracles, such as healing the sick, raising the dead, causing the lame to walk, the blind to receive their sight, and the deaf to hear, and curing all manner of diseases.

"And he shall cast out devils, or the evil spirits which dwell in the hearts of the children of men.

"And lo, he shall suffer temptations, and pain of body, hunger, thirst, and fatigue, even more than man can suffer, except it be unto death; for behold, blood cometh from every pore, so great shall be his anguish for the wickedness and the abominations of his people.

"And he shall be called Jesus Christ, the Son of God, the Father of heaven and earth, the Creator of all things from the beginning; and his mother shall be called Mary" (Mosiah 3:5–8).

• What are some ancient prophecies about Jesus Christ?

He Was the Only Begotten of the Father

• What did Jesus Christ inherit from His Father? What did He inherit from His mother?

The story of the birth and life of the Savior is found in the New Testament in the books of Matthew, Mark, Luke, and John. From their accounts we learn that Jesus was born of a virgin named Mary. She was engaged to marry Joseph when an angel of the Lord appeared to her. The angel told her that she was to be the mother of the Son of God. She asked him how this was possible (see Luke 1:34). He told her, "The Holy Ghost shall come upon thee, and the power of the Highest shall overshadow thee: therefore also that holy thing which shall be born of thee shall be called the Son of God" (Luke 1:35). Thus, God the Father became the literal Father of Jesus Christ.

Jesus is the only person on earth to be born of a mortal mother and an immortal Father. That is why He is called the Only Begotten Son. He inherited divine powers from His Father. From His mother He inherited mortality and was subject to hunger, thirst, fatigue, pain, and death. No one could take the Savior's life from Him unless He willed it. He had power to lay it down and power to take up His body again after dying. (See John 10:17–18.)

when they get old. By definition, a resurrected person never dies again.

We are all begotten children of God, because we were His children in the spirit world before we came here. But Jesus is His only child begotten in the flesh of mortality. Jesus has dual parentage, an immortal Father and a mortal mother. That is why He had the powers He needed to have in order to satisfy God's laws when He atoned for our sins. He needed to have the power over life and death or he could not have suffered enough to pay for our sins and still live. It was this very power that enabled Him to raise Himself from the dead and live forever as a resurrected person.

He Led a Perfect Life

• What does the Savior's life mean for us?

From His youth, Jesus obeyed all that was required of Him by our Heavenly Father. Under the guidance of Mary and Joseph, Jesus grew much as other children grow. He loved and obeyed the truth. Luke tells us, "And the child grew, and waxed strong in spirit, filled with wisdom: and the grace of God was upon him" (Luke 2:40; see also D&C 93:12–14).

By the time He was 12 years old, Jesus had grown in His understanding that He had been sent to do the will of His Father. He went with His parents to Jerusalem. When His parents were returning home, they discovered that He was not with their group. They went back to Jerusalem to look for Him. "After three days they found him in the temple, sitting in the midst of the doctors, and they were hearing him, and asking him questions" (Joseph Smith Translation, Luke 2:46). "And all that heard him were astonished at his understanding and answers" (Luke 2:47).

Joseph and Mary were relieved to find Him, but "they were amazed: and his mother said unto him, Son, why hast thou thus dealt with us? behold, thy father and I have sought thee sorrowing." Jesus answered her, saying, "Wist ye not that I must be about my [Heavenly] Father's business?" (Luke 2:48–49).

In order to fulfill His mission, Jesus was to do the will of His Father in Heaven. "I do nothing of myself," He declared, "but as my Father hath taught me, I speak these things. … I do always those things that please him" (John 8:28–29).

Jesus was always the perfect example of obedience to God. He put our Father in Heaven's will before His own will in all things. That is why Jesus is able to tell us to do as He has done and follow Him in all things, because He was always obedient to our Father in Heaven.

When Jesus was 30 years old, He came to John the Baptist to be baptized in the Jordan River. John was reluctant to baptize Jesus because he knew that Jesus was greater than he. Jesus asked John to baptize Him in order "to fulfil all righteousness." John did baptize the Savior, immersing Him completely in the water. When Jesus was baptized, His Father spoke from heaven, saying, "This is my beloved Son, in whom I am well pleased." The Holy Ghost descended, as shown by the sign of the dove. (See Matthew 3:13–17.)

Jesus waited until the age of 30 because Jewish law required a person to be 30 years old before they could begin a ministry and become a teacher.

John was a great prophet sent to prepare the way for Jesus's ministry. John taught the people about the coming of Jesus and prepared their minds to believe Him when he began His ministry.

Soon after Jesus was baptized, He fasted for 40 days and 40 nights to be with God. After that, Satan came to tempt Him. Jesus firmly resisted all of Satan's temptations and then commanded Satan to leave. (See Matthew 4:1–11; see also Joseph Smith Translation, Matthew 4:1, 5–6, 8–9, 11.) Jesus Christ remained sinless, the one perfect being to ever walk the earth (see Hebrews 4:15; 1 Peter 2:21–22).

To be sinless means that Jesus never put His will before God's will. He never did anything that violated one of God's commandments or put Him above another person. In other words, He never took advantage of anyone or acted selfishly in any way. He was always humble and meek, wanting only to be obedient to the will of God, and to do good always. His greatest joy was to be of service to others.

• Which accounts from the Savior's life are especially meaningful to you?

He Taught Us How to Love and Serve One Another

• How did the Savior teach us how to love and serve one another?

After His fast and His encounter with Satan, Jesus began His public ministry. He came to earth not only to die for us but also to teach us how to live. He taught that there are two great commandments: first, to love God with all our heart, mind, and strength; and second, to love others as we love ourselves (see Matthew 22:36–39). His life is an example of how we should obey these two commandments. If we love God, we will trust and obey Him, as Jesus did. If we love others, we will help them meet their physical and spiritual needs.

Jesus spent His life serving others. He cured them of diseases. He made the blind see, the deaf hear, and the lame walk. Once when He was healing the sick, it became late and the people were hungry. Instead of sending them away, He blessed five loaves of bread and two fishes and miraculously was able to feed a multitude of 5,000 people. (See Matthew 14:14–21.) He taught that whenever we find people hungry, cold, naked, or lonely, we should help them all we can. When we help others, we are serving the Lord. (See Matthew 25:35–46.)

Jesus loved others with all His heart. Often His heart was so full of compassion that He wept. He loved little children, the elderly, and the humble, simple people who had faith in Him. He loved those who had sinned, and with great compassion He taught them to repent and be baptized. He taught, "I am the way, the truth, and the life" (John 14:6).

Jesus even loved those who sinned against him and were unrepentant. At the end of His life, as He hung on the cross, He prayed to the Father for the soldiers who had crucified Him, pleading, "Father, forgive them; for they know not what they do" (Luke 23:34). He taught, "This is my commandment, That ye love one another, as I have loved you" (John 15:12).

• In what ways can we show the Lord that we love Him?

He Organized the Only True Church

• Why did the Savior organize His Church and ordain Apostles?

Jesus wanted His gospel taught to people all over the earth, so He chose twelve Apostles to testify of Him. They were the original leaders of His Church. They received the

It is important to remember that loving others as we love God means helping others meet their physical needs, not just their spiritual needs. God helps us meet our physical needs too. Love is about caring for both the physical and spiritual parts of us.

This part of Jesus showed how much he wanted to relieve people of their suffering. His only desire is that we find happiness. Once we are relieved of our physical suffering we are more likely to listen to what will bring us happiness. He understood that we are a mix of both physical and spiritual needs, and he addressed both of those sets of needs.

Jesus loves us because He understands our true worth and value as children of God. Our choices and our behavior do not take away from our true worth. This is how He is able to love us even when we are acting very unlovable. We are commanded to learn to love each other in this same way. Yes, it takes lots of practice.

Being an apostle was more than just a title. With the calling of being an Apostle came a bestowal of God's priesthood or power as well. This is why they were able to bless and heal the sick, have revelations, raise the dead, etc. The priesthood is what gave them the gift of the Holy Ghost. As the holders of God's power they were able to perform the ordinances of salvation, like baptism in Jesus's name and it was recognized as valid by God. When authority to act in His name and do the works they had seen Him do. Those who received authority from them were also able to teach, baptize, and perform other ordinances in His name. After His death, they continued to do His work until the people became so wicked that they killed the Apostles.

He Redeemed Us from Our Sins and Saved Us from Death

• As you study this section, take time to ponder the events of the Atonement.

For teachers: Pondering invites the Spirit. Consider asking class members or family members to quietly read the final two sections of the chapter, thinking about their feelings for the Savior. Then invite those who feel comfortable doing so to share their thoughts with the class.

Near the end of His mortal ministry, Jesus prepared to make the ultimate sacrifice for all the sins of mankind. He had been condemned to die because He had testified to the people that He was the Son of God.

The night before His Crucifixion, Jesus went to a garden called Gethsemane. Soon He was weighed down by deep sorrow and wept as He prayed. Latter-day Apostle Orson F. Whitney was permitted to see the Savior's suffering in a vision. Seeing the Savior weep, he said: "I was so moved at the sight that I also wept, out of pure sympathy. My whole heart went out to Him; I loved Him with all my soul, and longed to be with Him as I longed for nothing else" ("The Divinity of Jesus Christ," Improvement Era, Jan. 1926, 224–25; see also Ensign, Dec. 2003, 10). Jesus "went a little further, and fell on his face, and prayed, saying, O my Father, if it be possible, let this cup pass from me: nevertheless not as I will, but as thou wilt" (Matthew 26:39).

In a modern revelation the Savior described how great His suffering was, saying it caused Him "to tremble because of pain, and to bleed at every pore, and to suffer both body and spirit" (D&C 19:18). He suffered "according to the flesh," taking upon himself our pains, sicknesses, infirmities, and sins (see Alma 7:10–13). No mortal person can comprehend just how great this burden was. No other person could have endured such agony of body and spirit. "He descended below all things … that he might be in all and through all things, the light of truth" (D&C 88:6).

the last of the Apostles was killed there were no more priesthood holders who held the priesthood keys or the right to administer the priesthood. The church continued, but without the power of the priesthood.

Notice that Jesus never actually did anything worthy of death. All the charges they used to sentence Him to death were made up by those who wanted Him dead.

We normally think of Christ's suffering as just paying for our sins, our disobedience to God's laws. But His suffering was more than that. He suffered "according to the flesh" which means that there was no physical form of suffering He did not experience, nothing we could go through He did not suffer as well. He did this so he could understand the full extent of our mortal suffering. He wanted to have a complete understanding of what every one of us must endure while here, so in the garden He was given that experience.

There is nothing we can suffer physically that He has not already suffered, and more. At some point in His paying for our sins and experiencing our personal sufferings, He experienced so much pain and anguish that he began to sweat great drops of blood. Such suffering would have killed any mortal man, but no one could take His life, he had to give it up of His own free will, so He allowed Himself to continue to suffer so He could experience the full breadth of the mortal experience.

But His suffering was not yet complete. The following day, Jesus was beaten, humiliated, and spit upon. He was required to carry His own cross; then He was lifted up and nailed to it. He was tortured in one of the cruelest ways men have ever devised. After suffering on the cross, He cried out in agony, "My God, my God, why hast thou forsaken me?" (Mark 15:34). In Jesus's bitterest hour, the Father had withdrawn from Him so Jesus could finish suffering the penalty for the sins of all mankind that Jesus might have complete victory over the forces of sin and death (see James E. Talmage, Jesus the Christ, 3rd ed. [1916], 660–61).

When the Savior knew that His sacrifice had been accepted by the Father, He exclaimed in a loud voice, "It is finished" (John 19:30). "Father, into thy hands I commend my spirit" (Luke 23:46). He bowed His head and voluntarily gave up His spirit. The Savior was dead. A violent earthquake shook the earth.

Some friends took the Savior's body to a tomb, where it lay until the third day. During this time His spirit went and organized the missionary work to other spirits who needed to receive His gospel (see 1 Peter 3:18–20; D&C 138). On the third day, a Sunday, He returned to His body and took it up again. He was the first to overcome death. The prophecy had been fulfilled "that he must rise again from the dead" (John 20:9).

Shortly after His Resurrection, the Savior appeared to the Nephites and established His Church in the Americas. He taught the people and blessed them. This moving account is found in 3 Nephi 11 through 28.

His Sacrifice Showed His Love for His Father and for Us
Jesus taught: "Greater love hath no man than this, that a man lay down his life for his friends. Ye are my friends, if ye do whatsoever I command you" (John 15:13–14). He willingly and humbly went through the sorrow in Gethsemane and the suffering on the cross so we could receive all the blessings of the plan of salvation. To receive these blessings, we must come unto Him, repent of our sins, and love Him with all our hearts. He said:

"And this is the gospel which I have given unto you—that I came into the world to do the will of my Father, because my Father sent me.

"And my Father sent me that I might be lifted up upon the cross; and after that I had been lifted up upon the cross, that I might draw all men unto me … that they may be judged according to their works. …

The Church was organized the same way in the Americas as it was in Jerusalem. It was His Church, after all, and its leaders had His priesthood authority to bless the lives of those who belonged to the Church.

We show Jesus how much we love Him by keeping His commandments.

When we say that Jesus was born to die, we mean that He came into mortality with the mission to atone for our sins, which could only be accomplished through His ultimate death. It was through His death that He was able to resurrect His body and open the way for all of us to be resurrected as well. The resurrection was the other part of His mission.

We may not be able to atone for sins or resurrect ourselves, but Jesus has told us we are capable of living

"For the works which ye have seen me do that shall ye also do. …

"Therefore, what manner of men ought ye to be? Verily I say unto you, even as I am" (3 Nephi 27:13–15, 21, 27; italics added).

• What are your feelings as you ponder the Savior's sacrifice for you?

Additional Scriptures and Other Sources
• 2 Nephi 25:12 (the Only Begotten of the Father in the flesh)
• Moses 6:57 (Jesus Christ named as the Only Begotten)
• Matthew, Mark, Luke, John (life and teachings of Jesus Christ)
• Matthew 10:1–8; Luke 9:1–2 (Apostles ordained with power and authority)
• Matthew 26–28; Mark 14–16; Luke 22–24; John 18–20 (Jesus in the garden; betrayed, crucified, and resurrected)
• "The Living Christ: The Testimony of the Apostles," Ensign, Apr. 2000, 2–3

our lives like He lived His. We need to learn to be obedient to God in all things.

Page 47

Chapter 12

The Atonement
Gospel Principles, (2011), 59–66

The Atonement Is Necessary for Our Salvation

• Why is the Atonement necessary for our salvation?

For teachers: Simple charts and pictures can help class members or family members understand principles and doctrines. Consider making a chart with two columns, one labeled Results of the Fall and the other labeled Blessings of the Atonement. Use information from this chapter to fill in the chart.

Jesus Christ "came into the world … to be crucified for the world, and to bear the sins of the world, and to sanctify the world, and to cleanse it from all unrighteousness; that through him all might be saved" (D&C 76:41–42). The great sacrifice He made to pay for our sins and overcome death is called the Atonement. It is the most important event that has ever occurred in the history of mankind: "For it is expedient that an atonement should be made; for according to the great plan of the Eternal God there must be an atonement made, or else all mankind must unavoidably perish; … yea, all are fallen and are lost, and must perish except it be through the atonement" (Alma 34:9).

The Fall of Adam brought two kinds of death into the world: physical death and spiritual death. Physical death is separation of the body and spirit. Spiritual death is separation from God. If these two kinds of death had not been overcome by Jesus Christ's Atonement, two consequences would have resulted: our bodies and our spirits would have been separated forever, and we could not have lived again with our Heavenly Father (see 2 Nephi 9:7–9).

By the word "fall" we refer to Adam and Eve going from a state of grace, agreement, being justified within the laws of God, to a state of violation of the laws of God. Where they used to walk and talk with God in the garden, after breaking the commandment and eating the fruit they were no longer allowed to be in God's presence and had to driven from the garden. So not only did they experience a spiritual death, a separation from God, but they became mortal so now they would also experience a physical death or separation of their spirits from their bodies. Unless someone else came along to repair this breach in mortal man's relationship with God, Adam and Eve and all their posterity would be separated from God for eternity, never to see their Father's face again. Christ's atoning sacrifice repaired this breach between us and God and made it possible for us to someday return to live with Him again.

But our wise Heavenly Father prepared a wonderful, merciful plan to save us from physical and spiritual death. He planned for a Savior to come to earth to ransom (redeem) us from our sins and from death. Because of our sins and the weakness of our mortal bodies, we could not ransom ourselves (see Alma 34:10–12). The one who would be our Savior would need to be sinless and to have power over death.

The two conditions that had to exist to pay the price for our sins was the redeemer had to be sinless and he had to have power over life and death, in the eternal sense. If Jesus had committed any sins He would have been in the same problem we are in, in violation of God's laws. Fortunately he was without sin.

Jesus Christ Was the Only One Who Could Atone for Our Sins

• Why was Jesus Christ the only one who could atone for our sins?

There are several reasons why Jesus Christ was the only person who could be our Savior. One reason is that Heavenly Father chose Him to be the Savior. He was the Only Begotten Son of God and thus had power over death. Jesus explained: "I lay down my life, that I might take it again. No man taketh it from me, but I lay it down of myself. I have power to lay it down, and I have power to take it again" (John 10:17–18).

Jesus also qualified to be our Savior because He is the only person who has ever lived on the earth who did not sin. This made Him a worthy sacrifice to pay for the sins of others.

Christ Suffered and Died to Atone for Our Sins

• As you read this section, imagine yourself in the Garden of Gethsemane or at the cross as a witness of the suffering of Jesus Christ.

The Savior atoned for our sins by suffering in Gethsemane and by giving His life on the cross. It is impossible for us to fully understand how He suffered for all of our sins. In the Garden of Gethsemane, the weight of our sins caused Him to feel such agony that He bled from every pore (see D&C 19:18–19). Later, as He hung upon the cross, Jesus suffered painful death by one of the most cruel methods known to man.

How Jesus loves us, to suffer such spiritual and physical agony for our sake! How great the love of Heavenly Father that He would send His Only Begotten Son to suffer and die for the rest of His children. "For God so loved the world, that he gave his only begotten Son, that whosoever believeth in him should not perish, but have everlasting life" (John 3:16).

The Atonement and Resurrection Bring Resurrection to All

On the third day after His Crucifixion, Christ took up His body again and became the first person to be resurrected. When His friends went to seek Him, the angels who guarded His tomb told them, "He is not here: for he is risen, as he said" (Matthew 28:6). His spirit had reentered His body, never to be separated again.

Christ thus overcame physical death. Because of His Atonement, everyone born on this earth will be resurrected (see 1 Corinthians 15:21–22). Just as Jesus was

It was Christ's heavenly parentage that allowed Him to have power over life and death. His Father was an eternal being, and Jesus inherited that power as a mortal. He could die because of His mother's heritage, but He had to choose to die. No one could kill Jesus. And just as He could die at will, He could also take up His body again in resurrected form at will. Our Father in Heaven planned for it to be this way so Jesus could open the door for us to be resurrected as well.

Our Heavenly Father had no intention of leaving Adam and Eve and their posterity abandoned and alone in the eternities. He had planned for our redemption through the sacrifice of Jesus. This was all part of the great plan presented to us in the pre-earth life at the grand council in heaven.

As mentioned in the last lesson, the difference between being raised from the dead and being resurrected is that those raised from the dead will die eventually. Those who resurrected, our spirits will be reunited with our bodies, "that they can die no more ... , never to be divided" (Alma 11:45). This condition is called immortality. All people who have ever lived will be resurrected, "both old and young, both bond and free, both male and female, both the wicked and the righteous" (Alma 11:44).

For teachers: Object lessons can help class members and family members understand principles and doctrines. To explain death and resurrection, consider this object lesson: Put your hand in a glove. Explain that a hand in a glove can be compared to a person's spirit in his or her body. Take off the glove. Explain that this is like physical death—the spirit (the hand) and the body (the glove) are separated. Then put the glove back on your hand. Explain that this is like resurrection—the spirit and body are reunited.

• How has your knowledge of the Resurrection helped you?

The Atonement Makes It Possible for Those Who Have Faith in Christ to Be Saved from Their Sins

• Think about how the parable in this section helps us understand the Atonement. Whom do the people in the parable represent in our lives?

The Savior's Atonement makes it possible for us to overcome spiritual death. Although all people will be resurrected, only those who accept the Atonement will be saved from spiritual death (see Articles of Faith 1:3).

We accept Christ's Atonement by placing our faith in Him. Through this faith, we repent of our sins, are baptized, receive the Holy Ghost, and obey His commandments. We become faithful disciples of Jesus Christ. We are forgiven and cleansed from sin and prepared to return and live forever with our Heavenly Father.

The Savior tells us, "For behold, I, God, have suffered these things for all, that they might not suffer ... even as I" (D&C 19:16–17). Christ did His part to atone for our sins. To make His Atonement fully effective in our lives, we must strive to obey Him and repent of our sins.

President Boyd K. Packer of the Council of the Twelve gave the following illustration to show how Christ's Atonement makes it possible to be saved from sin if we do our part.

"Let me tell you a story—a parable.

"There once was a man who wanted something very much. It seemed more important than anything else in his life. In order for him to have his desire, he incurred a great debt.

are resurrected will never die again. The nature of the body is different when you are resurrected. Resurrected bodies are immortal.

"He had been warned about going into that much debt, and particularly about his creditor. But it seemed so important for him to do what he wanted to do and to have what he wanted right now. He was sure he could pay for it later.

"So he signed a contract. He would pay it off some time along the way. He didn't worry too much about it, for the due date seemed such a long time away. He had what he wanted now, and that was what seemed important.

"The creditor was always somewhere in the back of his mind, and he made token payments now and again, thinking somehow that the day of reckoning really would never come.

"But as it always does, the day came, and the contract fell due. The debt had not been fully paid. His creditor appeared and demanded payment in full.

"Only then did he realize that his creditor not only had the power to repossess all that he owned, but the power to cast him into prison as well.

"'I cannot pay you, for I have not the power to do so,' he confessed.

"'Then,' said the creditor, 'we will exercise the contract, take your possessions, and you shall go to prison. You agreed to that. It was your choice. You signed the contract, and now it must be enforced.'

"'Can you not extend the time or forgive the debt?' the debtor begged. 'Arrange some way for me to keep what I have and not go to prison. Surely you believe in mercy? Will you not show mercy?'

"The creditor replied, 'Mercy is always so one-sided. It would serve only you. If I show mercy to you, it will leave me unpaid. It is justice I demand. Do you believe in justice?'

"'I believed in justice when I signed the contract,' the debtor said. 'It was on my side then, for I thought it would protect me. I did not need mercy then, nor think I should need it ever. Justice, I thought, would serve both of us equally as well.'

"'It is justice that demands that you pay the contract or suffer the penalty,' the creditor replied. 'That is the law. You have agreed to it and that is the way it must be. Mercy cannot rob justice.'

"There they were: One meting out justice, the other pleading for mercy. Neither could prevail except at the expense of the other.

"'If you do not forgive the debt there will be no mercy,' the debtor pleaded.

"'If I do, there will be no justice,' was the reply.

"Both laws, it seemed, could not be served. They are two eternal ideals that appear to contradict one another. Is there no way for justice to be fully served, and mercy also?

"There is a way! The law of justice can be fully satisfied and mercy can be fully extended—but it takes someone else. And so it happened this time.

"The debtor had a friend. He came to help. He knew the debtor well. He knew him to be shortsighted. He thought him foolish to have gotten himself into such a predicament. Nevertheless, he wanted to help because he loved him. He stepped between them, faced the creditor, and made this offer.

"'I will pay the debt if you will free the debtor from his contract so that he may keep his possessions and not go to prison.'

"As the creditor was pondering the offer, the mediator added, 'You demanded justice. Though he cannot pay you, I will do so. You will have been justly dealt with and can ask no more. It would not be just.'

"And so the creditor agreed.

"The mediator turned then to the debtor. 'If I pay your debt, will you accept me as your creditor?'

"'Oh yes, yes,' cried the debtor. 'You save me from prison and show mercy to me.'

"'Then,' said the benefactor, 'you will pay the debt to me and I will set the terms. It will not be easy, but it will be possible. I will provide a way. You need not go to prison.'

"And so it was that the creditor was paid in full. He had been justly dealt with. No contract had been broken.

"The debtor, in turn, had been extended mercy. Both laws stood fulfilled. Because there was a mediator, justice had claimed its full share, and mercy was fully satisfied" (in Conference Report, Apr. 1977, 79–80; or Ensign, May 1977, 54–55).

Our sins are our spiritual debts. Without Jesus Christ, who is our Savior and Mediator, we would all pay for our sins by suffering spiritual death. But because of Him, if we will keep His terms, which are to repent and keep His commandments, we may return to live with our Heavenly Father.

It is wonderful that Christ has provided us a way to be healed from our sins. He said:

"Behold, I have come unto the world ... to save the world from sin.

"Therefore, whoso repenteth and cometh unto me as a little child, him will I receive, for of such is the kingdom of God. Behold, for such I have laid down my life, and have taken it up again; therefore repent, and come unto me ye ends of the earth, and be saved" (3 Nephi 9:21–22).

• Ponder how you can show gratitude for the gift of the Atonement.

The Savior has told us that if we love Him we will keep His commandments. Keeping and living the commandments is the only way we can demonstrate to God that we are grateful for His sacrifice on our behalf.

Additional Scriptures
• Alma 34:9–16 (Atonement necessary; sacrifice of God)
• 2 Nephi 9:7–12 (the Atonement saves us from physical and spiritual death)
• Romans 5:12–17 (by one came death, by one came life)
• Helaman 14:15–18 (purpose of Jesus's death)
• Articles of Faith 1:3 (all may be saved)
• 1 Peter 1:18–20 (Jesus was foreordained)
• Matthew 16:21 (Jesus's sacrifice was necessary)
• Luke 22:39–46 (Jesus's suffering in the garden)
• 1 John 1:7 (Jesus cleanses from sin)
• 2 Nephi 9:21–22 (the Savior suffered for all people)
• Mosiah 16:6–8 (resurrection possible only through Jesus)
• Alma 11:40–45; Mormon 9:12–14 (all to be resurrected)
• Isaiah 1:18 (sins shall be made white)
• 1 Corinthians 15:40–44; Alma 40:23 (description of the Resurrection)

Chapter 13

The Priesthood
Gospel Principles, (2011), 67–71

What Is the Priesthood?

For teachers: This chapter is organized under five headings. Each heading is a question about the priesthood. You could use these questions as a guide for your lesson. If the classroom setup allows for small group discussion, consider dividing class members into groups of two to four. Assign each group one of the sections of the chapter (in large classes, some sections may be assigned to more than one group). Have each group do the following: (1) Read and discuss their assigned section. (2) Find scriptures that help answer the question in the section heading. (3) Share personal experiences that relate to the section. Then ask class members to share some of these experiences with the entire class.

The priesthood is the eternal power and authority of God. Through the priesthood He created and governs the heavens and the earth. By this power the universe is kept in perfect order. Through this power He accomplishes His work and glory, which is "to bring to pass the immortality and eternal life of man" (Moses 1:39).

Our Heavenly Father delegates His priesthood power to worthy male members of the Church. The priesthood enables them to act in God's name for the salvation of the human family. Through it they can be authorized to preach the gospel, administer the ordinances of salvation, and govern God's kingdom on earth.

• Think about the significance of God allowing worthy men and boys to hold His priesthood.

Why Do We Need the Priesthood on the Earth?

We must have priesthood authority to act in the name of God when performing the sacred ordinances of the gospel, such as baptism, confirmation, administration of the sacrament, and temple marriage. If a man does not have the priesthood, even though he may be sincere, the Lord will not recognize ordinances he performs (see Matthew 7:21–23; Articles of Faith 1:5). These important

We don't really know exactly what the priesthood is. To say the priesthood is the "eternal power and authority of God" is over simplifying the mighty power of the priesthood. Unfortunately, we can't comprehend more than that, so this is the definition we live with. Another example of something over simplified might be the answer to the question, "What is a spaceship?" One might answer, "It is something that gets you from point A to point B." It is obviously much more than that, but to one who has never seen a spaceship, what would be the point in getting into details?

How does one quantify or fully describe the power and authority of God? We know it is how He governs and controls the universe, but we don't really have any concept of what that entails. The priesthood is a power beyond our imagining.

We do not govern anything in the universe (stars and planets for example) with the priesthood power we have. But we do participate in the process of bringing to pass the eternal life of man by the service we render to our brothers and sisters by virtue of the priesthood we bear. This is done through blessings and priesthood ordinances, like the bestowal of the gift of the Holy Ghost.

"The priesthood enables them to act in God's name for the salvation of the human family." All use of the priesthood is in Christ's name. Even the service we render to others on our own efforts is done in behalf of Christ, whose priesthood we bear or carry.

There is no more powerful force in the universe than the priesthood. A boy, ordained as a Deacon, has more power to affect change in this world than any other force in nature or politics. Deacons have the right to ministering angels. Who else, besides another priesthood holder has the ability to call on the angels to help and minister to them?

The only part of the priesthood power we have been given has to do with those ordinances that have to be performed in mortality. Baptisms and sealings, for example, have to be done in mortality. To wield a power such as this requires the holder of the priesthood receive it in the proper way, through the proper channel. God does not allow just anyone to use His power, even if it is for good. It must be used and passed on to others in the manner God has specified or He won't recognize the right of the person to act in His name.

ordinances must be performed on the earth by men holding the priesthood.

Men need the priesthood to preside in The Church of Jesus Christ of Latter-day Saints and to direct the work of the Church in all parts of the world. When Christ lived on the earth, He chose His Apostles and ordained them so that they could lead His Church. He gave them the power and authority of the priesthood to act in His name. (See Mark 3:13–15; John 15:16.)

The priesthood is what gives us the gift of the Holy Ghost and all spiritual gifts. It is through the gift of the Holy Ghost that men are able to preside or govern the Lord's Church or His affairs here in mortality. Through the Holy Ghost Christ still speaks to the leaders of His Church and to all those who have been placed in positions of authority to govern or lead others among the membership of the church.

Another reason the priesthood is needed on the earth is so we can understand the will of the Lord and carry out His purposes. God reveals His will to His authorized priesthood representative on the earth, the prophet. The prophet, who is President of the Church, serves as the spokesman for God to all members of the Church and all people on the earth.

It is the gift of the Holy Ghost that grants us the ability to receive revelation or knowledge from God. This knowledge is what we use to help spiritually save the lives of our brothers and sisters around the world, in addition to our own life.

• Why is it essential for a man to have proper authority when he performs an ordinance?

Just as a community doesn't recognize anyone in a police uniform, except those who have passed the training and certifications required to be one, so too God does not recognize just anyone as His representative. He said in the Old Testament when Aaron was called to be a priesthood holder that those called had to be called of God by one already having authority, by the laying on of hands. If it happens any other way it is not of God.

How Do Men Receive the Priesthood?

The Lord has prepared an orderly way for His priesthood to be given to His sons on the earth. A worthy male member of the Church receives the priesthood "by the laying on of hands by those who are in authority, to preach the Gospel and administer in the ordinances thereof" (Articles of Faith 1:5).

This is the same way men received the priesthood long ago, even in the days of Moses: "And no man taketh this honour unto himself, but he that is called of God, as was Aaron" (Hebrews 5:4). Aaron received the priesthood from Moses, his priesthood leader (see Exodus 28:1). Only those who hold the priesthood can ordain others, and they can do so only when authorized by those who hold the keys for that ordination (see chapter 14 in this book).

It is not enough to want the priesthood. To get the priesthood requires someone in authority who already holds that priesthood. It has to be passed along by the laying on of hands, and by the permission of one who has the keys or rights to administer the use of the priesthood in that person's area.

Men cannot buy and sell the power and authority of the priesthood. Nor can they take this authority upon themselves. In the New Testament we read of a man named Simon who lived when Christ's Apostles presided over the Church. Simon became converted and was baptized into the Church. Because he was a skillful magician, the people believed he had the power of God. But Simon did not have the priesthood, and he knew it.

The priesthood is not a commodity to be bought and sold. The priesthood is a sacred privilege that requires a life-long commitment to service in the Lord's name and in His church.

Simon knew that the Apostles and the other priesthood leaders of the Church had the true power of God. He saw them use their priesthood to do the Lord's work, and he wanted this power for himself. He offered to buy the priesthood. (See Acts 8:9–19.) But Peter, the chief Apostle, said, "Thy money perish with thee, because thou hast thought that the gift of God may be purchased with money" (Acts 8:20).

• Why is it significant that "no man taketh this honour [of the priesthood] unto himself"?

The priesthood power controls the universe. What would happen if wicked or selfish men were allowed to take upon themselves this power to do with it what they chose? The Lord has been very clear that only those who are called and are willing to serve Him in humility will be allowed to have access to His power.

How Do Men Properly Use the Priesthood?

The priesthood should be used to bless the lives of our Heavenly Father's children here on earth. Priesthood holders should preside in love and kindness. They should not force their families and others to obey them. The Lord has told us that the power of the priesthood cannot be controlled except in righteousness (see D&C 121:36). When we try to use the priesthood to gain wealth or fame or for any other selfish purpose, "behold, the heavens withdraw themselves; the Spirit of the Lord is grieved; and when it is withdrawn, Amen to the priesthood or the authority of that man" (D&C 121:37).

Remember that we don't really know how the priesthood works, except that the Lord has told us that if we will obey certain rules with regards to using His power He will cause things to happen for our benefit. For example, when a priesthood holder presides or governs his household in kindness and love, and not force and tyranny, the Lord sends His Spirit to that home to bless the lives of all in the house. Peace and love abounds in the home, and the children learn to cooperate and care for each other. These results are things we cannot take personal credit for since we don't know how they happen. We just know that the Lord has promised that as we honor His priesthood he will honor us and those we come in contact with by giving us blessings too numerous to count.

When a man uses the priesthood "by persuasion, by long-suffering, by gentleness and meekness, and by love unfeigned" (D&C 121:41), he can do many wonderful things for his family and others. He can baptize, confirm, and administer the sacrament when authorized by those who hold the keys for those ordinances. He can bless the sick. He can give priesthood blessings to his family members to encourage and protect them when they have special needs. He can also help other families with these ordinances and blessings when asked to do so.

The description of how to use the priesthood found in D&C 121:41 shows us how Jesus uses His priesthood power. The blessings of the priesthood can only be found when the priesthood is used in this way. The priesthood operates on the principles and virtues of righteousness and love. When we try to use our priesthood in a selfish way we violate the very core of what the priesthood is all about, and that offends the Holy Ghost and the priesthood power of that man is withdrawn from him. He may remain for a time with the authority to use the priesthood, but his ability to do good with it fades until all the power is gone.

Men use priesthood authority to preside in the Church in such callings as branch president, bishop, quorum president, stake president, and mission president. Men and women who hold positions in the Church as officers and teachers work under the direction of priesthood leaders and under the guidance of the Holy Ghost.

To preside means to govern. A Bishop presides over his congregation like a pastor or priest is responsible for his congregation. The main difference is that the LDS Bishop has the priesthood of God to use to bless the lives over whom he governs. The protestant pastor or Catholic bishop does not have the priesthood to use in his/her duties.

What Blessings Come When We Use the Priesthood Properly?

It is through the exercise of the priesthood of God that the sons of God learn to be like Christ. This is where we learn how to be giving, self-sacrificing, and loving. The use of the priesthood teaches us patience, humility, the ability to

The Lord has promised great blessings to righteous priesthood holders who use the priesthood to bless others:

"Then shall thy confidence wax strong in the presence of God; and the doctrine of the priesthood shall distil upon thy soul as the dews from heaven.

"The Holy Ghost shall be thy constant companion, and thy scepter an unchanging scepter of righteousness and truth; and thy dominion shall be an everlasting dominion, and without compulsory means it shall flow unto thee forever and ever" (D&C 121:45–46).

President David O. McKay promised every man who uses the priesthood in righteousness that he "will find his life sweetened, his discernment sharpened to decide quickly between right and wrong, his feelings tender and compassionate, yet his spirit strong and valiant in defense of right; he will find the priesthood a never failing source of happiness—a well of living water springing up unto eternal life" (Teachings of Presidents of the Church: David O. McKay [2003], 116).

• What are some of the blessings you have received through the priesthood?

Additional Scriptures
• D&C 84; 107 (revelations on priesthood, including the oath and covenant of the priesthood in D&C 84:33–40)
• D&C 20:38–67 (duties of the priesthood explained)

follow the directions of the Holy Spirit, and how to care for others. This is why our confidence grows stronger as we learn to approach the Lord in prayer for the welfare of others. We gain confidence that we are living worthily of His blessings. We come to know that we are truly obedient to the commandments and are living our lives in a manner that pleases God.

God's kingdom is one set up on the principle of love. He does not force anyone to serve Him or worship Him. People do it because they love Him. This is why the scripture says that as we learn to live our lives like Christ lives His, we will gain the constant companionship of the Holy Spirit and our symbol or scepter of righteousness will last forever and our power in the priesthood will flow to us without force for eternity.

Chapter 14

Priesthood Organization
Gospel Principles, (2011), 72–80

For most of the world's history only selected men were allowed to hold the priesthood. It is only in this last dispensation of the gospel that every worthy male member is not only allowed, but expected to hold the priesthood and be a spiritual leader.

The Priesthood Is on the Earth Today

The Church of Jesus Christ of Latter-day Saints is governed by the priesthood. The priesthood, which is always associated with God's work, "continueth in the church of God in all generations, and is without beginning of days or end of years" (D&C 84:17). It is upon the earth today. Men young and old are baptized into the Church, and when they are judged worthy they are ordained to the priesthood. They are given the authority to act for the Lord and do His work on the earth.

Two Divisions of Priesthood

• How did the Melchizedek and Aaronic Priesthoods get their names?

For teachers: Use questions at the beginning of a section to start a discussion and send class members or family members to the text to find more information. Use questions at the end of a section to help class members or family members ponder and discuss the meaning of what they have read and apply it in their lives.

The priesthood is divided into two parts: the Melchizedek Priesthood and the Aaronic Priesthood (see D&C 107:1). "The first is called the Melchizedek Priesthood … because Melchizedek was such a great high priest.

Melchizedek was the king of Salem, that later was named Jerusalem. Abraham came to Melchizedek to pay his tithing. Because of his great righteousness Melchizedek was known as the prince of peace (Alma 13:18). This also happens to be a title by which the Savior is known.

"Before his day it was called the Holy Priesthood, after the Order of the Son of God.

"But out of respect or reverence to the name of the Supreme Being, to avoid the too frequent repetition of his name, they, the church, in ancient days, called that priesthood after Melchizedek, or the Melchizedek Priesthood" (D&C 107:2–4; italics in original).

By "appendage" is meant that the Aaronic Priesthood is but a small part of the Melchizedek Priesthood. Any Melchizedek Priesthood holder also holds all the rights to the Aaronic Priesthood.

The lesser priesthood is an appendage to the Melchizedek Priesthood. It is called the Aaronic Priesthood because it was conferred on Aaron and his sons throughout all their generations. Those who hold the Aaronic Priesthood have authority to administer the outward ordinances of the sacrament and baptism. (See D&C 20:46; 107:13–14, 20.)

Those holding the Melchizedek Priesthood have the power and authority to lead the Church and direct the preaching of the gospel in all parts of the world. They administer all the spiritual work of the Church (see D&C 84:19–22; 107:8). They direct the work done in the temples; they preside over wards, branches, stakes, and missions. The

Those holding the Aaronic Priesthood perform the ordinances of the sacrament and baptism, but are in charge of all physical needs fo the Saints. They care for the chapels, care for the members' physical needs, and preach and teach the gospel to the members of the church. They

Lord's chosen prophet, the President of the Church, is the presiding high priest over the Melchizedek Priesthood (see D&C 107:65–67).

collect the tithes and offerings of the church. That is why the office of Bishop is in the Aaronic Priesthood.

The Stake President and those above him are responsible for the spiritual welfare of all members of the church, which is a Melchizedek Priesthood function. Because the Bishop also presides over the spiritual welfare of the ward, he has to be a high priest in the Melchizedek Priesthood to be called as a Bishop.

Keys of the Priesthood

• What is the difference between the priesthood and the keys of the priesthood? Which priesthood leaders receive keys?

There is a difference between being ordained to an office in the priesthood and receiving keys of the priesthood. President Joseph F. Smith taught:

"The Priesthood in general is the authority given to man to act for God. Every man ordained to any degree of the Priesthood has this authority delegated to him.

"But it is necessary that every act performed under this authority shall be done at the proper time and place, in the proper way, and after the proper order. The power of directing these labors constitutes the keys of the Priesthood. In their fulness, the keys are held by only one person at a time, the prophet and president of the Church. He may delegate any portion of this power to another, in which case that person holds the keys of that particular labor. Thus, the president of a temple, the president of a stake, the bishop of a ward, the president of a mission, the president of a quorum, each holds the keys of the labors performed in that particular body or locality. His Priesthood is not increased by this special appointment; … the president of an elders' quorum, for example, has no more Priesthood than any member of that quorum. But he holds the power of directing the official labors performed in the … quorum, or in other words, the keys of that division of that work" (Teachings of Presidents of the Church: Joseph F. Smith [1998], 141; italics in original).

Think of the keys of the priesthood as the rights of administration. These rights include deciding who can hold the priesthood based on worthiness, who can perform ordinances in their jurisdiction and when they can be performed. They preside over meetings and councils and receive revelation for their area of stewardship in the church.

Keys are attached to callings, not people. When a Bishop is called to the position he is given the keys of that office for the people in his ward. When he is released, though he will always be a Bishop, the keys or rights to administer the priesthood activities in his ward, are passed on to the next Bishop. The same goes for any quorum president, either in the Melchizedek or Aaronic Priesthood, the president of the quorum is given keys for as long as they hold that calling. When they are released, the keys are taken from them and given to the next president.

• How do priesthood keys safeguard the Church?

The keys being passed along by assignment brings a level of continuity to the Church. It makes it so that people cannot randomly decide they will baptize someone. Because they cannot perform the main ordinances of the church without consent of the one holding the keys for that ordinance, only those who should perform ordinances can, and they can only perform them when and where the one with the keys says they can. This provides order in the Lord's Church, and prevents anyone from taking privileges upon themselves that they are not worthy of having.

The Offices and Duties of the Aaronic Priesthood

• In what ways do Aaronic Priesthood holders serve?

When the Aaronic Priesthood is conferred on a man or boy, he is ordained to an office in that priesthood. The offices in the Aaronic Priesthood are deacon, teacher, priest, and bishop. Each office carries duties and responsibilities. Each quorum is presided over by a quorum president, who teaches the members their duties and asks them to fill assignments.

Some men join the Church or become active after they have passed the usual age to receive the offices of this priesthood. They are usually ordained to an office in the Aaronic Priesthood and can soon be ordained to other offices as they remain worthy.

Deacon

A young man who has been baptized and confirmed a member of the Church and is worthy may be ordained to the office of deacon when he is 12 years old. The deacons are usually assigned to pass the sacrament to members of the Church, keep Church buildings and grounds in good order, act as messengers for priesthood leaders, and fulfill special assignments such as collecting fast offerings.

A deacon's quorum can have up to 12 members. If there are more than 12 deacons in a ward the Bishop may create a second quorum of deacons, each with its own presidency.

Teacher

A worthy young man may be ordained a teacher when he is 14 years old or older. Teachers have all the duties, rights, and powers of the office of deacon plus additional ones. Teachers in the Aaronic Priesthood are to help Church members live the commandments (see D&C 20:53–59). To help fulfill this responsibility, they are usually assigned to serve as home teachers. They visit the homes of Church members and encourage them to live the principles of the gospel. They have been commanded to teach the truths of the gospel from the scriptures (see D&C 42:12). Teachers also prepare the bread and water for the sacrament service.

Teachers quorums can have up to 24 teachers.

Priest

A worthy young man may be ordained a priest when he is 16 years old or older. Priests have all the duties, rights, and powers of the offices of deacon and teacher plus some additional ones (see D&C 20:46–51). A priest may baptize. He may also administer the sacrament. He may ordain other priests, teachers, and deacons. A priest may take charge of meetings when there is no Melchizedek Priesthood holder present. He is to preach the gospel to those around him.

Priests quorums can have up to 48 priests. The Bishop is the president of the priest's quorum. Notice that only the priest may ordain other boys to positions within the Aaronic Priesthood. They are also able to perform the first two ordinances of the gospel, baptism and the sacrament.

Bishop

A bishop is ordained and set apart to preside over the Aaronic Priesthood in a ward. He is the president of the priests quorum (see D&C 107:87–88). When he is acting in his Aaronic Priesthood office, a bishop deals primarily with temporal matters, such as administering finances and records and directing care for the poor and needy (see D&C 107:68).

A bishop is also ordained a high priest so he can preside over all members in the ward (see D&C 107:71–73; 68:15). A bishop is a judge in Israel (see D&C 107:74) and interviews members for temple recommends, priesthood ordinations, and other needs. It is his right to have the gift of discernment.

The gift of discernment allows the Bishop to understand when people are telling the truth or lying. It helps him to know when people are in need or not. It is a gift that reveals truth and needs. This gift also helps the Bishop come to understand how to help people in the best possible way, even people he doesn't know.

• How have you been blessed through the service of Aaronic Priesthood holders?

The Offices and Duties of the Melchizedek Priesthood

• In what ways do Melchizedek Priesthood holders serve?

The offices of the Melchizedek Priesthood are elder, high priest, patriarch, Seventy, and Apostle.

Elder

Elders are called to teach, expound, exhort, baptize, and watch over the Church (see D&C 20:42). All Melchizedek Priesthood holders are elders. They have the authority to bestow the gift of the Holy Ghost by the laying on of hands (see D&C 20:43). Elders should conduct meetings of the Church as they are led by the Holy Ghost (see D&C 20:45; 46:2). Elders may administer to the sick (see D&C 42:44) and bless little children (see D&C 20:70). Elders may preside over Church meetings when there is no high priest present (D&C 107:11).

Just as all Melchizedek Priesthood holders hold the Aaronic Priesthood, so too do they hold all the offices below them in the Melchizedek Priesthood. A High Priest is also an Elder. Each calling adds more responsibility to the shoulders of the one accepting the call. The Prophet has all the responsibilities of all the other priesthood callings, but also has responsibilities no other office in the priesthood has since he is responsible for directing the work of the world-wide Church.

High Priest

A high priest is given the authority to officiate in the Church and administer spiritual things (see D&C 107:10, 12). He may also officiate in all lesser offices (see D&C 68:19). Stake presidents, mission presidents, high councilors, bishops, and other leaders of the Church are ordained high priests.

Once you are a high priest all the offices listed in the paragraph to the left are just callings one is called to perform. The only exception is the office of a Bishop, that requires an ordination. Once a bishop, always a bishop, whether or not you are actively filling that calling.

Patriarch

Patriarchs are ordained by General Authorities, or by stake presidents when they are authorized by the Council of the

Patriarchs are normally called for life. Once a patriarch, you are released from all other callings and responsibilities in the priesthood and in the ward. Giving patriarchal blessings requires revelation, and hence there

Twelve, to give patriarchal blessings to members of the Church. These blessings give us some understanding of our callings on earth. They are the word of the Lord personally to us. Patriarchs are also ordained high priests. (See D&C 107:39–56.)

Seventy

Seventies are special witnesses of Jesus Christ to the world and assist in building up and regulating the Church under the direction of the First Presidency and Quorum of the Twelve Apostles (see D&C 107:25, 34, 38, 93–97).

Apostle

An Apostle is a special witness of the name of Jesus Christ in all the world (see D&C 107:23). The Apostles administer the affairs of the Church throughout the world. Those who are ordained to the office of Apostle in the Melchizedek Priesthood are usually set apart as members of the Quorum of the Twelve Apostles. Each one is given all the keys of the kingdom of God on earth, but only the senior Apostle, who is President of the Church, actively exercises all of the keys. The others act under his direction.

is a lot of fasting and prayer involved by the patriarch. Without revelation the blessing cannot be given, so usually when someone goes in to receive their blessing they go fasting and praying, as does the patriarch.

The office of the seventy used to be one that many members of each ward had. The Church changed that and consolidated the office of seventy to special quorums that assist the quorum of the twelve apostles in administering the affairs of the Church throughout the world. The number of quorums of seventy change with the increase in needs for the church.

This means there are 12 apostles in the Quorum of the Twelve, and three more apostles in the Quorum of the First Presidency. That makes 15 apostles in all. Apostles advance based on tenure in the quorum. The senior apostle currently serves as the President of the Church, THE Prophet. The prophet calls two members of the quorum to be his counselors in the Quorum of the First Presidency. The apostle that is next in seniority, based on the order in which they were called to the apostleship, is the president of the quorum of the twelve apostles. We refer to him as President (_____). If the second most senior apostle is called into the quorum of the first presidency then the third most senior apostle becomes the Acting President of the Quorum of the Twelve Apostles. We call him President as well. There are always four men we refer to as President: the Prophet, each of his two counselors, and the president of the quorum of the twelve.

• How have you been blessed through the service of Melchizedek Priesthood holders?

The Quorums of the Aaronic Priesthood

The Lord has instructed that the holders of the priesthood be organized into quorums. A quorum is a body of brethren holding the same priesthood office.

There are three quorums of the Aaronic Priesthood:
1. The deacons quorum, which consists of up to 12 deacons (see D&C 107:85). The presidency of the deacons quorum is called by the bishop from among the quorum members.
2. The teachers quorum, which consists of up to 24 teachers (see D&C 107:86). The presidency of the teachers quorum is called by the bishop from among the quorum members.
3. The priests quorum, which consists of up to 48 priests (see D&C 107:87–88). It is presided over by the bishop of the ward to which the quorum belongs. The bishop is a high priest and thus also belongs to the high priests quorum.

A quorum is meant to be a brotherhood of those with the same calling in the priesthood. They are to love and support each other and help to bear each other's burdens.

Whenever the number specified for a quorum is exceeded, the quorum may be divided.

The Quorums of the Melchizedek Priesthood

At the general Church level, the members of the First Presidency form a quorum, as do the Twelve Apostles. The Seventies are also organized in quorums.

You guessed it, each quorum of the seventy hold up to seventy men.

At the local Church level—in wards and branches and stakes and districts—Melchizedek Priesthood bearers are organized into the following quorums:

Elders Quorum

Each elders quorum "is instituted for standing ministers; nevertheless they may travel, yet they are ordained to be standing ministers" (D&C 124:137). They do most of their work near their homes. The quorum is to consist of up to 96 elders, presided over by a quorum presidency. When this number is exceeded, the quorum may be divided.

When there is no high priest present to conduct or preside over a meeting then the Elder's Quorum President or one of his counselors may step in and preside or conduct the meeting.

High Priests Quorum

Each quorum includes all high priests residing within the boundaries of a stake, including patriarchs and bishops. The stake president and his counselors are the presidency of this quorum. The high priests in each ward are organized into a group with a group leader.

There is no upper limit on the number of high priests in a quorum. Because the Stake Presidency is the head of the stake quorum of high priests, each ward has a high priest group leader who is assisted by two assistants. The high priest group leader is different from a quorum president in that he does not hold any keys of administration. Only presidents hold keys. The last sentence in the paragraph to the left is no longer valid. As of April, 2018 General Conference, all high priests in the ward meet with the Elder's Quorum as a body of priesthood holders. Currently, the only active members of the high priest quorum are the members of the bishopric, stake presidency, and the stake patriarch. But even these attend the Elder's Quorum each Sunday. The Stake President is still the president of the Stake High Priests Quorum.

Importance of Priesthood Quorums

• How can priesthood quorums help strengthen individuals and families?

When ordained to the priesthood, a man or boy automatically becomes a member of a priesthood quorum. From then on through life, it is expected that he will hold membership in a quorum of the priesthood according to his office (see Boyd K. Packer, "What Every Elder Should Know—and Every Sister as Well: A Primer on Principles of Priesthood Government," Ensign, Feb. 1993, 9).

If a priesthood quorum functions properly, the members of the quorum are encouraged, blessed, fellowshipped, and taught the gospel by their leaders. Even though a man may be released from Church callings, such as teacher, quorum president, bishop, high councilor, or stake president, his membership in his quorum does not change. Membership

In a properly functioning quorum, the brotherhood among the members of the quorum should provide physical, emotional, social, and spiritual support to each member of the quorum. These men serve together, pray together, work together, and conduct God's business together. It is a sacred brotherhood when the quorum in a quorum of the priesthood should be regarded as a sacred privilege.

Auxiliaries to the Priesthood
• How can auxiliaries to the priesthood help strengthen individuals and families?

All organizations in the Church work under the direction of priesthood leaders and help them carry out the work of the Lord. For example, the presidencies in a ward's Relief Society, Young Women, Young Men, Primary, and Sunday School organizations serve under the direction of the bishopric. These organizations are called auxiliaries to the priesthood.

• What role do you have as an individual in helping priesthood quorums and auxiliaries be successful?

Additional Scriptures
• Alma 13:1–19 (manner in which men were ordained to the priesthood)
• Matthew 16:19; D&C 68:12 (Apostles given priesthood keys and power; what they seal on earth is sealed in heaven)
• D&C 20:38–67 (duties of elders, priests, teachers, deacons)
• D&C 84; 107 (revelations on the priesthood)
• 1 Corinthians 12:14–31 (all offices of the priesthood are important)

understands its true role in the lives of the members of the quorum.

The auxiliaries perform for the members of each auxiliary what the quorum does for the quorum members. The primary is in charge of teaching the little children and helping them feel close to the Savior. The auxiliaries are meant to strengthen what is already being taught in the home. They are not meant to be the only source of teaching of gospel principles to the members of the church. They are specifically meant to be support structures to what happens in the individual homes.

Chapter 15
The Lord's Covenant People

Gospel Principles, (2011), 81–86

The Nature of Covenants

• What is a covenant? Why are Latter-day Saints called a covenant people?

From the beginning, the Lord has made covenants with His children on earth. When His people make covenants (or promises) with Him, they know what He expects of them and what blessings they may expect from Him. They can better carry out His work on earth. The people who covenant with the Lord and with whom the Lord makes covenants are known as the Lord's covenant people. Members of the Church are part of the Lord's covenant people.

Within the gospel, a covenant means a sacred agreement or mutual promise between God and a person or a group of people. In making a covenant, God promises a blessing for obedience to particular commandments. He sets the terms of His covenants, and He reveals these terms to His prophets. If we choose to obey the terms of the covenant, we receive promised blessings. If we choose not to obey, He withholds the blessings, and in some instances a penalty also is given.

For example, when we join the Church we make several covenants with God (see chapter 20 in this book). We covenant with the Savior at baptism to take upon ourselves His name. He promises that "as many as repent and are baptized in my name, which is Jesus Christ, and endure to the end, the same shall be saved" (D&C 18:22). We covenant with the Lord as we partake of the sacrament (see chapter 23 in this book). We promise to take His name upon ourselves, to remember Him, and to obey His commandments. We are promised that the Holy Spirit will be with us. (See D&C 20:77–79.) When we receive temple ordinances, we make other sacred covenants and are promised exaltation for faithful obedience (see D&C 132; see also chapter 47 in this book).

God has also made special covenants with particular persons or groups. He made special covenants with Adam, Enoch, Noah, the children of Israel, and Lehi (see Moses 6:31–36, 52; Genesis 9:9–17; Exodus 19:5–6; 2 Nephi 1). He made a special covenant with Abraham and his descendants that blesses members of the Church and all nations of the earth today.

• Think about the covenants you have made with God and the blessings He has promised you for keeping these covenants.

When the Lord wants to bless His people He makes a contract with them. In exchange for their adherence to the terms of his promise He will give them certain blessings or abilities. All covenants are designed to bring us joy and bless our lives in a way we could not achieve on our own. This means that being a covenant maker with God is a special treat because it makes possible blessings not available anywhere else in the world.

The covenant made with Abraham is referred to in a couple of different ways. It is known as the Abrahamic covenant, and also as the New and Everlasting Covenant of Marriage. This is the covenant we make in the temple that allows us to be married for all eternity, and not just for time while we are in mortality. The covenant of eternal marriage is the highest covenant in the temple ceremony.

The main blessing promised us when we are baptized and confirmed a member of God's Church is the gift of the Holy Ghost. He promises to send that member of the

God's Covenant with Abraham and His Descendants

• What is the Abrahamic covenant?

Abraham, an Old Testament prophet, was a very righteous man (see the picture in this chapter). He refused to worship his father's idols. He kept all of the Lord's commandments. Because of Abraham's righteousness, the Lord made a covenant with him and his descendants.

The Lord promised Abraham that he would have numberless descendants. He promised that all of them would be entitled to receive the gospel, the blessings of the priesthood, and all of the ordinances of exaltation. These descendants, through the power of the priesthood, would carry the gospel to all nations. Through them, all the families of the earth would be blessed (see Abraham 2:11). God further promised that if they were righteous He would establish His covenant with all generations of Abraham's children (see Genesis 17:4–8).

• How do the commandments and promises in the Abrahamic covenant apply to us? (Consider how this question applies in different settings, such as at home, in the workplace, in the community, or as missionaries.)

Members of the Church Are a Covenant People
• What blessings and responsibilities come to God's covenant people today?

For teachers: You can help class members or family members think more deeply about a question by giving them time to ponder. After they have had enough time, ask for their responses.

The blood descendants of Abraham are not the only people whom God calls His covenant people. In speaking to Abraham, God said, "As many as receive this Gospel shall be called after thy name, and shall be accounted thy seed [lineage], and shall rise up and bless thee, as their father" (Abraham 2:10). Thus, two groups of people are included in the covenant made with Abraham: (1) Abraham's righteous blood descendants and (2) those adopted into his lineage by accepting and living the gospel of Jesus Christ (see 2 Nephi 30:2).

Godhead to teach us, comfort us, guide us, and open our minds to truth. What a wonderful promise!

We usually read references to the Abrahamic covenant in the scriptures when they refer to the God of Abraham, Isaac, and Jacob. God renewed the covenant made with Abraham with each of his descendants to show that the covenant really is meant to be available to all of Abraham's posterity. This covenant is available only to those of Abraham's family. Fortunately, all those who make covenants with the Lord are spiritually adopted into Abraham's lineage if they are not already a blood descendant. So in effect, the blessings of this covenant are available to anyone, anywhere who is willing to make and keep this covenant with God.

There is a pattern of families in the gospel of Christ. Adam and Eve were married by the Lord before they left the garden of Eden. Noah and his family were the only ones saved in the flood. The blessings of eternal families came through the family of a righteous man and woman, the family of Abraham and Sarah. Even though the blessings are available to all the people of the earth who are willing to accept these covenants, the Lord brings them into a family, the family of Abraham, a righteous man. How fitting, since the purpose of the Abrahamic covenant is to create eternal families.

When we are baptized into the Church, we enter into the covenant the Lord made with Abraham, Isaac, and Jacob (see Galatians 3:26–29). If we are obedient, we inherit the blessings of that covenant. We have the right to receive help and guidance from the Holy Ghost. Worthy males have the right to hold the priesthood. Families can receive the blessings of the priesthood. We can gain eternal life in the celestial kingdom. There are no greater blessings than these.

Along with the blessings we receive as the Lord's covenant people, we have great responsibilities. The Lord promised Abraham that through his descendants the gospel would be taken to all the earth. We are fulfilling this responsibility through the full-time missionary program of the Church and the missionary work done by the members. This opportunity to preach the gospel to all the world belongs only to the Lord's Church and His covenant people.

As the Lord's covenant people, we should keep His commandments. The Lord said, "I, the Lord, am bound when ye do what I say; but when ye do not what I say, ye have no promise" (D&C 82:10). If we reject our covenant after accepting the gospel, the covenant becomes void and we will stand condemned before God (see D&C 132:4). He has said: "Refrain from sin, lest sore judgments fall upon your heads. For of him unto whom much is given much is required; and he who sins against the greater light shall receive the greater condemnation" (D&C 82:2–3).

The main blessings of the Abrahamic covenant are as follows:

Baptism, which is the gateway ordinance to the Celestial kingdom.

Gift of the Holy Ghost, which is the member of the Godhead who is sent to teach us everything we need to know and learn to become worthy to live with God again someday.

Priesthood - the authority to act in God's name. All the blessings of the covenant are available only because of the presence of God's authority through the priesthood power.

Temple ordinances, which include eternal marriage and the creation of eternal families.

Do you see the pattern here? All these covenants are meant only for those who want to go to the Celestial kingdom. If you are not interested in the Celestial kingdom, in living with Christ and our Father in Heaven, and with your eternal family, then you have no need of all these covenants. These covenants are meant and designed to groom us for a celestial inheritance.

If we are to receive the blessings of the Celestial kingdom and become like God then we will have to learn to live like Him. This is where the responsibilities come in. With great privileges come great responsibilities. We, as covenant makers, are held to a higher standard than anyone else in the world because we are being given greater blessings than any other people in the world. One of the primary responsibilities of this covenant is to help spread the gospel message of Christ to all of God's children. This is what we do when we engage in missionary work. We are sharing Christ's message of salvation for the rest of God's family.

Even though other Christian churches do missionary work, they do not have the Lord's priesthood, nor are they covenant makers or heirs to the Celestial kingdom. That responsibility is ours alone because we share in the responsibilities of the Abrahamic covenant.

Making a contract with God is a serious thing. At least it is to Him. As pointed out in the lesson (to the left) breakers of the covenant are not only left without any promise of blessings, but they also enter condemnation from the Lord for violating the covenants they made with Him.

The covenants of the Abrahamic family line are the highest covenants we can make with God. As such they carry with them both the highest blessings of joy and the highest punishments for violating the covenants. The Lord will not be mocked. To enter into a covenant relationship with Him then violate that covenant is a serious matter. But the good news is that if you have no intention of baling on the covenants you made then you have only joy in the eternal worlds to look forward to.

The New and Everlasting Covenant

• What do we promise to do when we accept the gospel? What blessings does Heavenly Father give us as we keep these promises?

The fulness of the gospel is called the new and everlasting covenant. It includes the covenants made at baptism, during the sacrament, in the temple, and at any other time. The Lord calls it everlasting because it is ordained by an everlasting God and because the covenant will never be changed. He gave this same covenant to Adam, Enoch, Noah, Abraham, and other prophets. In this sense it is not new. But the Lord calls it new because each time the gospel is restored after being taken from the earth, it is new to the people who receive it (see Jeremiah 31:31–34; Ezekiel 37:26).

When we accept the new and everlasting covenant, we agree to repent, be baptized, receive the Holy Ghost, receive our endowments, receive the covenant of marriage in the temple, and follow and obey Christ to the end of our lives. As we keep our covenants, our Heavenly Father promises us that we will receive exaltation in the celestial kingdom (see D&C 132:20–24; see also chapter 47 in this book).

The greatness of that promise is hard for mortals to understand. The commandments He gives are for our benefit, and as we are faithful we may forever share the blessings and beauties of heaven and earth. We may live in His presence and partake of His love, compassion, power, greatness, knowledge, wisdom, glory, and dominions.

Up to this point I have made it sound almost ominous to be brave enough to accept the covenants that make up the new and everlasting covenant. But look at how simple it actually is. When we get baptized we promise to be good to each other, to remember the Lord and try our best to be a good representative of Christ wherever we are each day. We also promise to care for the poor and the needy. That's not so hard, now is it?

The help God gives us is in the Holy Ghost and the sacrament. By repenting each week so we take the sacrament worthily, and by learning to follow the promptings from the Holy Ghost we become better people. Over time we become more Christlike. The Lord knows we will make mistakes along the way. He has built in mercy and helps to give us hope and to lift us up along our path. Yes, the consequences of these covenants are eternal in duration, but the rewards are worth every effort we make on our part to be worthy of those blessings in the end.

• What does being the Lord's covenant people have to do with how we dress, act, and keep the commandments of God?

Additional Scriptures and Other Sources

• 1 Peter 2:9–10 (peculiar people)
• D&C 54:4–6 (effects of covenants kept and broken)
• D&C 132:7 (covenants made by proper authority)
• D&C 133:57–60 (purpose of covenants)
• D&C 35:24 (promises for obedience to covenants)
• Hebrews 8:6 (Jesus Christ is the mediator of a better covenant)
• Bible Dictionary, "Covenant," 651

Chapter 16

The Church of Jesus Christ in Former Times

Gospel Principles, (2011), 87–93

Some Features That Identify the Church of Jesus Christ

"We believe in the same organization that existed in the Primitive Church, namely, apostles, prophets, pastors, teachers, evangelists, and so forth" (Articles of Faith 1:6).

Jesus established His Church when He was on the earth. It was called the Church of Jesus Christ (see 3 Nephi 27:8), and the members were called Saints (see Ephesians 2:19–20).

For teachers: Consider inviting each member of your family or class to study one of the six features that identify the Church—the italicized headings such as Revelation and Authority from God. (In large classes, some members will be assigned the same feature. In families and small classes, some members may be assigned more than one feature.) When they have had time to study, invite them to discuss what they have learned.

Revelation

When Jesus established His Church, He personally instructed and directed its leaders. He, in turn, received His instructions from His Father in Heaven. (See Hebrews 1:1–2.) Thus the Church of Jesus Christ was directed by God and not by men. Jesus taught His followers that revelation was the "rock" upon which He would build His Church (see Matthew 16:16–18).

Before Jesus ascended into heaven after His Resurrection, He told His Apostles, "I am with you alway, even unto the end of the world" (Matthew 28:20). True to His word, He continued to guide them from heaven. He sent the Holy Ghost to be a comforter and a revelator to them (see Luke 12:12; John 14:26). He spoke to Saul in a vision (see Acts 9:3–6). He revealed to Peter that the gospel should be taught not only to the Jews but to the whole world (see Acts 10). He revealed many glorious truths to John, which are written in the book of Revelation. The New Testament records many other ways in which Jesus revealed His will to guide His Church and enlighten His disciples.

Authority from God

The ordinances and principles of the gospel cannot be administered and taught without the priesthood. The Father gave this authority to Jesus Christ (see Hebrews 5:4–6),

An important side note: A feature is the same as a function. What you call that function is not as important as what that function does. For example, in one generation the one responsible for the welfare of the congregation is called an evangelist, and in another generation that same position is called a patriarch. If the function of the evangelist and the patriarch are the same then that church still has the same feature in both generations.

Some have mistakenly believed that Jesus built His church on a person, Peter, whose name meant stone. But Jesus would never build and base His church on a human. He built his church on principles of righteousness. In this case, the church is built on the rock of revelation. Without revelation the Lord's Church cannot function or stand. It requires ongoing revelation to exist. That is the way Jesus designed it.

Jesus could not be with the Church "unto the end of the world" if all they had was their memory of what He had said while in mortality. Too much was happening and too many changes were coming about in the world. They needed their Lord's constant guidance, which He gave them through the Holy Ghost in the way of revelation.

Notice that Jesus continued to give the leaders of His Church revelations that taught them what they needed to do in order to direct the Saints to overcome their trials and difficult circumstances.

Jesus set the pattern for how the Church would be run through the priesthood. God chose Jesus. Jesus chose the apostles. The apostles, under the direction of Jesus, through the Holy Ghost, chose other leaders and filled positions and callings within the church. We do not who in turn ordained His Apostles and gave them the power and authority of the priesthood (see Luke 9:1–2; Mark 3:14). He reminded them, "Ye have not chosen me, but I have chosen you, and ordained you" (John 15:16).

That there might be order in His Church, Jesus gave the greatest responsibility and authority to the Twelve Apostles. He appointed Peter chief Apostle and gave him the keys to seal blessings both on earth and in heaven (see Matthew 16:19). Jesus also ordained other officers with specific duties to perform. After He ascended into heaven, the pattern of appointment and ordination was continued. Others were ordained to the priesthood by those who had already received that authority. Jesus made it known through the Holy Ghost that He approved of those ordinations (see Acts 1:24).

The Church Organization

The Church of Jesus Christ was a carefully organized unit. It was compared to a building that was "built upon the foundation of the apostles and prophets, Jesus Christ himself being the chief corner stone" (Ephesians 2:20).

Jesus appointed other priesthood leaders to assist the Apostles in the work of the ministry. He sent officers called Seventies in pairs to preach the gospel (see Luke 10:1). Other officers in the Church were evangelists (patriarchs), pastors (presiding leaders), high priests, elders, bishops, priests, teachers, and deacons (see chapter 14 in this book). These officers were all necessary to do missionary work, perform ordinances, and instruct and inspire Church members. These officers helped the members come to a "unity of the faith, and of the knowledge of the Son of God" (Ephesians 4:13).

The Bible does not tell us everything about the priesthood or the organization and government of the Church. However, enough of the Bible has been preserved to show the beauty and perfection of the Church organization. The Apostles were commanded to go into all the world and preach (see Matthew 28:19–20). They could not stay in any one city to supervise new converts. Therefore, local priesthood leaders were called and ordained, and the Apostles presided over them. The Apostles and other Church leaders visited and wrote letters to the various branches. Thus, our New Testament contains letters written by Paul, Peter, James, John, and Jude, giving counsel and instruction to the local priesthood leaders.

The New Testament shows that this Church organization was intended to continue. For example, the death of Judas left only eleven Apostles. Soon after Jesus had ascended into heaven, the eleven Apostles met together to choose someone to take the place of Judas. Through revelation from the Holy Ghost, they chose Matthias. (See Acts

choose the callings we want. Instead, we are called by those in authority over us to serve in positions within the church. That is the eternal pattern.

After Jesus left the apostles to guide the Church, they had to rely on revelation and inspiration (pretty much the same thing) to know who to call to fill vacancies in the positions of the church. They relied on the Holy Ghost to do this. The Holy Ghost is the great revelator. His purpose is to reveal truth and to testify of God and Christ and to teach us all how to return to our heavenly home. When Jesus was with the apostles they did not have the gift of the Holy Ghost. He did not enter into the Church until the Day of Pentecost. Ever after that day it has been the Holy Ghost who connects all the Saints with the will of Christ and the Father.

Often times when we think of the ministry of Jesus we think only of Jesus and the apostles. But the church Jesus set up had many positions in it. Every position had a purpose and filled a need for the spiritual welfare of the members of the church.

The Apostles, as ones sent forth to the world to testify of Christ, couldn't do what they were called to do and still manage the needs of the growing church. The Saints were divided up into congregations or churches. Each one needed leaders to watch over and teach the Saints. As you read the letters of the Apostles to the Saints in various places through Asia Minor, notice that the letters are addressed to the Saints through their leaders. The letter went to the leaders, who in turn, taught the doctrine to the members of their respective churches.

The Apostles had been taught by Jesus that a great apostasy would take place, but even knowing it was going to happen, the Church was set up as though it would last forever. The timing of the apostasy was not known, so they worked as though it was not going to happen for a

1:23–26.) Jesus had set a pattern for twelve Apostles to govern the Church. It seemed clear that the organization was to continue as He had established it.

First Principles and Ordinances

The Apostles taught two basic principles: faith in the Lord Jesus Christ and repentance. After new converts had faith in Jesus Christ as the Son of God and their Redeemer and had repented of their sins, they received two ordinances: baptism by immersion and the laying on of hands for the gift of the Holy Ghost (see Acts 19:1–6). These were the first principles and ordinances of the gospel. Jesus had taught, "Except a man be born of water and of the Spirit, he cannot enter into the kingdom of God" (John 3:5).

Ordinances Performed for the Dead

Jesus has provided for everyone to hear the gospel, whether on earth or after death. Between His death and Resurrection, Jesus went among the spirits of those who had died. He organized missionary work among those who were dead. He appointed righteous messengers and gave them power to teach the gospel to all the spirits of people who had died. This gave them an opportunity to accept the gospel. (See 1 Peter 3:18–20; 4:6; D&C 138.) Living members of His Church then performed ordinances in behalf of the dead (see 1 Corinthians 15:29). Ordinances such as baptism and confirmation must be done on earth.

Spiritual Gifts

All faithful members of the Church were entitled to receive gifts of the Spirit. These were given to them according to their individual needs, capacities, and assignments. Some of these gifts were faith, including the power to heal and to be healed; prophecy; and visions. (The gifts of the Spirit are discussed in more detail in chapter 22.) Spiritual gifts always exist in the true Church of Jesus Christ (see 1 Corinthians 12:4–11; Moroni 10:8–18; D&C 46:8–29). Jesus told His disciples that these signs or spiritual gifts always follow them that believe (see Mark 16:17–18). Many of His disciples performed miracles, prophesied, or beheld visions through the power of the Holy Ghost.

• Why does the Church of Jesus Christ need these six features?

long, long time. For this reason, as one member died or left the church another was called by revelation to take his place.

The gospel contains all the laws and ordinances needed for us to return to live with our Father in Heaven. The most basic and fundamental of these laws and ordinances is faith and repentance, and then baptism and the receipt of the Holy Ghost. These are the most basic and necessary of all the principles of the gospel and the most fundamental of the ordinances. The focus of the Apostles is to get the world to do these things. The local leaders of the Church will help us prepare for the blessings of the temple and will help us grow beyond these fundamentals, but everyone has to work through the fundamental first before moving on to other principles and ordinances.

God requires the same thing for salvation from each of us, whether in mortality or out of mortality. The problem is that most of His children weren't in mortality when the gospel message was available to be taught. This is why Jesus had to set up missionary work in the spirit world after His crucifixion. He needed to send His priesthood leaders in to preach to those who left mortality without having had the gospel preached to them.

But once the dead accept the gospel, how are they to be baptized, which is an earthly ordinance? The answer is in the temple practice of baptizing living people in behalf of those who have already lived on earth, but now cannot be baptized for themselves. This practice of baptisms for the dead was practiced in the original church. This is why we do family history work. It is to identify our family members who need to have this saving work done for them in the temples.

Spiritual gifts have always existed among those who have faith in Christ. If the gifts stop it is because faith in Christ has ceased to be.

Here are the six features of the Lord's Church:
1. Revelation
2. Authority from God
3. Church organization
4. First principles and ordinances

5. Ordinances performed for the dead
6. Spiritual gifts

The Church of Jesus Christ in the Americas

After Jesus was resurrected, He visited the people in the Americas and organized His Church among them, teaching the people for three days and then returning often for some time thereafter (see 3 Nephi 11–28). Then He left them and ascended into heaven. For over 200 years they lived righteously and were among the happiest people whom God had created (see 4 Nephi 1:16).

As wonderful as the miracles of the New Testament are, the miracles Jesus performed for those in the Americas were even more amazing. Read 3 Nephi 11 - 28. These chapters will touch your heart over the tenderness of Jesus for His people.

Apostasy from the True Church

• What does the term apostasy mean?

Apostasy is to desert or depart from one's religion or principles. It is to abandon that which you have been taught and turn away from it.

Throughout history, evil people have tried to destroy the work of God. This happened while the Apostles were still alive and supervising the young, growing Church. Some members taught ideas from their old pagan or Jewish beliefs instead of the simple truths taught by Jesus. Some rebelled openly. In addition, there was persecution from outside the Church. Church members were tortured and killed for their beliefs. One by one, the Apostles were killed or otherwise taken from the earth. Because of wickedness and apostasy, the apostolic authority and priesthood keys were also taken from the earth. The organization that Jesus Christ had established no longer existed, and confusion resulted. More and more error crept into Church doctrine, and soon the dissolution of the Church was complete. The period of time when the true Church no longer existed on earth is called the Great Apostasy.

The letters from the apostles to the leaders throughout the church make frequent reference to those who were deliberately and constantly trying to destroy the church from within. They would pretend to be Jews from Jerusalem, claim authority then preach false doctrine to lead the members astray. They tried to get the members of the church, especially those who were not Jews, to live Jewish laws and lifestyle. They perverted the truth wherever they could. The apostles were constantly correcting the Saints over these perversions of doctrine and practice.

When the Apostles were alive they could regulate the beliefs of the Church, but as they were killed and not able to assemble to replace those who had died, there was less and less ability to correct the spiritual course of the Church. Finally, with the death of the last Apostle, there was no one left to correct the false doctrine and put a stop to false practices. The movement toward spiritual apostasy was in full force, with nothing to stop it.

Soon pagan beliefs dominated the thinking of those called Christians. The Roman emperor adopted this false Christianity as the state religion. This church was very different from the church Jesus organized. It taught that God was a being without form or substance.

These people lost the understanding of God's love for us. They did not know that we are His children. They did not understand the purpose of life. Many of the ordinances were changed because the priesthood and revelation were no longer on the earth.

Remember that the Apostles held the keys, the right to administer the priesthood. When they died those rights to revelation died with them. There was no more revelation in the church. It became the church of men, not of God.

The emperor chose his own leaders and sometimes called them by the same titles used by priesthood leaders in the true Church of Christ. There were no Apostles or other priesthood leaders with power from God, and there were no spiritual gifts. The prophet Isaiah had foreseen this condition, prophesying, "The earth also is defiled under the inhabitants thereof; because they have transgressed the laws, changed the ordinance, broken the everlasting covenant" (Isaiah 24:5). It was the Church of Jesus Christ no longer; it was a church of men. Even the name had been changed. In the Americas, apostasy also occurred (see 4 Nephi).

A Restoration Foretold

• What prophecies in the Old and New Testaments foretold the Restoration?

God had foreseen the Apostasy and prepared for the gospel to be restored. The Apostle Peter spoke of this to the Jews: "He shall send Jesus Christ, which before was preached unto you: whom the heaven must receive until the times of restitution of all things, which God hath spoken by the mouth of all his holy prophets since the world began" (Acts 3:20–21).

John the Revelator had also foreseen the time when the gospel would be restored. He said, "I saw another angel fly in the midst of heaven, having the everlasting gospel to preach unto them that dwell on the earth, and to every nation, and kindred, and tongue, and people" (Revelation 14:6).

Just as the Apostles had prophesied of the apostasy that would come to the church, they also prophesied that in the last days the Savior would restore the Church to the earth once again. In that day He would restore all that was lost and all the covenants God had ever made with His children would be revealed once again.

• Why was the Restoration necessary?

The Lord needs a people in place and prepared to meet Him when He comes the second time. His kingdom needs to be set up and already running so when He returns the kingdom can be expanded and not have to be set up from scratch. The restoration of Christ's church through Joseph Smith began the final dispensation of time. This is the restoration of Christ's Church on the earth and will not be taken from the earth ever again. This time, unlike every other time God has revealed His word to His children, His people will not reject Him.

• Consider the blessings that have come to you because the Church of Jesus Christ has been restored to the earth.

Additional Scriptures

• Ephesians 2:19 (members called Saints)
• 1 Corinthians 12:12–31 (Church likened to a body)
• Luke 10:1; Acts 14:23; Titus 1:7; 1 Timothy 2:7 (officers of the Church identified)
• John 8:26–29 (the Father directs Jesus)
• Luke 9:1; James 1:17; 5:14–15 (spiritual gifts)
• Mosiah 27:13 (apostasy comes as a result of transgression)
• 2 Peter 2:1; Matthew 24:9–12; John 16:1–3; Amos 8:11; 2 Thessalonians 2:3–4 (Apostasy predicted)
• Daniel 2:44–45; Matthew 24:14; Acts 3:19–21; Micah 4:1; Isaiah 2:2–4 (Restoration predicted)
PREVIOUS

Chapter 17

The Church of Jesus Christ Today

Gospel Principles, (2011), 94–100

This opening question needs to be understood in order to understand the need for the restoration. The apostasy wasn't a mistake, it was a deliberate sabotage of Christ's Church and doctrine by those who fought against the Church. Satan used man's thirst for power and position to do the rest of the damage.

The Church of Jesus Christ Was Taken from the Earth

• Why was the Church of Jesus Christ removed from the earth shortly after the Savior's death and Resurrection?

When Jesus lived on the earth, He established His Church, the only true Church. He organized His Church so the truths of the gospel could be taught to all people and the ordinances of the gospel could be administered correctly with authority. Through this organization, Christ could bring the blessings of salvation to mankind.

The names of the offices used in the original church may have been different from what we call them today. They spoke a different language, and the names of callings in the church we know of today are translations in the 1600s of the old languages used to record the events of the original church. The name of a position in the church doesn't change the function of the position. Both the original Church and the restored Church have the same basic functions needed to save mankind, namely apostles and prophets, etc.

After the Savior ascended into heaven, men changed the ordinances and doctrines that He and His Apostles had established. Because of apostasy, there was no direct revelation from God. The true Church was no longer on the earth. Men organized different churches that claimed to be true but taught conflicting doctrines. There was much confusion and contention over religion. The Lord had foreseen these conditions of apostasy, saying there would be "a famine in the land, not a famine of bread, nor a thirst for water, but of hearing the words of the Lord. … They shall … seek the word of the Lord, and shall not find it" (Amos 8:11–12).

The Jews in Jerusalem actually sent people out to the various churches to infiltrate them and try to destroy them from the inside. The sect of Jesus believers was a real threat to the Jewish leaders. It undermined their power base. So not only did all the churches have to deal with converted pagans who were still clinging, in many ways, to their pagan beliefs, but they had Jews who were trying to destroy the church by leading people astray as well. With the death of the apostles, who were the only ones capable of setting straight all doctrinal questions, the church was bound to be led astray eventually. All miracles ceased. There was no more gift of the Holy Ghost, because they lost the priesthood power. They could perform the duties in their offices of the priesthood, but they no longer had the keys or rights from God to administer in His priesthood. Those keys were held by the apostles, and they were dead. Without the keys of the priesthood no one had the authority to baptize or give the gift of the Holy Ghost.

• How does the famine spoken of in Amos 8:11–12 affect people?

Spiritual nourishment, like physical food, is something everyone craves, even if they can't identify it as such. Without the truth to bring comfort to our souls, we search and search, looking for someone who can teach us what will help us have confidence and direction in our lives. There are those who will gladly tell us what they think we want to hear, for a price. So churches are born, and people wander from church to church seeking the truth, but generally leaving unfulfilled and unsatisfied in the end. Nothing can satisfy our souls like the pure truth found only in Christ's gospel.

The Lord Promised to Restore His True Church

• What were some of the conditions in the world that prepared the way for the Restoration of the gospel?

After centuries of spiritual and intellectual darkness (interestingly referred to as the dark ages), the Renaissance happened. This was a rebirth of enlightenment in all areas. Intellectual advances were made and celebrated, a spiritual reawakening took place throughout Europe and elsewhere. People began to question the church and challenge its teachings, claiming that what was being taught was not doctrine taught in the Bible. People began to look forward to the day that God would once again reveal His truth and restore His original church. But a land that was free to practice religion without persecution was needed. When America, the United States was born, finally there was a country that guaranteed religious liberty, a place that would be safe for the Lord to restore His church once again.

The Savior promised to restore His Church in the latter days. He said, "I will proceed to do a marvellous work among this people, even a marvellous work and a wonder" (Isaiah 29:14).

For many years people lived in spiritual darkness. About 1,700 years after Christ, people were becoming more and more interested in knowing the truth about God and religion. Some of them could see that the gospel Jesus taught was no longer on the earth. Some recognized that there was no revelation and no true authority and that the Church that Christ organized did not exist on the earth. The time had arrived for the Church of Jesus Christ to be restored to the earth.

• In what ways is the Restoration of the fulness of the gospel a "marvellous work"?

The world had been in spiritual darkness and ignorance for so many centuries that it was going to take a long string of miracles for the Lord to restore His church once again. Satan had prejudiced the people against anyone who might claim revelation. So even though many wanted the true church restored, they did not understand that revelation is the backbone of that restoration.

New Revelation from God

• When Joseph Smith received his First Vision, what did he learn about God?

In the spring of 1820, one of the most important events in the history of the world occurred. The time had come for the marvelous work and wonder of which the Lord had spoken. As a young boy, Joseph Smith wanted to know which of all the churches was the true Church of Jesus Christ. He went into the woods near his home and prayed humbly and intently to his Heavenly Father, asking which church he should join. On that morning a miraculous thing happened. Heavenly Father and Jesus Christ appeared to Joseph Smith. The Savior told him not to join any church because the true Church was not on the earth. He also said that the creeds of present churches were "an abomination in his sight" (Joseph Smith—History 1:19; see also verses

One of Satan's top priorities in perverting the doctrines of Christ's church was to destroy their understanding of who God is. Without a proper understanding of who they worship, the people could not exercise proper faith, preventing miracles and answers to most prayers. By destroying the definition of God Satan put the people in chains that bound them spiritually.

The power behind Joseph's first vision is that all the lies and deception about God and His nature were shattered. There was no someone with firsthand knowledge of the nature of God. Joseph could see for himself that God had a body. He could see that the Father and the Son were

7–18, 20). Beginning with this event, there was again direct revelation from the heavens. The Lord had chosen a new prophet. Since that time the heavens have not been closed. Revelation continues to this day through each of His chosen prophets. Joseph was to be the one to help restore the true gospel of Jesus Christ.

• Why was the First Vision one of the most important events in the history of the world?

two different people. The non-biblical doctrine of the Trinity was exposed for what it is, a false tradition that did not come from God. With that one simple visit Joseph knew more about God than any person then living.

The First Vision corrected more than 1700 years of false teachings. It also began the process of restoring the Savior's church again to the earth. This last dispensation is the last time the Lord will restore His truth to man before He comes to reign personally on the earth for a thousand years. The last dispensation has been prophesied about since the days of Adam. All the prophets have wished they could experience the blessings of those who would live just prior to Christ's second coming. They all wished they could be alive in our day and time.

Authority from God Was Restored
• Why was the restoration of the Aaronic and Melchizedek Priesthoods necessary?

In restoring the gospel, God again gave the priesthood to men. John the Baptist came in 1829 to confer the Aaronic Priesthood on Joseph Smith and Oliver Cowdery (see D&C 13; 27:8). Then Peter, James, and John, the presidency of the Church in ancient times, came and gave Joseph and Oliver the Melchizedek Priesthood and the keys of the kingdom of God (see D&C 27:12–13). Later, additional keys of the priesthood were restored by heavenly messengers such as Moses, Elias, and Elijah (see D&C 110:11–16). Through the Restoration, the priesthood was returned to the earth. Those who hold this priesthood today have the authority to perform ordinances such as baptism. They also have the authority to direct the Lord's kingdom on earth.

For teachers: Bearing testimony invites the Spirit. As part of this lesson, bear your testimony of the Restoration and give others the opportunity to do the same.

The backbone of Christ's Church is revelation. To have revelation you need the gift of the Holy Ghost, which can only be given by those who hold the Lord's priesthood.

We believe that we were foreordained by our Father in Heaven to perform certain tasks here in mortality. Many of the prophets were given the responsibility of overseeing certain parts of God's work in mortality. They were given the keys over that part of the gospel. John the Baptist held the keys, the rights to administer in the ordinance of baptism. Peter, James, and John were given the keys of the Melchizedek priesthood by the Savior. Moses, Elias, and Elijah all had specific keys. All of them needed to transfer those keys to Joseph Smith so he could rightfully perform all the ordinances and do all that was required to begin a new dispensation of the gospel. Revelation, through the priesthood power, made it possible for this transfer of priesthood keys.

Christ's Church Was Organized Again
• What events led to the organization of the Church on the earth again?

On April 6, 1830, the Savior again directed the organizing of His Church on the earth (see D&C 20:1). His Church is called The Church of Jesus Christ of Latter-day Saints (see D&C 115:4). Christ is the head of His Church today, just as He was in ancient times. The Lord has said that it is "the only true and living church upon the face of the whole earth, with which I, the Lord, am well pleased" (D&C 1:30).

From the day of the First Vision at the age of 14 until the day the Church was legally and officially organized, the Lord sent messengers to Joseph to teach him his responsibilities and to give him a better understanding of the gospel plan.

What makes this a living church is that the members are growing, maturing, allowing the church itself to grow and mature. As the Saints prepare themselves spiritually the Lord is able to reveal the next step in their progress. As the world becomes more wicked the Lord reveals to the prophet what the members of the Church need to do to stay safe from the temptations and sins of the world. It is revelation that gives the Church life.

Joseph Smith was sustained as prophet and "first elder" of the Church (see D&C 20:2–4). Later the First Presidency was organized, and he was sustained as President. When the Church was first organized, only the framework was set up. The organization would develop as the Church continued to grow.

The Church was organized with the same offices as were in the ancient Church. That organization included apostles, prophets, seventies, evangelists (patriarchs), pastors (presiding officers), high priests, elders, bishops, priests, teachers, and deacons. These same offices are in His Church today (see Articles of Faith 1:6).

A prophet, acting under the direction of the Lord, leads the Church. This prophet is also the President of the Church. He holds all the authority necessary to direct the Lord's work on earth (see D&C 107:65, 91). Two counselors assist the President. Twelve Apostles, who are special witnesses of the name of Jesus Christ, teach the gospel and regulate the affairs of the Church in all parts of the world. Other general officers of the Church with special assignments, including the Presiding Bishopric and the Quorums of the Seventy, serve under the direction of the First Presidency and the Twelve.

The offices of the priesthood include apostles, seventies, patriarchs, high priests, bishops, elders, priests, teachers, and deacons. These are the same offices that existed in the original Church.

The Church has grown much larger than it was in the days of Jesus. As it has grown, the Lord has revealed additional units of organization within the Church. When the Church is fully organized in an area, it has local divisions called stakes. A stake president and his two counselors preside over each stake. The stake has 12 high councilors who help do the Lord's work in the stake. Melchizedek Priesthood quorums are organized in the stake under the direction of the stake president (see chapter 14 in this book). Each stake is divided into smaller areas called wards. A bishop and his two counselors preside over each ward.

In areas of the world where the Church is developing, there are districts, which are like stakes. Districts are divided into smaller units called branches, which are like wards.

Important Truths Were Restored
• What important truths have been brought back with the Restoration of the Church?

The Church today teaches the same principles and performs the same ordinances as were performed in the days of Jesus. The first principles and ordinances of the gospel are faith in the Lord Jesus Christ, repentance,

All the members of the church in Joseph's day were new to the church. They had all come from either the Catholic church or a protestant church. Everyone was new to the teachings of Christ's gospel. It took time and effort for them to learn how the gospel worked, and to grow into a cohesive body of Saints.

Just as Joseph Smith held all the keys or rights to administer in the priesthood in all things, so too does the current prophet. The keys of the priesthood are still here and are being used by the prophet.

It shouldn't be surprising that the truths the Lord restored are vastly different from what the other churches teach. These truths were lost more than 1700 years ago. We should expect to be surprised occasionally by discovering what was lost or changed in the original church.

All throughout the New Testament, after Christ ascended to heaven, these four principles and ordinances of the gospel were taught almost exclusively by the apostles.

baptism by immersion, and the laying on of hands for the gift of the Holy Ghost (see Articles of Faith 1:4). These precious truths were returned in their fulness when the Church was restored.

Through the gift and power of God, Joseph Smith translated the Book of Mormon, which contains the plain and precious truths of the gospel. Many other revelations followed and have been recorded as scripture in the Doctrine and Covenants and the Pearl of Great Price (see chapter 10 in this book).

The Book of Mormon was prepared by the Lord over a two thousand year period as an instruction book for those of us living in the last days. He inspired the prophets to record key events and teachings that would be relevant to us in this dispensation of time. The book is meant to help keep us safe and prepare us for the trials of the last days.

Other important truths that the Lord restored include the following:
1. Our Heavenly Father is a real being with a tangible, perfected body of flesh and bones, and so is Jesus Christ. The Holy Ghost is a personage of spirit.
2. We existed in premortal life as spirit children of God.
3. The priesthood is necessary to administer the ordinances of the gospel.
4. We will be punished for our own sins and not for Adam's transgression.
5. Children do not need to be baptized until they are accountable (eight years old).
6. There are three kingdoms of glory in the heavens, and through the grace of the Lord Jesus Christ, people will be rewarded according to their actions on earth and according to the desires of their hearts.
7. Family relationships can be eternal through the sealing power of the priesthood.
8. Ordinances and covenants are required for salvation and are available for both the living and the dead.

• How have these truths influenced you and others?

The Church of Jesus Christ Will Never Be Destroyed
• What is the mission of the Church?

Since its restoration in 1830, The Church of Jesus Christ of Latter-day Saints has grown rapidly in membership. There are members in nearly every country in the world. The Church will continue to grow. As Christ said, "This Gospel of the Kingdom shall be preached in all the world, for a witness unto all nations" (Joseph Smith—Matthew 1:31). The Church will never again be taken from the earth. Its mission is to take the truth to every person. Thousands of years ago, the Lord said He would "set up a kingdom, which shall never be destroyed: and the kingdom shall not be left to other people, … and it shall stand for ever" (Daniel 2:44).

Do not be confused, the numbers of members of the Lord's Church will always be in the minority. We will never be in the majority until the Lord comes. But He has promised to protect us and help us, and if need be, fight for us.

• How have you helped in the work of the kingdom of God?

What can you do to continue this work?

Additional Scriptures

• Acts 3:19–21; Revelation 14:6; Daniel 2:44–45; Isaiah 2:2–4; 2 Nephi 3:6–15 (Restoration foretold)
• D&C 110; 128:19–21; 133:36–39, 57–58 (Restoration of the gospel)
• Ephesians 2:20 (Jesus Christ the cornerstone of the Church)
• D&C 20:38–67 (duties of officers of the Church)
• Matthew 24:14 (gospel to be preached to all nations)

Chapter 18

Faith in Jesus Christ

Gospel Principles, (2011), 101–6

What Is Faith?

For teachers: This chapter is organized under four section headings. Each heading is a question about faith. You could use these questions as a guide for your lesson. If the classroom setup allows for small group discussion, consider dividing class members into groups of four. Ask each group to divide the sections of the chapter among themselves. Then invite each person to do the following with his or her assigned section: (1) Read it. (2) Find scriptures that help answer the question in the section heading. (3) Think about personal experiences that relate to the section. (4) Share thoughts about the section with the other group members.

Faith in the Lord Jesus Christ is the first principle of the gospel. It is a spiritual gift, and it is necessary to our salvation. King Benjamin declared, "Salvation cometh to none … except it be through repentance and faith on the Lord Jesus Christ" (Mosiah 3:12).

Faith is a "hope for things which are not seen, which are true" (Alma 32:21; see also Hebrews 11:1). Faith is a principle of action and power that motivates our day-to-day activities.

Would we study and learn if we did not believe we could obtain wisdom and knowledge? Would we work each day if we did not hope that by doing so we could accomplish something? Would a farmer plant if he did not expect to harvest? Each day we act upon things we hope for when we cannot see the end result. This is faith. (See Hebrews 11:3.)

Many scriptural stories tell how great things were accomplished through faith.

By faith Noah built an ark and saved his family from the flood (see Hebrews 11:7). Moses parted the waters of the Red Sea (see Hebrews 11:29). Elijah called down fire from heaven (see 1 Kings 18:17–40). Nephi called for a famine (see Helaman 11:3–5). He also asked the Lord to end the famine (see Helaman 11:9–17). Seas have been calmed,

Spiritual gifts are abilities we receive because of the grace of God. No one is born with a huge endowment of faith already in place. Faith is something that we practice in small incremental steps. Some naturally start mortality with more faith than others, but we all have to learn to exercise faith. As we choose to use our faith the Lord grants us the ability to use more faith, and hence our capacity for faith grows.

Though belief is part of faith, faith is far more than just belief. Faith requires action and resolve. We refer to faith as a principle of power because as we exercise our faith we become stronger spiritually. Faith actually can cause things in the physical world to behave differently. By faith the prophets moved mountains and turned rivers in their courses. By faith they caused famines and pestilences, and by faith caused them to stop. Faith can heal and bring answers to prayers.

The key word in the paragraph to the left is "expectation." Why would anyone plant a seed if they did not expect it to grow? Why would we trust someone if we did not expect they were safe to trust? This expectation of a positive result is where our hope comes from.

visions opened, and prayers answered, all through the power of faith.

As we carefully study the scriptures, we learn that faith is a strong belief of truth within our souls that motivates us to do good. This causes us to ask: In whom should we have faith?

It is important to remember that trust in truth is faith, but trust in anything not based in truth is fantasy. Praying to God is exercising expectation and having hope in something that is true, therefore it will produce good results. But if I sprinkle myself with glitter, clap my hands and say I believe in fairies, no amount of jumping is going to get me to fly.

• Think about your everyday activities. What are things you act upon each day that you cannot see the end results of? How does faith move you to action?

Setting your alarm clock is an act of faith. Setting an appointment is an act of faith. Mailing a letter is an act of faith. Signing a contract is an act of faith. Trusting that what your friend just told you is true is an act of faith.

Why Should We Have Faith in Jesus Christ?
We must center our faith in the Lord Jesus Christ.

Why should we center our faith in Christ? Why not someone else? Let's face it, if we center our faith in a mortal sooner or later they will disappoint us. God, on the other hand, cannot lie or he would cease to be God. His honesty is one of the things that makes him completely trustworthy.

To have faith in Jesus Christ means to have such trust in Him that we obey whatever He commands. As we place our faith in Jesus Christ, becoming His obedient disciples, Heavenly Father will forgive our sins and prepare us to return to Him.

It takes practice and life lessons to learn for ourselves that we can trust the Lord to honor all his promises to us. The more we place our trust and faith in God, the more we can be forgiven of our sins. Faith is a principle of power only because it requires action on our part. We cannot place our faith in Christ without obeying His commandments. It is through this obedience that he is able to forgive us of our sins.

The Apostle Peter preached that "there is none other name under heaven given among men, whereby we must be saved" (Acts 4:12; see also Mosiah 3:17). Jacob taught that men must have "perfect faith in the Holy One of Israel [Jesus Christ], or they cannot be saved in the kingdom of God" (2 Nephi 9:23). Through faith in the Savior and through repentance, we make His Atonement fully effective in our lives. Through faith we can also receive strength to overcome temptations (see Alma 37:33).

Remember that faith placed in anything other than perfect reliability (Christ and God) will not be able to produce the level of trust/faith required for us to become the people we need to be in order to find salvation. Since we need faith to overcome weaknesses and temptation, our faith has to be in a power that is unassailable, without fault. Only God has that quality.

We cannot have faith in Jesus Christ without also having faith in our Heavenly Father. If we have faith in Them, we will also have faith that the Holy Ghost, whom They send, will teach us all truth and will comfort us.

Having faith in Christ means also having faith in all the members of the Godhead. They are a package deal. We cannot have faith in one and refuse to have faith in either of the other two. They are united in the purpose of saving us and bringing us home. Now we have three people in whom we can have absolute faith.

• How can faith in Jesus Christ influence us in our Church callings? in our family relationships? in our jobs? How does faith in Jesus Christ influence our hope for eternal life?

How Can We Increase Our Faith in Jesus Christ?

An important aspect of faith that we sometimes don't think about is that faith is a deliberate decision to believe

Knowing of the many blessings that come through exercising faith in Jesus Christ, we should seek to increase our faith in Him. The Savior said, "If ye have faith as a grain of mustard seed, … nothing shall be impossible unto you" (Matthew 17:20). A mustard seed is very small, but it grows into a large tree.

How can we increase our faith? The same way we increase or develop any other skill. How do we develop skills in woodcarving, weaving, painting, cooking, making pottery, or playing a musical instrument? We study and practice and work at it. As we do so, we improve. So it is with faith. If we want to increase our faith in Jesus Christ, we must work at it. The prophet Alma compared the word of God to a seed that must be nurtured by faith:

"But behold, if ye will awake and arouse your faculties, even to an experiment upon my words, and exercise a particle of faith, yea, even if ye can no more than desire to believe, let this desire work in you, even until ye believe in a manner that ye can give place for a portion of my words.

"Now, we will compare the word unto a seed. Now, if ye give place, that a seed may be planted in your heart, behold, if it be a true seed, or a good seed, if ye do not cast it out by your unbelief, that ye will resist the Spirit of the Lord, behold, it will begin to swell within your breasts; and when you feel these swelling motions, ye will begin to say within yourselves—It must needs be that this is a good seed, or that the word is good, for it beginneth to enlarge my soul; yea, it beginneth to enlighten my understanding. …

"Now behold, would not this increase your faith?" (Alma 32:27–29).

then act wholeheartedly on that belief, exercising every expectation that what we have chosen to believe will turn out to be correct. Think about that last sentence for a moment. It doesn't matter how small the task, if you consciously choose to accept the promise of the Lord then act on that promise as though nothing in the world can stop it from coming true - nothing, then you need to acknowledge later on that what you exercised your faith in really did happen, exactly as you believed it would. This confirms to yourself that what you chose to believe in was based on the truth. The next time you need to believe something a little harder to do, you can think back on your experiment and know that you have proven the Lord before, so you will prove Him once again. This is how we exercise faith deliberately. This is how our faith grows through experience with God. After all, it is the Lord who said, "Prove me now herewith …" (Malachi 3:10). He wants us to test Him, to prove Him so He can show us that He is trustworthy.

Increasing faith is not done blindly. We need to know what we are exercising our faith in. We need to be aware of when we are proving the Lord and in what we are proving the Lord. We will make much faster gains in our faith if we are aware of when we are placing our faith in Christ. Being aware of when we are exercising our faith in him will help us become aware of how we are actually placing our faith and trust in him on a daily basis. This is as it should be. This is what we mean when we say we should center our faith in Christ.

The desire to believe is how we start the process of exercising faith. At first, if we have no faith at all, if we are at least willing to want to have faith, the Lord can work with that and prove to us that he is worthy of our trust. But we must make the first move. God will never force himself on us, he can only work with those who are willing and desirous of working with him.

Alma here is teaching us to be aware of what we are testing. If the missionaries have come to me and promised that I would receive a witness of the Book of Mormon if I do the following things, A, B, and C, and I do them then when I go to the Lord in prayer, expecting to receive an answer because I have done what I was told to do in order to get my answer, I should expect an answer. How that answer comes is up to God, but I should expect an answer. This is often where we need to exercise our belief and expectation. Sometimes the Lord doesn't answer our prayers at the moment we ask for something. We need to continue in faith until the answer comes. This is how the Lord, in turn, tests our resolve and our willingness to trust Him. The answer will always come, but it will come in the Lord's own way and in His own time.

So we can increase our faith in God by acting on our desire to have faith in Him.

We can also increase our faith by praying to Heavenly Father about our hopes, desires, and needs (see Alma 34:17–26). But we must not suppose that all we have to do is ask. We are told in the scriptures that "faith, if it hath not works, is dead, being alone" (James 2:17). The following story is about a man whose faith was shown by his works.

This man wanted to study the scriptures, but he could not read. He prayed for Heavenly Father to help him learn to read. In time a teacher came to his village, and he asked the teacher to help him. He learned the alphabet. He studied sounds and learned to put the letters together to make words. Soon he was reading simple words. The more he practiced, the more he learned. He thanked the Lord for sending the teacher and for helping him learn to read. This man has increased his faith, humility, and knowledge to such a degree that he has served as a branch president in the Church.

Faith is a principle of power because it causes change. Without our accompanying action and changes of behavior, based on the trust and expectation we are placing in the Lord, our "faith" will produce nothing. Without action on our part faith is nothing more than mislabeled belief.

Some might read this story and say, "But anyone who is willing to put forth the work would be able to learn to read." Oh ye of little faith. We don't know what the man's capacity to learn was. We don't know what his past opportunities had been or his future ones for that matter. We don't know how much, at his age, he would have been able to have accomplished on his own. He put his trust in God and gave the Lord credit for all the opportunities and blessings that came into his life. He learned, through something as simple as learning to read (okay, maybe not so simple) that if he trusted in the Lord the Lord would give him the capacity and the opportunities he hadn't had before to do what he couldn't do before.

Giving credit to the Lord for all things good in our lives is never a mistake. That practice will always lead to greater faith and ability. Giving the Lord credit for all good things pleases the Lord and helps us. There is no downside to this practice.

President Spencer W. Kimball explained, "There must be works with faith. How foolish it would be to ask the Lord to give us knowledge, but how wise to ask the Lord's help to acquire knowledge, to study constructively, to think clearly, and to retain things that we have learned" (Faith Precedes the Miracle [1972], 205; italics in original).

Faith involves doing all we can to bring about the things we hope and pray for. President Kimball said: "In faith we plant the seed, and soon we see the miracle of the blossoming. Men have often misunderstood and have reversed the process." He continued by explaining that many of us want to have health and strength without keeping the health laws. We want to have prosperity without paying our tithes. We want to be close to the Lord but don't want to fast and pray. We want to have rain in due season and to have peace in the land without observing the Sabbath as a holy day and without keeping the other commandments of the Lord. (See Teachings of Presidents of the Church: Spencer W. Kimball [2006], 142.)

An important way to increase our faith is to hear and study the word of the Lord. We hear the word of the Lord at our Church meetings. We can study His word in the scriptures.

"And as all have not faith, seek ye diligently and teach one another words of wisdom; yea, seek ye out of the best books words of wisdom; seek learning, even by study and also by faith" (D&C 88:118).

• What relationship do you see between our faith and our actions?

What Are Some Blessings That Follow Faith?
Through the gift of faith, miracles are wrought, angels appear, other gifts of the Spirit are given, prayers are answered, and men become the sons of God (see Moroni 7:25–26, 36–37).

"When faith comes it brings ... apostles, prophets, evangelists, pastors, teachers, gifts, wisdom, knowledge, miracles, healings, tongues, interpretation of tongues, etc. All these appear when faith appears on the earth, and disappear when it disappears from the earth; for these are the effects of faith. ... And he who possesses it will, through it, obtain all necessary knowledge and wisdom, until he shall know God, and the Lord Jesus Christ, whom he has sent—whom to know is eternal life" (Lectures on Faith [1985], 83).

Why did apostles and prophet, miracles and spiritual gifts disappear from the original Church? It is because they redefined God into a being that doesn't exist. The first principle of faith is that you must place your faith in something that is true. The original Church changed the definition of God into something equivalent to the fairy analogy I gave earlier. No amount of belief in what is not correct will produce the desired outcome. They were taught that what they believed in was the truth, but because they had altered reality by redefining God, it was no longer possible to properly exercise faith in God. The power source was gone because they believed in a false tradition rather than the truth. That is why the Lord needed to restore His Church once again, so people could exercise their faith productively. All those spiritual gifts that existed in the original Church are here again, because we once again have the truth. We can now exercise faith in God as He really is.

• What are some stories from the scriptures in which people have become stronger because they had faith in Jesus Christ? How have you seen this happen in your own life?

Additional Scriptures
• Hebrews 11; Alma 32 (nature of faith explained)
• Exodus 14:19–22 (parting the waters of the Red Sea)
• Genesis 6–8 (Noah and the flood)
• Matthew 8:5–33 (sick healed, tempest calmed, miracles of faith)
• Mark 5:25–34 (healed by faith)
• Romans 10:17 (faith comes by hearing the word of God)

Chapter 19

Repentance
Gospel Principles, (2011), 107–13

We All Need to Repent
• What is sin? What effects do our sins have on us?

Faith in Jesus Christ naturally leads to repentance. There has been the need for repentance in the world from the time of Adam to the present day. The Lord instructed Adam, "Wherefore teach it unto your children, that all men, everywhere, must repent, or they can in nowise inherit the kingdom of God, for no unclean thing can dwell there, or dwell in his presence" (Moses 6:57).

We come to earth for the purpose of growing and progressing. This is a lifelong process. During this time we all sin (see Romans 3:23). We all have need to repent. Sometimes we sin because of ignorance, sometimes because of our weaknesses, and sometimes because of willful disobedience. In the Bible we read that "there is not a just man upon earth, that doeth good, and sinneth not" (Ecclesiastes 7:20) and that "if we say that we have no sin, we deceive ourselves, and the truth is not in us" (1 John 1:8).

What is sin? James said, "To him that knoweth to do good, and doeth it not, to him it is sin" (James 4:17). John described sin as "all unrighteousness" (1 John 5:17) and "the transgression of the law" (1 John 3:4).

That is why the Lord said, "All men, everywhere, must repent" (Moses 6:57). Except for Jesus Christ, who lived a perfect life, everyone who has lived upon the earth has sinned. Our Heavenly Father in His great love has provided us this opportunity to repent of our sins.

Becoming Free from Our Sins through Repentance
• What is repentance?

Repentance is the way provided for us to become free from our sins and receive forgiveness for them. Sins slow our spiritual progression and can even stop it. Repentance makes it possible for us to grow and develop spiritually again.

These are the questions that will be answered in this section.

Faith is an action word as well as a noun. Faith, as an action word is the effort we put into our trust in Christ. We trust that He can save us, change us, help us, and will always love us. To this end we keep the commandments and work hard to be like Him. This is how we demonstrate our faith or belief in Christ. As we demonstrate our trust and love in Christ by obeying His commandments, He in turn forgives us of the sins we commit. This is why "faith in Jesus Christ naturally leads to repentance."

Sin is our lot in life. We cannot avoid it, but we can minimize it by turning to Christ and repenting of our sins. To repent is to work toward change so we don't commit our sins again. He helps us overcome those parts of our weaknesses of personality that cause us to sin. He strengthens us and helps us be better people. We may not be able to avoid all sin in this life, but at least He gives us a way to clean up the results of our sins, even the accidental ones.

Between these three scripture references we get a pretty full description of what sin is. Sin can come from committing a wrong, not doing what is right, or from any form of not living any law (social or spiritual) strictly.

Obedience to God's laws teaches us how to live like Christ. They teach us how to behave as Jesus behaves. This invites the Spirit to come and help us, to change us, and to teach us how to be better than we currently are.

Sin prevents the Spirit from fully helping us, thus slowing down our spiritual progress and keeping us from becoming close to God. It is repentance that heals that breech between us and the Spirit so He can help us learn how to be and do better each day.

The privilege of repenting is made possible through the Atonement of Jesus Christ. In a way we do not fully understand, Jesus paid for our sins. President Joseph Fielding Smith said of this:

"I have suffered pain, you have suffered pain, and sometimes it has been quite severe; but I cannot comprehend pain ... that would cause the blood, like sweat, to come out upon the body. It was something terrible, something terrific. ...

"... There was no man ever born into this world that could have stood under the weight of the load that was upon the Son of God, when he was carrying my sins and yours and making it possible that we might escape from our sins" (Doctrines of Salvation, sel. Bruce R. McConkie, 3 vols. [1954–56], 1:130–31; italics in original).

Repentance sometimes requires great courage, much strength, many tears, unceasing prayers, and untiring efforts to live the commandments of the Lord.

Repentance will always, at some point, require that each of us acknowledge our weaknesses and face them. As we accept our failings and take them to the Lord and pray for strength to overcome them, we will have to exert great energy and sincerity to fully own our fault and admit our wrongs. Repentance requires great humility and patience in the process of repenting. Repenting doesn't happen overnight, it takes time and effort that sometimes can take months (years in some cases) to complete.

The patience required to repent is not so much for the Lord, but for ourselves. We need to be willing to give ourselves enough time to fully embrace the changes required to completely repent of something we have identified as needing to change in our lives. The Lord is plenty patient with us, as long as we don't give up on ourselves.

Principles of Repentance
• What are the principles of repentance?

For teachers: Writing a list can generate interest and help learners focus their attention. As you discuss the principles of repentance with class members or family members, you may want to ask someone to write the principles on the board or on a large piece of paper.

President Spencer W. Kimball declared: "There is no royal road to repentance, no privileged path to forgiveness. Every man must follow the same course whether he be rich or poor, educated or untrained, tall or short, prince or pauper, king or commoner" (Teachings of Presidents of the Church: Spencer W. Kimball [2006], 38; italics in original).

I don't know how comforting this is, but we all have to travel the same road to repent. There are no shortcuts, not privileges given to some and not to others. Everyone must go through the same process to be forgiven. The principle of repentance is a universal cure for what ails us.

We Must Recognize Our Sins

To repent, we must admit to ourselves that we have sinned. If we do not admit this, we cannot repent.

Alma counseled his son Corianton, who had been unfaithful in his missionary calling and had committed serious sins: "Let your sins trouble you, with that trouble which shall bring you down unto repentance. … Do not endeavor to excuse yourself in the least point" (Alma 42:29–30). The scriptures advise us further not to justify our sinful practices (see Luke 16:15–16).

My mother used to tell me that "a little guilt never hurt anybody." We cannot afford to excuse our behavior even in the smallest degree. To excuse our behavior and not fully own up to what we have done is to pridefully defend our disobedience. To repent we must fully embrace what we have done and recognize that there is no valid excuse for disobedience. Period.

We cannot hide any act of our lives from ourselves or from the Lord.

Remember, God already knows how much we have sinned. The recognition step is for our benefit. We are only learning to recognize what He already knows.

We Must Feel Sorrow for Our Sins

In addition to recognizing our sins, we must feel sincere sorrow for what we have done. We must feel that our sins are terrible. We must want to unload and abandon them. The scriptures tell us, "All those who humble themselves before God, and desire to be baptized, and come forth with broken hearts and contrite spirits, and … have truly repented of all their sins … shall be received by baptism into his church" (D&C 20:37).

I can feel sorry for things I have done wrong, but have no desire to change. I can feel sorry for poor decisions, but plan on repeating them again in the future. This is common among those who have addictions.

Godly sorrow is different in that we begin to recognize how offensive our behavior is to the Lord. Our love for God creates a sense of sorrow in our souls that makes us want to never hurt Him like that again.

Sometimes, when we have been heavily into a sin, it is difficult to develop godly sorrow. The Spirit can help us learn godly sorrow if we pray for help in developing this kind of sorrow for our sin. This may be something that the Spirit helps us develop over time, but in the meanwhile we need to refrain from committing that sin or we put ourselves back at the beginning of the process.

This process of learning how to repent, how to feel as we should, is what makes repentance a gift from God. The Spirit will teach us how to be forgiven of those things that are holding up our souls from progressing and becoming more like God. We need to learn to rely on and seek for the Spirit's company and for His help each and every day. Without it we cannot fully repent.

• Study 2 Corinthians 7:9–10 and Mormon 2:10–14. In what ways do you think "godly sorrow" is different from expressions of regret?

We Must Forsake Our Sins

Our sincere sorrow should lead us to forsake (stop) our sins. If we have stolen something, we will steal no more. If we have lied, we will lie no more. If we have committed adultery, we will stop. The Lord revealed to the Prophet Joseph Smith, "By this ye may know if a man repenteth of

If you are forsaken, you are left alone, abandoned, by yourself. And not just to be alone by yourself, but to have had someone you depended on leave you and go away from you leaving you without any help or hope. This is to be forsaken.

his sins—behold, he will confess them and forsake them" (D&C 58:43).

When we forsake a sin, we abandon it on the side of the road. We leave it and never look at it or for it again. It ceases to be of any importance in our lives. We replace that sin with something else that takes all our love and attention. This is what it means to forsake a sin.

The catch to forsaking sin is that we have to replace it with something else. You cannot leave a void or hole in your life. If you don't fill it with something worthwhile then Satan will try to fill it with something from his side of life. Forsaking of sin must be accompanied by embracing something else, something worthwhile and uplifting. We have to replace evil with good.

We Must Confess Our Sins

Confessing our sins is very important. The Lord has commanded us to confess our sins. Confession relieves a heavy burden from the sinner. The Lord has promised, "I, the Lord, forgive sins, and am merciful unto those who confess their sins with humble hearts" (D&C 61:2).

The Lord, like all of us, has habits and patterns in how He lives. One of His patterns is the requirement that all things be verbally or physically stated. There is no ambiguity or confusion when things are done this way. All is clear.

In order for us to be forgiven of our sin, we must not only recognize our sin for what it truly is, and forsake it, but we must also verbally confess our understanding of the sin to God or to a priesthood leader (depending on the seriousness of the sin). Then we must follow that verbal confession with physically living a different way. Repentance is meaningless if we live our life the same way after repenting as we did before repenting. If nothing has changed then no repentance has taken place.

We must confess all our sins to the Lord. In addition, we must confess serious sins—such as adultery, fornication, homosexual relations, spouse or child abuse, and the sale or use of illegal drugs—which might affect our standing in the Church, to the proper priesthood authority. If we have sinned against another person, we should confess to the person we have injured. Some less serious sins involve no one but ourselves and the Lord. These may be confessed privately to the Lord.

Often we might feel we have completely embrace our guilt in a sin, but when it comes time to put it into words we discover that we have been holding back. We may still be harboring a desire to hide parts of the sin or are still wanting to justify parts of the sin or reasons for the sin. This is the beauty of confession, it reveals any remaining ties we have to the sin.

Since humility is a big part of repenting, part of the test of true repentance is to go to those whom we may have injured because of our sin and fully disclosing our guilt. In the process of telling someone from whom I have stolen something, I must be careful not to hide any of the facts, cover up any of my wrong deeds, or verbally or emotionally minimize the effects of what I have done that hurt the other person. Part of the process of repenting is to restore trust. If I try to minimize or hide anything in my confession to God or the person I am trying to make amends to then I have just betrayed them and lied to them once again.

When we go to someone with a broken heart and a contrite spirit that means we hold nothing back. We bare our soul and plainly beg for forgiveness. It doesn't matter if the other person forgives us. The point is that you made the effort to repair the damage you did. What they do with that effort is between them and the Lord.

We Must Make Restitution

Part of repentance is to make restitution. This means that as much as possible we must make right any wrong that we have done. For example, a thief should give back what he has stolen. A liar should make the truth known. A gossip who has slandered the character of a person should work to restore the good name of the person he has harmed. As we do these things, God will not mention our sins to us when we are judged (see Ezekiel 33:15–16).

If I am truly sorry for damaging someone's reputation, asking for forgiveness will not be enough. I must endeavor to do all in my power to restore that which I damaged. This means I may have to go public and tell people what I did wrong and apologize to others for the damage I caused this person in hurting their reputation. Sometimes it takes years of mending to fully fix what we break in a careless moment.

An important principle we all need to learn better is that we chose our behavior, but we cannot choose what is required to repent of our bad behavior. We may not like that something we did as a teenager follows us the rest of our life, but we really don't have any control over consequences. There are natural laws of behavior and physics that happen because of the choices we make. If I choose to smoke for a year, but I repent and stop, that doesn't mean that I am guaranteed I won't get lung cancer in 30 years. I chose to smoke, and now the laws of nature will take their course. I have to accept the consequences for my behavior, even the unpleasant ones or the ones that seem unfair or unduly harsh. It is part of go to the Lord with a broken heart and a contrite spirit.

We Must Forgive Others

A vital part of repentance is to forgive those who have sinned against us. The Lord will not forgive us unless our hearts are fully cleansed of all hate, bitterness, and bad feelings against other people (see 3 Nephi 13:14–15). "Wherefore, I say unto you, that ye ought to forgive one another; for he that forgiveth not his brother his trespasses standeth condemned before the Lord; for there remaineth in him the greater sin" (D&C 64:9).

In Matthew 18:23-35 the parable of the master who forgave the servant's debt demonstrates this principle of forgiving others. As you read these verses, put your name in for the first servant who is pleading for forgiveness. The point of the parable is that each of us has great sin. The sins of those who have hurt us are tiny compared to what the Lord is forgiving in us. If we are so selfish and stingy, and unwilling to forgive a brother or sister who has sinned against us then the Lord says He will not forgive us.

Is not the point of seeking forgiveness from God that we rely on His generosity and kindness to forgive our disobedience? How can we expect Him to be so generous with us if we are so mean to others in the presence of such kindness? We are required to forgive others as part of our own forgiveness.

This is one of the patterns of behavior that typify or are typical of God. Goodness (and all that is good comes from God) never just affects one soul. Goodness by its very nature spreads to all those around whom the goodness is shown. This is what is happening when we seek for forgiveness. As we are forgiven we must also forgive others. The joy and gladness that comes into our life spills over into the lives of others in kind-hearted gestures and a loving heart. This is how goodness replicates or copies itself.

We Must Keep the Commandments of God

To make our repentance complete we must keep the commandments of the Lord (see D&C 1:32). We are not fully repentant if we do not pay tithes or keep the Sabbath day holy or obey the Word of Wisdom. We are not repentant if we do not sustain the authorities of the Church and do not love the Lord and our fellowmen. If we do not pray and are unkind to others, we are surely not repentant. When we repent, our life changes.

President Kimball said: "First, one repents. Having gained that ground he then must live the commandments of the Lord to retain his vantage point. This is necessary to secure complete forgiveness" (Teachings of Presidents of the Church: Spencer W. Kimball, 43).

• How do the teachings in this section differ from the false idea that repentance is the performance of a list of simple steps or routine actions?

This can be a hard concept to come to grips with, since it requires acceptance of the whole repentance package. Repentance isn't just about this one sin. To truly repent we must be seeking to fix the whole person, all of us. Every part of my life must be on the table for fixing, not just one habit or crime against God. The Lord requires all of my heart, not just a sliver of my soul.

I can't repent of all my sins at once, but I need to understand that my repentance will be a life-long endeavor, and it will include all parts of my life that are out of sync with my creator.

When we repent we undergo deeply personal internal changes of heart. This is something you cannot put on a checklist. These changes change our lives for the better, and there is no time line associated with repentance. Each sin is going to take as long as it takes to be forgiven. There is no list that says sin A takes a day and sin B takes a week to be forgiven. It is what it is, and when we choose to repent we accept that we will be at this process for as long as it takes to fix our mistakes. It becomes a life choice, not a task.

How Repentance Helps Us
• In what ways does repentance help us?

As we repent, the Atonement of Jesus Christ becomes fully effective in our lives, and the Lord forgives our sins. We become free from the bondage of our sins, and we find joy.

Alma recounted his experience of repenting from his sinful past:

"My soul was harrowed up [troubled] to the greatest degree and racked with all my sins.

"Yea, I did remember all my sins and iniquities, for which I was tormented with the pains of hell; yea, I saw that I had rebelled against my God, and that I had not kept his holy commandments.

"… So great had been my iniquities, that the very thought of coming into the presence of my God did rack my soul with inexpressible horror.

"… It came to pass that as I was … harrowed up by the memory of my many sins, behold, I remembered also to have heard my father prophesy … concerning the coming of one Jesus Christ, a Son of God, to atone for the sins of the world.

"Now, as my mind caught hold upon this thought, I cried within my heart: O Jesus, thou Son of God, have mercy on me. …

"And now, behold, when I thought this, I could remember my pains no more. …

"And oh, what joy, and what marvelous light I did behold; yea, my soul was filled with joy as exceeding as was my pain!

"… There can be nothing so exquisite and sweet as was my joy" (Alma 36:12–14, 17–21).

• How did repentance and forgiveness bring Alma joy?

The Dangers of Procrastinating Our Repentance
• What are some possible consequences of procrastinating our repentance?

The prophets have declared that "this life is the time for men to prepare to meet God" (Alma 34:32). We should repent now, every day. When we get up in the morning, we should examine ourselves to see whether the Spirit of God is with us. At night before we go to sleep, we should review our acts and words of the day and ask the Lord to help us recognize the things for which we need to repent. By repenting every day and having the Lord forgive our sins, we will experience the daily process of becoming perfect. As with Alma, our happiness and joy can be sweet and exquisite.

The most obvious problem associated with procrastinating our repentance is that we don't know how long we have to live in mortality. Repentance is designed to be done while we still have a body. Once we die and leave our bodies to return to the spirit world, repentance becomes a thousand times more difficult. If Satan really wants to nail us all he has to do is convince us that the need to repent can be looked at, or felt at a later time. As long as we are willing to put off repenting then we are just guarantying that we will go into the next life unprepared and unrepentant. Not good. As mentioned earlier, repenting needs to become a lifestyle choice. It needs to be something we do on a daily basis. This is the only way we can become clean and remain clean from our sins.

Additional Scriptures
• Matthew 9:10–13; Luke 13:3; Ezekiel 18:30 (repent or perish)
• Alma 7:21 (no unclean thing can dwell in God's presence)
• 2 Corinthians 7:9–10 (godly sorrow)
• Mosiah 4:10–12 (steps to repentance)
• Isaiah 1:18; Mosiah 26:28–32 (repentance brings forgiveness)
• D&C 58:42 (sins remembered no more)
• 2 Nephi 9:23 (repentance necessary to salvation)
• 2 Nephi 2:21 (repent while in the flesh)
• D&C 19:15–20 (the Lord has commanded us to repent so we will not have to suffer as He did)

Chapter 20

Baptism
Gospel Principles, (2011), 114–19

The Commandment to Be Baptized
• Why must we be baptized?

For teachers: Use questions at the beginning of a section to start a discussion and send class members or family members to the text to find more information. Use questions at the end of a section to help class members or family members ponder and discuss the meaning of what they have read and apply it in their lives.

Today, as in the days of Jesus, there are certain principles and ordinances of the gospel that we must learn and obey. A gospel principle is a true belief or teaching. An ordinance is a rite or a ceremony. The first two principles of the gospel are faith in the Lord Jesus Christ and repentance. Baptism is the first ordinance of the gospel. One of the instructions the Lord gave His Apostles was, "Go ye therefore, and teach all nations, baptizing them in the name of the Father, and of the Son, and of the Holy Ghost: teaching them to observe all things whatsoever I have commanded you" (Matthew 28:19–20).

We Must Be Baptized for the Remission of Our Sins

When we place our faith in Jesus Christ, repent, and are baptized, our sins are forgiven through the Atonement of Jesus Christ.

From the scriptures we learn that John the Baptist "did baptize in the wilderness, and preach the baptism of repentance for the remission of sins" (Mark 1:4). The Apostle Peter taught, "Repent, and be baptized every one of you in the name of Jesus Christ for the remission of sins" (Acts 2:38). Following Paul's conversion, Ananias said to him, "Arise, and be baptized, and wash away thy sins" (Acts 22:16).

We Must Be Baptized to Become Members of the Church of Jesus Christ

"All those who humble themselves before God, and desire to be baptized … that … have truly repented of all their sins … shall be received by baptism into his church" (D&C 20:37).

We Must Be Baptized before We Can Receive the Gift of the Holy Ghost

SIDE NOTE: As mentioned in the last lesson, the Lord requires physical responses to the commitments we make with Him. Sometimes this may be a simple confession in prayer, or a gesture or action like eating a piece of sacramental bread. Sometimes He requires more. In the case of baptism, the first of all the covenants we make with God, He requires that we be "all in." The Lord symbolically requires that we give up our old life through a complete submersion under water. We'll talk about that more in a moment. Baptism is the only covenant we make with the Lord that requires the use of our whole body.

When we come to the Lord and desire to be part of His kingdom and Church on the earth, he requires the ordinance of baptism. This symbol of full and complete repentance is necessary to be forgiven of all our sins and to then receive the gift of the Holy Ghost. Baptism is God's requirement, not the requirement of men. The Lord also specifies how the baptism is to be done, and by whom and by what authority. Baptism is not something God takes lightly.

The main requirement to be baptized is that the one desiring to be baptized has repented for all their sins. They have made a concerted effort to clean up their life and live like Christ wants them to live. It doesn't require that the person be perfect, just in a state of constant repentance.

The most useful blessing we can receive in this life is the gift of the Holy Ghost. Baptism is the prerequisite to receiving this gift.

The Lord said, "If thou wilt turn unto me, and ... repent of all thy transgressions [sins], and be baptized, even in water, in the name of mine Only Begotten Son, ... ye shall receive the gift of the Holy Ghost" (Moses 6:52).

We Must Be Baptized to Show Obedience

Jesus Christ was without sin, yet He was baptized. He said His baptism was necessary "to fulfil all righteousness" (Matthew 3:15). The prophet Nephi explained that the Lord told him, "Follow me, and do the things which ye have seen me do ... with full purpose of heart, acting no hypocrisy and no deception before God, but with real intent, repenting of your sins, witnessing unto the Father that ye are willing to take upon you the name of Christ, by baptism" (2 Nephi 31:12–13).

We Must Be Baptized to Enter the Celestial Kingdom

Jesus said, "Whoso believeth in me, and is baptized ... shall inherit the kingdom of God. And whoso believeth not in me, and is not baptized, shall be damned" (3 Nephi 11:33–34). Baptism is the gateway through which we enter the path to the celestial kingdom (see 2 Nephi 31:17–18).

Jesus demonstrated for us that it doesn't matter how good you are, the requirement to enter the kingdom of God is the same for everyone. All must be baptized and accept the covenant associated with baptism in order to enter the Lord's Church and receive His gift to each of us of the Holy Ghost.

The lower kingdoms of glory, the Terrestrial and the Telestial, require no covenants at all to enter. Only those who want to go to the Celestial kingdom are required to make sacred covenants with God. It is with these who want to return to live with God that He makes covenants. The covenants come with special spiritual blessings as well as with special requirements of behavior. Baptism offers people more than what the world has to offer. Baptism offers us the path back to our Heavenly Parents.

The Correct Mode of Baptism
• How should we be baptized?

There is only one correct mode of baptism. Jesus revealed to the Prophet Joseph Smith that a person having the proper priesthood authority to baptize "shall go down into the water with the person who has presented himself or herself for baptism. ... Then shall he immerse him or her in the water, and come forth again out of the water" (D&C 20:73–74). Immersion is necessary. The Apostle Paul taught that being immersed in water and coming out again is symbolic of death, burial, and resurrection. After baptism we start a new life. Paul said:

"Know ye not, that so many of us as were baptized into Jesus Christ were baptized into his death?

"Therefore we are buried with him by baptism into death: that like as Christ was raised up from the dead by the glory of the Father, even so we also should walk in newness of life.

"For if we have been planted together in the likeness of his death, we shall be also in the likeness of his resurrection" (Romans 6:3–5).

Baptism by immersion by a person having the proper authority is the only acceptable way of being baptized.

We have the example in the New Testament of how John baptized Jesus in the Jordan River, but we don't have anything in the New Testament that specifically details how baptism is to be done to satisfy the demands of God for this ordinance. That is why we rely on the revelation given to Joseph Smith that confirms what we read in the New Testament about how baptism is supposed to be done.

As I mentioned earlier, baptism is for those who are "all in." Those who desire baptism are ready and willing to start a whole new kind of life as disciples of Christ.

Baptism is symbolic of the death, burial, and resurrection of Christ. As Christ arose from the dead a new creature in God, so too when we are pulled from the water we arise a new creature in Christ. We begin a new life as a disciple and follower after truth.

Baptism, as a covenant with God, does no one any good if the one performing this sacred covenant does not have authority from God to perform it. God is offended by those who pretend to represent Him and do His work without any input from Him. God's priesthood power and authority is necessary for the ordinance to be recognized as valid before God.

• Why is authority to perform a baptism important?

• In what ways is baptism by immersion like the burial and Resurrection of the Savior?

Baptism at the Age of Accountability
• Who should be baptized?

Every person who has reached eight years of age and is accountable (responsible) for his or her actions should be baptized. Some churches teach that little children should be baptized. This is not in keeping with the teachings of the Savior. When Jesus spoke of little children, He said, "Of such is the kingdom of heaven" (Matthew 19:14).

After centuries of teaching that children are innocent before God until they reach the age of accountability, finally the scientific community has caught up. They have now proven that children don't know right from wrong and are not capable of making moral choices accurately until about the age of eight. This is what the Lord has been saying for thousands of years.

The prophet Mormon said that it is mockery before God to baptize little children, because they are not capable of sinning. Likewise, baptism is not required of people who are mentally incapable of knowing right and wrong (see Moroni 8:9–22).

Accountability doesn't not just include little children and babies. Any adult or person who is incapable of understanding the consequences or the moral implications of their choices are considered to be innocent before God and therefore have no need for baptism. Baptism is for the remission or forgiveness of sins. Those who are innocent are without sin in the eyes of God. Christ's atoning sacrifice pays for anything the innocent may do. They are automatically saved in the kingdom of God.

All other people are to be baptized. We must receive the ordinance of baptism and remain true to the covenants we make at that time.

• What might you say to a friend who believes that infants need to be baptized?

We Make Covenants When We Are Baptized
Many scriptures teach about baptism. In one of these scriptures, the prophet Alma taught that faith and repentance are steps that prepare us for baptism. He taught that when we are baptized we make a covenant with the Lord. We promise to do certain things, and God promises to bless us in return.

It is important to remember that all covenants in the Church come from God. He sets the terms and the blessings or punishments. These covenants are not negotiable or debatable. The Lord has designed each covenant we need to make for our maximum benefit. To try to give anything less than full commitment to a covenant from the Lord is to hurt ourselves by denying ourselves important blessings.

Alma explained that we must want to be called the people of God. We must be willing to help and comfort each other. We must stand as witnesses of God at all times and in all things and in all places. As we do these things and are baptized, God will forgive our sins. Alma told the people who believed his teachings about the gospel:

"Behold, here are the waters of Mormon. ... And now, as ye are desirous to come into the fold of God, and to be called his people, ... what have you against being baptized in the name of the Lord, as a witness before him that ye have entered into a covenant with him, that ye will serve him and keep his commandments, that he may pour out his

When we have received a testimony of the Book of Mormon and that Joseph Smith is a prophet of God, our hearts are filled with happiness. We become excited to become a member of Christ's church so we can learn as much truth as we can. This is why we are willing to commit to four promises in the baptismal covenant to come into the fold of God, etc. (see the next paragraph for the four promises.)

Spirit more abundantly upon you?" (Mosiah 18:8, 10). The people clapped their hands for joy and said it was their desire to be baptized. Alma baptized them in the Waters of Mormon. (See Mosiah 18:7–17.)

Alma taught that when we are baptized we make covenants with the Lord to:
1. Come into the fold of God.
2. Bear one another's burdens.
3. Stand as witnesses of God at all times and in all places.
4. Serve God and keep His commandments.

When we are baptized and keep the covenants of baptism, the Lord promises to:
1. Forgive our sins (see Acts 2:38; D&C 49:13).
2. Pour out His Spirit more abundantly upon us (see Mosiah 18:10).
3. Give us daily guidance and the help of the Holy Ghost (see Acts 2:38; D&C 20:77).
4. Let us come forth in the First Resurrection (see Mosiah 18:9).
5. Give us eternal life (see Mosiah 18:9).

• What do you think it means to bear one another's burdens? to stand as a witness of God at all times and in all places?

The promises the Lord makes in return for our commitment to serve Him and keep His commandments are not stingy or cheap. He offers us eternal life, which is the kind of life He lives. The gift of the Holy Ghost is most generous. The Holy Ghost is a member of the Godhead. He is sending a God to be our tutor and companion to teach us how to live so we can learn to become like Him. This is a win/win proposition. We get to return and live with our Father in Heaven, and He gets another one of His children back forever and ever. Everyone is happy!

Baptism Gives Us a New Beginning
With baptism we begin a new way of life. That is why we call it a rebirth. Jesus said that unless we are born of the water and of the Spirit, we cannot enter the kingdom of God (see John 3:3–5). This principle was explained clearly to Adam:

"Inasmuch as ye were born into the world by water, and blood, and the spirit, which I have made, and so became of dust a living soul, even so ye must be born again into the kingdom of heaven, of water, and of the Spirit, and be cleansed by blood, even the blood of mine Only Begotten" (Moses 6:59).

The Apostle Paul said that after our baptism we should begin a new life: "We are buried with him by baptism; … even so we also should walk in newness of life" (Romans 6:4). One of the great blessings of baptism is that it provides us with a new start on our way toward our eternal goal.

• How was your baptism a new beginning?

Arising in a newness of life is not just a metaphor for starting a new project. When we come out of the water, having committed ourselves to obey Christ in all things, we have committed to become a different person. Baptism marks the beginning of the trail, the path that leads to eternal life with God. This is the path He laid out and defined. We cannot get on it or travel this path unless we go through His gate to get onto the path. That gate is the ordinance and covenant of baptism by immersion by one of His authorized priesthood holders.

Additional Scriptures
• 2 Nephi 31:4–7 (purpose and necessity of baptism)
• 3 Nephi 11:21–27; D&C 20:72–74 (how to perform a baptism)
• Acts 2:38–39 (be baptized for the remission of sins)
• Moroni 8:8–12; D&C 20:71–72 (baptism is not required of little children; baptism is required of all who repent)

• Alma 7:14–16 (baptism is cleansing, entering into a covenant of eternal life)

Chapter 21
The Gift of the Holy Ghost
Gospel Principles, (2011), 120–24

The Holy Ghost
In chapter 7 we learned that the Holy Ghost is a member of the Godhead. He is "a personage of Spirit" (D&C 130:22). He does not have a body of flesh and bones. His influence can be everywhere at once. His mission is to bear witness of the Father and the Son and of all truth. Furthermore, the Holy Ghost purifies, or sanctifies, us to prepare us to dwell in the presence of God. The Holy Ghost purifies our hearts so we no longer have the desire to do evil.

There is a difference between the Holy Ghost and the gift of the Holy Ghost. In this chapter we will learn what the gift of the Holy Ghost is and how we can receive this great gift from God.

For teachers: You may want to invite class members or family members to participate in one or more of the following activities: (1) Read the additional scriptures listed at the end of the chapter, and discuss how the Holy Ghost helps us through our mortal journey. (2) Tell about some of the blessings that have come into their lives because they have the gift of the Holy Ghost. (3) Discuss what parents can do to help their children understand the gift of the Holy Ghost and how the Holy Ghost communicates with us.

The Gift of the Holy Ghost
• What is the difference between the Holy Ghost and the gift of the Holy Ghost?

The gift of the Holy Ghost is the privilege—given to people who have placed their faith in Jesus Christ, been baptized, and been confirmed as members of the Church—to receive continual guidance and inspiration from the Holy Ghost.

Joseph Smith said we believe in the gift of the Holy Ghost being enjoyed now as much as it was enjoyed in the days of the first Apostles. We believe in this gift in all its fulness, power, greatness, and glory. (See Teachings of Presidents of the Church: Joseph Smith [2007], 97–98.)

A person may be temporarily guided by the Holy Ghost without receiving the gift of the Holy Ghost (see D&C 130:23). However, this guidance will not be continuous unless the person is baptized and receives the laying on of hands for the gift of the Holy Ghost. We read in Acts 10

It is not uncommon to come to the conclusion that the role of the Holy Ghost must be minimal, after all, He is not the Christ, nor is He God the Father. What we forget is that it is through the Holy Ghost that God and Christ teach us. Without the Holy Ghost there would be no revelation. The Spirit or Holy Ghost is the member of the Godhead who acts as our personal guide through life. He tutors us, reveals things to us, helps us understand, and prompts us to do the right things. He helps us recognize all truth for what it is. It is also through His power that our hearts are changed and purified, and the peace of Christ is conveyed to our souls.

The Holy Ghost can be felt by anyone in the world who exercises faith in Christ. He can also influence anyone for good. It is the continual companionship, as opposed to the occasional visit from the Holy Ghost that makes this gift special. In order to make the changes necessary for us to return to our Father in Heaven, we all require the constant companionship of this celestial tutor. There is no way to return to God without this gift.

The Holy Ghost is the great revelator. He reveals new knowledge to us, testifies of truth, and clarifies our understanding. He prompts us to do good and changes our hearts, helping us to be more forgiving and to live more Christlike lives.

The gift of the Holy Ghost can only be given by someone who holds God's priesthood. The only time the gift is given is right after baptism as soon as you are confirmed by the priesthood as a new member of Christ's Church. No one in the world but members of Christ's Church (The that the Roman soldier Cornelius received inspiration from the Holy Ghost so that he knew the gospel of Jesus Christ was true. But Cornelius did not receive the gift of the Holy Ghost until after he was baptized. The Prophet Joseph Smith taught that if Cornelius had not received baptism and the gift of the Holy Ghost, the Holy Ghost would have left him (see Teachings of Presidents of the Church: Joseph Smith, 97).

Today people who are not members of the Church learn by the power of the Holy Ghost that the Book of Mormon is true (see Moroni 10:4–5). But that initial testimony leaves them if they do not receive the gift of the Holy Ghost. They do not receive the continuing assurance that can come to those who have the gift of the Holy Ghost.

Receiving the Gift of the Holy Ghost
• What must we do to receive the constant companionship of the Holy Ghost?

After people are baptized, they are confirmed members of the Church and given the gift of the Holy Ghost by the laying on of hands. The Lord said, "Whoso having faith you shall confirm in my church, by the laying on of the hands, and I will bestow the gift of the Holy Ghost upon them" (D&C 33:15).

Every worthy elder of the Church, when authorized, may give the gift of the Holy Ghost to another person. However, there is no guarantee that the person will receive inspiration and guidance from the Holy Ghost just because the elders have laid their hands on his or her head. Each person must "receive the Holy Ghost." This means that the Holy Ghost will come to us only when we are faithful and desire help from this heavenly messenger.

To be worthy to have the help of the Holy Ghost, we must seek earnestly to obey the commandments of God. We must keep our thoughts and actions pure.

Recognizing the Influence of the Holy Ghost
The Holy Ghost usually communicates with us quietly. His influence is often referred to as a "still small voice" (see 1 Kings 19:9–12; Helaman 5:30; D&C 85:6). President Boyd K. Packer explained: "The Holy Ghost speaks with a voice that you feel more than you hear. … While we speak of 'listening' to the whisperings of the Spirit, most often one describes a spiritual prompting by saying, 'I had a feeling …'" He continued: "This voice of the Spirit speaks gently, prompting you what to do or what to say, or it may

Church of Jesus Christ of Latter-day Saints) has the gift of the Holy Ghost. For all others in the world, the Holy Ghost will work with them to help steer them to the Lord's Church, but His visits to them are only fleeting. It requires the power of the priesthood to be entitled to His constant companionship.

This gift is the greatest gift God can give His children in this life. The Holy Ghost becomes our guiding light who leads us back to God.

We are each commanded by the priesthood to "receive the Holy Ghost" but it is a personal decision to do so. To receive the Holy Ghost the member must seek for His witness, pray for His company, and thank the Lord continually for the Holy Ghost's guidance from day to day. Just because we have been given the privilege of having His company doesn't mean He moves in and takes over our lives. We still have to live in such a way as to be inviting and comfortable to Him. If we live in sin He will withdraw from us, leaving us on our own. Offending the Holy Ghost leaves us exposed to the temptations and wiles of Satan.

Doing anything that is good and praiseworthy will please the Holy Ghost and encourage Him to be with us. The more we practice listening to Him the more He can bless us.

Sometimes the Spirit of God (Holy Ghost) has to "club" us over the head to get our attention. More often than not He will influence us by giving us a good feeling about an action or course to take. My mother always taught me that if we always act on our first impulse to do good then the Lord will see that we can be counted on to always follow the Spirit, for our first instinct to be like Christ is our best course of action.

How the Spirit influences us is a very individual thing. He will communicate with us in whatever way works best for caution or warn you" (in Conference Report, Oct. 1994, 77; or Ensign, Nov. 1994, 60).

us. His promptings may be an initial desire to do good, which if ignored may come a second time or may not. It may come as a feeling to do something in a particular way. We may have a thought come into our head that we normally wouldn't think of. If acted on these thoughts will turn out to be blessings to us. Sometimes we get a warmth in our chest that confirms a decision as correct. We may actually hear a voice, though for most people this is rare.

The point is that there are as many ways for the Spirit to speak to God's children as there are children to communicate with. He will tailor each communication to best suit your needs at the time. As you practice learning how to listen to Him the method of communication will become refined. You may find that words seem to flow into your mind when you need to say something, whether you were planning on saying something or not. Sometimes when giving a blessing I have had words come into my head and I couldn't go on with the blessing until those exact words had been recited to the person. As soon as I had said what the Spirit put there, new words would follow. It is an amazing experience.

One of God's Greatest Gifts
• What blessings can we receive through the gift of the Holy Ghost?

The gift of the Holy Ghost is one of God's greatest gifts to us. Through the Holy Ghost we may know that God lives, that Jesus is the Christ, and that His Church has been restored to the earth. We may have the promptings of the Holy Ghost to show us all the things we should do (see 2 Nephi 32:5). The Holy Ghost sanctifies us to prepare us for God's presence. We may enjoy the gifts of the Spirit (see chapter 22 in this book). This great gift from our Heavenly Father can also bring peace to our hearts and an understanding of the things of God (see 1 Corinthians 2:9–12).

The Holy Ghost is the source of all revelation. To experience the peace of Christ throughout our lives we need the Holy Ghost. To receive witnesses of the truth for things we cannot prove we need the Holy Ghost. To comprehend the mysteries of God we need the Holy Ghost. He is our link to our Father in Heaven and Christ. He helps us understand their personalities so we can learn to become like them.

• Why is the gift of the Holy Ghost one of God's greatest gifts to us?

Additional Scriptures
• 1 Corinthians 3:16–17; D&C 130:22–23 (the Holy Ghost dwells with the faithful)
• Acts 19:1–7 (gift of the Holy Ghost bestowed anciently)
• Moroni 8:25–26 (how to receive the Holy Ghost)
• Moroni 10:5 (the Holy Ghost is a witness to truth)
• Mosiah 5:2 (the Holy Ghost changes hearts)
• Alma 5:54 (the Holy Ghost sanctifies)

Chapter 22

The Gifts of the Spirit
Gospel Principles, (2011), 125–32

The Gifts of the Spirit
• What spiritual gifts does the Lord give us?

Following baptism, each of us had hands laid on our heads to receive the gift of the Holy Ghost. If we are faithful, we can have His influence continually with us. Through Him, each of us can be blessed with certain spiritual powers called gifts of the Spirit. These gifts are given to those who are faithful to Christ. "All these gifts come from God, for the benefit of the children of God" (D&C 46:26).They help us know and teach the truths of the gospel. They will help us bless others. They will guide us back to our Heavenly Father. To use our gifts wisely, we need to know what they are, how we can develop them, and how to recognize Satan's imitations of them.

"Through Him [meaning the Holy Ghost], each of us can be blessed with certain spiritual powers called gifts of the Spirit." Spiritual gifts are literally a gift we are given from God, through the ministrations of the Holy Ghost. There are many kinds of spiritual gifts available. Which gift(s) we receive is tailored to our specific talents and needs. All gifts are to be used for the benefit of others. There is no such thing as a gift that only benefits the holder of the gift. God does not work that way.

A few key points to remember here are:
1. We have to discover our gift(s)
2. We have to develop them just like any talent
3. There are counterfeits out there used by Satan
4. We can seek additional gifts if we are currently using the ones we have been given

The scriptures mention many gifts of the Spirit. These gifts have been given to members of the true Church whenever it has been on the earth (see Mark 16:16–18). The gifts of the Spirit include the following:

This lesson talks about a limited number of spiritual gifts. If you go to lds.org and find the Conference talks you should be able to use the search term - spiritual gifts - and find several talks by the Brethren that enlarge this list considerably. Almost any virtuous behavior can be expanded into a spiritual gift.

For teachers: Consider asking each class member or family member to review the list of spiritual gifts in this chapter and choose two that they would like to learn more about. As part of the lesson, give them time on their own to study the paragraphs and scripture passages about the gifts they have chosen. When they have had time to study, ask them to share what they have learned.

The Gift of Tongues (D&C 46:24)

Sometimes it is necessary to communicate the gospel in a language that is unfamiliar to us. When this happens, the Lord can bless us with the ability to speak that language. Many missionaries have received the gift of tongues (see the picture in this chapter). For example, Elder Alonzo A. Hinckley was a missionary in Holland who understood and spoke very little Dutch even though he had prayed and studied hard. When he returned to a home he had visited before, a lady opened the door and spoke to him very angrily in Dutch. To his amazement he could understand every word. He felt a strong desire to bear his testimony to her in Dutch. He began to speak, and the words came out very clearly in Dutch. But when he returned to show his

The gift of tongues is the most prominent gift showcased in the New Testament. In many instances when the Holy Ghost was given to the gentiles, the first display of the Holy Ghost came in the form of people speaking in tongues. In a church that was expanding into new countries with many languages, this was a very helpful gift for them to have. As the Church matured, the frequency of this gift declined as the members developed other gifts and no longer needed the gift of tongues as much. The gift of tongues was also prevalent in the beginning of the restored gospel.

Now we find the gift of tongues most commonly among our missionaries who are learning new languages as they

Page 100

mission president that he could speak Dutch, the ability had left him. Many faithful members have been blessed with the gift of tongues. (See Joseph Fielding Smith, Answers to Gospel Questions, comp. Joseph Fielding Smith Jr., 5 vols. [1957–66], 2:32–33.)

spread the gospel message. No group of people on earth learn languages faster than the missionaries in the LDS church.

The Gift of Interpretation of Tongues (D&C 46:25)

This gift is sometimes given to us when we do not understand a language and we need to receive an important message from God. For example, President David O. McKay had a great desire to speak to the Saints in New Zealand without an interpreter. He told them that he hoped that the Lord would bless them that they could understand him. He spoke in English. His message lasted about 40 minutes. As he spoke, he could tell by the expression on many of their faces and the tears in their eyes that they were receiving his message. (See Answers to Gospel Questions, 2:30–31.)

The gift of the interpretation of tongues is a much more personal gift than the gift of tongues. The person speaks and people are able to understand, even though they speak a different language. This gift is often seen only on an "as needed" basis.

The Gift of Translation (D&C 5:4)

If we have been called by the leaders of the Church to translate the word of the Lord, we can receive a gift to translate beyond our natural ability. As with all gifts, we must live righteously, study hard, and pray to receive it. When we do these things, the Lord causes us to feel a burning inside concerning the correctness of the translation (see D&C 9:8–9). Joseph Smith had the gift of translation when he translated the Book of Mormon. This gift came to him only when he was in tune with the Spirit.

Translating is difficult work. When you translate you must not only give a word for word representation where possible, but everything you write or say must carry the original meaning as closely as the language and customs of the translated language will allow.

"We can receive a gift to translate beyond our natural ability." I have seen college students who have been called upon by the Church to help translate materials and scriptures into their native language. They were not trained linguists, and were usually fresh off their missions. Translating the word of God is perhaps the most difficult of all forms of translation, since the Lord speaks in symbols and stories that represent other things. This gift requires great sensitivity to the Spirit.

The Gift of Wisdom (D&C 46:17)

Some of us have been blessed with the ability to understand people and the principles of the gospel as they apply in our lives. We are told:

"If any of you lack wisdom, let him ask of God, that giveth to all men liberally, and upbraideth not; and it shall be given him.

"But let him ask in faith, nothing wavering. For he that wavereth is like a wave of the sea driven with the wind and tossed.

"For let not that man think that he shall receive any thing of the Lord" (James 1:5–7).

A wise person knows not only facts, but when and how to use them appropriately. Wisdom, but ability to know how to approach someone or a subject is a gift more of us should probably seek. Sometimes you will see someone teach a lesson or be in a discussion and suddenly start to say things or give counsel that you know full well is beyond their abilities. This is the gift of wisdom being revealed. This happens a lot with Bishops and in instructional classes at church. It also happens as parents counsel their children in righteousness.

The Lord said, "Seek not for riches but for wisdom, and behold, the mysteries of God shall be unfolded unto you" (D&C 6:7).

The Gift of Knowledge (D&C 46:18)

Everyone who becomes like Heavenly Father eventually knows all things. The knowledge of God and His laws is revealed by the Holy Ghost (see D&C 121:26). We cannot be saved if we are ignorant of these laws (see D&C 131:6).

The Lord revealed, "If a person gains more knowledge and intelligence in this life through his diligence and obedience than another, he will have so much the advantage in the world to come" (D&C 130:19). The Lord has commanded us to learn as much as we can about His work. He wants us to learn about the heavens, the earth, things that have happened or will happen, things at home and in foreign lands (see D&C 88:78–79). However, there are those who try to gain knowledge by their own study alone. They do not ask for the help of the Holy Ghost. They are those who are always learning but never arrive at the truth (see 2 Timothy 3:7). When we receive knowledge by revelation from the Holy Ghost, His Spirit speaks to our minds and our hearts (see D&C 6:15, 22–24; 8:2; 9:7–9).

The Gift of Teaching Wisdom and Knowledge (Moroni 10:9–10)

Some people are given a special ability to explain and testify of the truths of the gospel. This gift can be used when we teach a class. It can be used by parents to teach their children. This gift also helps us instruct others so they can understand the gospel.

The Gift of Knowing That Jesus Christ Is the Son of God (D&C 46:13)

This has been the gift of prophets and apostles who have been called as special witnesses of Jesus Christ. However, others are also given this gift. Every person can have a testimony through the whisperings of the Holy Spirit. President David O. McKay taught: "It is given unto some, says the Lord in the Doctrine and Covenants, to know by the Holy Ghost that Jesus is the Son of God and that He was crucified for the sins of the world [see D&C 46:13]. It is to these I refer who stand firm upon the rock of

Knowledge is a big subject. There are those who have a talent for being able to learn secular or worldly knowledge. We rely on the righteousness of these individuals to help us learn more about the world according to the principles of the gospel.

There are also people who have an ability to grasp spiritual relationships and hold onto them. They can take many parts of the gospel and can see how they all fit together to form grand principles of progression. These are the kinds of people you hope also have the gift of teaching wisdom and knowledge.

Since we cannot be saved in ignorance, we all need to study and learn all we can about everything we can. The Lord expects us to. It is an interesting statistic that the Church has discovered that those who have a higher level of education tend to remain more active in the Church over their lifetime. Education, whether formal or informal is important.

When we study we need to study to see how our learning fits in with the teachings of the gospel. In other words, our learning needs to be Spirit focused. If we are just learning to become an academic, then our knowledge will do us little good in the eternal view of things. If we are seeking truth through the Spirit while we study any subject, the Spirit can reveal all kinds of marvels to us.

Teaching is an art, not a science. To find someone who can make the gospel come alive and be meaningful is a wonderful thing. These are the people we want to just sit and listen to for hours at a time. They are wonderful to have question and answer sessions. Every teacher should seek for a measure of this gift. We can all improve our teaching, no matter how little teaching ability we think we have to start with. The Lord expects us to become better at what we are called to do. This means seeking the help of the Spirit to teach us how to be better.

It is a comfort to those who believe Jesus is the Christ, and that he was slain for the sins of the world to know that there are those who have gone beyond believing and know this for themselves. This is something we can all seek for, but for some it is given to them to be witnesses of these eternal truths. This is a highly responsible testimony to bear.

revelation in the testimony that they bear to the world"
(Teachings of Presidents of the Church: David O. McKay
[2003], 166).

The Gift of Believing the Testimony of Others (D&C 46:14)

By the power of the Holy Ghost we may know the truth of all things. If we want to know whether someone else is speaking the truth, we must ask God in faith. If the thing we are praying about is true, the Lord will speak peace to our minds (see D&C 6:22–23). In this way we can know when someone else, even the prophet, has received revelation. Nephi asked the Lord to let him see, feel, and know that his father's dream was true (see 1 Nephi 10:17–19).

The Savior said to Thomas, who doubted the Savior's resurrection, the blessed were they who saw Him and believed, but more blessed were they who didn't see Him and still believed the witness of those who had.

Very few of us will ever have spiritual witnesses of everything. It is important that we learn to believe in the testimony of others who have had a witness we have not yet received. Nephi was able to go to the Lord and receive the same revelation his father had, but most of us will need to rely on the testimony of the prophets without having the same revelations. If we seek after this gift the Lord will bear witness to our souls that what the prophets have told us is true.

The Gift of Prophecy (D&C 46:22)

Those who receive true revelations about the past, present, or future have the gift of prophecy. Prophets have this gift, but we too can have it to help us govern our own lives (see 1 Corinthians 14:39). We may receive revelations from God for ourselves and our own callings, but never for the Church or its leaders. It is contrary to the order of heaven for a person to receive revelation for someone over whom he or she does not preside. If we truly have the gift of prophecy, we will not receive any revelation that does not agree with what the Lord has said in the scriptures.

Every parent has the right to revelation for their own family. A Bishop has the right to revelation for his ward members. Satan has counterfeits so when we receive inspiration on behalf of someone else it is important that we vet that information or do a fact check.

1. Do I have the right to receive this kind of knowledge about that person or those people? If it is outside of my direct responsibility in my calling then I do not have the right to this information, therefore I need to question where this "inspiration" came from.
2. Does what I feel inspired about match up with the current teachings of the prophets? If not then what I have received, no matter how good it feels, is not from God. I need to fast and pray and possibly speak with my church leader.
3. Is whatever I have received doctrinally sound and taught clearly in the scriptures? If not then it is under suspicion.

Satan can also give revelation in his efforts to deceive. We always need to be aware of where our inspiration comes from and be sure it fits into the established patterns in the Lord's Church. The Lord WILL NOT deviate from those patterns.

The Gift of Healing (D&C 46:19–20)

Some have the faith to heal, and others have the faith to be healed. We can all exercise the faith to be healed when we are ill (see D&C 42:48). Many who hold the priesthood have the gift of healing the sick. Others may be given a knowledge of how to cure illness.

Have you ever met someone with a knack, a natural ability to know how to mix ingredients together or mix therapies together and affect healing in others? This is a talent that can be nurtured and developed. There are also those who have such strong belief in the priesthood ability of others or in the healing power of prayer that they can be blessed and be healed or can pray for others and they will be healed because of that faith.

The Gift of Working Miracles (D&C 46:21)

The Lord has blessed His people many times in miraculous ways. When the Utah pioneers planted their first crops, a

When we are on the Lord's errand, doing His work, and things so wrong, there is nothing wrong with seeking for help. We may receive inspiration on how to get around our difficulties or we may receive a miracle, an plague of locusts nearly destroyed them. The pioneers prayed that the Lord would save their crops, and He sent seagulls to devour the locusts. When we need help and ask in faith, if it is for our good the Lord will work miracles for us (see Matthew 17:20; D&C 24:13–14).

unexplainable event that will get us through to the other side of our efforts. In the example of the seagulls mentioned in the lesson, the Saints had done everything in their power, so when they prayed it was with the understanding that the Lord would have to deal with this problem because it was completely beyond anything they could control. The Lord could have done many things, but He chose to bring in seagulls to eat the locust to save their crops. Sometimes the Lord will alter the weather for the faithful, sometimes, like the parables of the loaves and fishes, our resources will stretch in a way we cannot explain until we are out of our troubles.

The secret to miracles is to never seek to have one for the sake of seeing one. Always leave how a problem is solved up to the Lord. If we see only one solution we can ask for it, but it is always up to the Lord to decide if we have been faithful enough to get the miracle we need to confirm our faith. But always believe. That is the key.

The Gift of Faith (Moroni 10:11)

The brother of Jared had great faith. Because of his faith, he received other gifts. His faith was so great that the Savior appeared to him (see Ether 3:9–15). Without faith, no other gift can be given. Moroni promises, "Whoso believeth in Christ, doubting nothing, whatsoever he shall ask the Father in the name of Christ it shall be granted him" (Mormon 9:21). We should seek to increase our faith, find out our gifts, and use them.

Having faith is the secret to receiving additional gifts, well that and exercising or practicing the gift(s) we have already been given. The Lord wants us to seek for more gifts.

Some people lack faith and deny that these gifts of the Spirit actually exist. Moroni says to them:

"And again I speak unto you who deny the revelations of God, and say that they are done away, that there are no revelations, nor prophecies, nor gifts, nor healings, nor speaking with tongues, and the interpretation of tongues;

"Behold I say unto you, he that denieth these things knoweth not the gospel of Christ; yea, he has not read the scriptures; if so, he does not understand them" (Mormon 9:7–8).

One of the great difficulties with spiritual gifts is acknowledging that we have one. First we must identify that we have one. Everyone has one, we have been promised that. Once we think we know what our gift might be then we need to seek opportunities through prayer, fasting, and daily activities, to use our gift so it gets stronger. Remember that all gifts are meant to bless the life of someone else. No gift is meant just for the recipient of the gift. If we do not find ways to bless the lives of others with whatever gift we can identify then that gift will eventually be taken away. Believe, believe, believe. If we believe the Lord loves each of us enough to give us a gift then we need to go find our gift and make good use of it.

• Why does the Lord give us spiritual gifts?

Just as all the parts of the body have their specialized function, they work together to complete the overall body and contribute to all that the body can accomplish. Each gift of the Spirit is the same thing, but for the body of Christ, which is the Church. We all have need of people who can teach, of people who can understand, of people who have the gift of belief and faith, etc. Because there are so many gifts available we all have the ability to contribute to the overall faith and performance of other members of the Church. We bless each other with our small but individually important contribution to each other's spiritual welfare.

We Can Develop Our Gifts
• How can we "seek … earnestly the best gifts"? (D&C 46:8).

The Lord has said: "For all have not every gift given unto them; for there are many gifts, and to every man is given a gift by the Spirit of God. To some is given one, and to some is given another, that all may be profited thereby" (D&C 46:11–12).

To develop our gifts, we must find out which gifts we have. We do this by praying and fasting. We should seek after the best gifts (see D&C 46:8). Sometimes patriarchal blessings will help us know which gifts we have been given.

Take the charge to find your gift seriously. This may take sitting down with others who know you and asking them to give their opinion as to what gift you may have. You may have several people tell you that a listening ear is a gift you possess. You may be told you are compassionate or that you are a great teacher of a particular art or form of craftsmanship. This is one way to find out what our gift might be. Once we feel comfortable with the knowledge that we actually do have a gift we can start seeking for additional gifts. Just remember that if the Lord blesses us with additional gifts we will be held accountable for what we do with those gifts. Be prepared to bless the lives of others with whatever gift you are given.

We must be obedient and faithful to be given our gifts. We then should use these gifts to do the work of the Lord. They are not given to satisfy our curiosity or to prove anything to us because we lack faith. Of spiritual gifts, the Lord said, "They are given for the benefit of those who love me and keep all my commandments, and him that seeketh so to do" (D&C 46:9).

• Think about some spiritual gifts that would strengthen you personally or help you serve the Lord and others. What will you do to seek these gifts?

Satan Imitates the Gifts of the Spirit
• How can we discern between the true gifts of the Spirit and Satan's imitations?

Satan can imitate the gifts of tongues, prophecy, visions, healings, and other miracles. Moses had to compete with Satan's imitations in Pharaoh's court (see Exodus 7:8–22). Satan wants us to believe in his false prophets, false healers, and false miracle workers. They may appear to be so real to us that the only way to know is to ask God for the gift of discernment. The devil himself can appear as an angel of light (see 2 Nephi 9:9).

There is nothing wrong with questioning where our gift comes from. When we are sure it comes from the Lord then run with it, play with it, enjoy it. Bless others with your gift as often as you can. Never be afraid to examine a gift to make sure you know who the author of that gift is. All good things come from God. If a gift violates, in any way, shape, or form, the commandments of God or the teachings of the scriptures or prophets then it becomes suspect. When in doubt, talk to your priesthood leaders.

Satan wants to blind us to the truth and keep us from seeking the true gifts of the Spirit. Mediums, astrologers, fortune tellers, and sorcerers are inspired by Satan even if they claim to follow God. Their works are abominable to the Lord (see Isaiah 47:12–14; Deuteronomy 18:9–10). We should avoid all associations with the powers of Satan.

We Must Be Careful with Our Gifts of the Spirit
• How can we respect the sacredness of spiritual gifts?

The Lord said, "A commandment I give unto them, that they shall not boast themselves of these things, neither speak them before the world; for these things are given unto you for your profit and for salvation" (D&C 84:73). We must remember that spiritual gifts are sacred (see D&C 6:10).

In return for giving us these gifts, the Lord asks that we "give thanks unto God in the Spirit for whatsoever blessing [we] are blessed with" (D&C 46:32).

This is a sort of catch 22, a lose/lose situation, if you will. We are told to seek after our gift. We are told to develop our gift and that it is for the benefit of others. We are told to then go seek additional gifts, which also require we bless the lives of others. But we are not allowed to boast or brag or discuss at length our gift(s). Our gift is between us and the Lord.

If we seek for gifts or to practice our gifts to be seen of men and receive the praise of others then we are going about it all wrong. These gifts are sacred responsibilities, sacred blessings given to us from our Father in Heaven to bless our lives and strengthen our faith and testimonies. We have to make sure we are treating these gifts as the sacred things they are.

Believe. Believe. Believe. Be grateful. Be grateful. Be grateful. Bless others. Bless others. Bless others.

Additional Scriptures
• 3 Nephi 29:6–7 (fate of those who deny gifts)
• Moroni 10:7–19 (gifts depend on faith)
• 3 Nephi 26:17; 27:20; D&C 84:64 (a gift given at baptism)
• 1 Corinthians 12 (gifts of the Spirit in the ancient Church of Jesus Christ)
• D&C 46:9–26 (gifts of the Spirit in the Church today)

Chapter 23

The Sacrament
Gospel Principles, (2011), 133–37

Christ Introduced the Sacrament
• What do the emblems of the sacrament teach about the Atonement of Jesus Christ?

Our Savior wants us to remember His great atoning sacrifice and keep His commandments. To help us do this, He has commanded us to meet often and partake of the sacrament.

The sacrament is a holy priesthood ordinance that helps remind us of the Savior's Atonement. During the sacrament, we partake of bread and water. We do this in remembrance of His flesh and His blood, which He gave as a sacrifice for us. As we partake of the sacrament, we renew sacred covenants with our Heavenly Father.

Shortly before His Crucifixion, Jesus Christ gathered His Apostles around Him in an upstairs room. He knew He would soon die on the cross. This was the last time He would meet with these beloved men before His death. He wanted them to always remember Him so they could be strong and faithful.

To help them remember, He introduced the sacrament. He broke bread into pieces and blessed it. Then He said, "Take, eat; this is in remembrance of my body which I give a ransom for you" (Joseph Smith Translation, Matthew 26:22). Next He took a cup of wine, blessed it, gave it to His Apostles to drink, and said, "This is in remembrance of my blood … , which is shed for as many as shall believe on my name, for the remission of their sins" (Joseph Smith Translation, Matthew 26:24; see also Matthew 26:26–28; Mark 14:22–24; Luke 22:15–20).

The Atonement of Jesus Christ is so important in the gospel plan that it is the only part of the entire plan of salvation that has a weekly ordinance associated with it. Part of our baptismal covenant is to "always remember Him." The sacrament helps us to stay focused on Christ by providing us with a weekly time that is set aside just for us to reflect and consider how we are doing in our obligations to always remember our Savior.

The instituting of the sacrament signaled the ending of the Mosaic Law. It was the last part of the gospel, the higher law, Christ gave the apostles before He died.

The word "ransom" here is important. By our sins we have sold ourselves into slavery, slavery to physical appetites, and slavery to Satan, the father of lies. The price Christ paid to buy the possibility of our release from our self-imposed captivity is the Atonement. The bread represents His flesh. He physically suffered in the flesh for our sins. He personally satisfied the demands of God's eternal justice in order to buy our souls from the grasp of eternal death and hell.

The water represents His blood. Christ's suffering caused such spiritual pain and suffering that he physically bled from every pore of his body. This shedding of His blood was the price He paid so we could be forgiven for the sins we commit. In this way His blood represents His sacrifice and payment for us and makes it possible for Him to spiritually purify and cleanse us from our sins.

There is only one condition for this saving and cleansing to take place, we must believe in Him and obey His commandments. Only then will he pardon our wrongs and mistakes.

After His Resurrection, the Savior came to the Americas and taught the Nephites the same ordinance (see 3 Nephi 18:1–11; 20:1–9). After the Church was restored in the latter days, Jesus once again commanded His people to partake of the sacrament in remembrance of Him, saying, "It is expedient that the church meet together often to partake of bread and wine in the remembrance of the Lord Jesus" (D&C 20:75).

How the Sacrament Is Administered

The scriptures explain exactly how the sacrament is to be administered. Members of the Church meet each Sabbath day to worship and partake of the sacrament (see D&C 20:75). The sacrament is administered by those who hold the necessary priesthood authority. A priest or Melchizedek Priesthood holder breaks bread into pieces, kneels, and blesses it (see D&C 20:76). A deacon or other priesthood holder then passes the sacrament bread to the congregation. Then the priest or Melchizedek Priesthood holder blesses the water, and it too is passed to the members. Jesus gave His disciples wine when He introduced the sacrament. However, in a latter-day revelation He has said that it doesn't matter what we eat and drink during the sacrament as long as we remember Him (see D&C 27:2–3). Today, Latter-day Saints drink water instead of wine.

Jesus has revealed the exact words for both sacrament prayers. We should listen carefully to these beautiful prayers and try to understand what we are promising and what is being promised to us. Here is the prayer that is offered to bless the bread:

"O God, the Eternal Father, we ask thee in the name of thy Son, Jesus Christ, to bless and sanctify this bread to the souls of all those who partake of it, that they may eat in remembrance of the body of thy Son, and witness unto thee, O God, the Eternal Father, that they are willing to take upon them the name of thy Son, and always remember him and keep his commandments which he has given them; that they may always have his Spirit to be with them. Amen" (D&C 20:77).

Here is the prayer that is offered to bless the water:

"O God, the Eternal Father, we ask thee in the name of thy Son, Jesus Christ, to bless and sanctify this wine [water] to the souls of all those who drink of it, that they may do it in remembrance of the blood of thy Son, which was shed for them; that they may witness unto thee, O God, the Eternal Father, that they do always remember him, that they may have his Spirit to be with them. Amen" (D&C 20:79).

The ordinance of the sacrament is performed very simply and reverently.

• Carefully review the sacrament prayers. Think about the meaning of each phrase.

The sacramental prayer can be broken into at least three parts:

1. We ask the Father, in Christ's name that what is being eaten or drunk will bless and sanctify the soul of each person who receives the sacrament.
2. The conditions for this blessing is that each person eats or drinks each part of the sacrament while remembering the Savior's body and blood sacrificed for them. Each person promises to take upon themselves the name of Christ and keep his commandments.
3. In exchange for doing this worthily, the Lord will give each person "his Spirit to be with them."

The sacramental prayer is one of the few ordinances in the Church that must be said word for word. If it is not said correctly then it has to be repeated until it is said correctly. The Bishop or Branch President is responsible for seeing that the prayer is reverently and correctly given. He is also responsible for overseeing the whole sacrament to make sure the congregation has the best possible experience.

The Covenants We Renew during the Sacrament

• What covenants do we renew during the sacrament? What blessings does the Lord promise us as we keep those covenants?

Each time we partake of the sacrament, we renew covenants with the Lord. A covenant is a sacred promise between the Lord and His children. The covenants we make are clearly stated in the sacramental prayers. It is important to know what those covenants are and what they mean.

We covenant that we are willing to take upon ourselves the name of Jesus Christ. By this we show we are willing to be identified with Him and His Church. We commit to serve Him and our fellowman. We promise that we will not bring shame or reproach upon that name.

Baptism is an adoption process. We are brought into the family of Christ. We become His sons and daughters, and He becomes our father. As such we have a filial or parent-child relationship with Him. We owe the same respect, allegiance, love, honor, and obedience to Christ that any child owes to the parent. We also take upon ourselves the family name, the name of Christ. This means that when we behave well, it reflects well on our parent and our family. When we misbehave we bring shame on ourselves and our family, and our parent. In this case, we bring that dishonor upon Christ, our parent and our Lord.

We covenant to always remember Jesus Christ. All our thoughts, feelings, and actions will be influenced by Him and His mission.

We promise to keep His commandments.

When we promise that we will always remember Him, it means that all our actions will be based on His teachings and His motives and morals. We have promised to keep the commandments He gave us. In exchange we are given the gift of the Holy Ghost, which is the constant companionship of the third member of the Godhead. It is the Spirit's role to teach us more of Christ, to soften and change our hearts, to open the eyes of our understanding so we can learn of God's ways, and to testify to us of all truth. He also comforts us and gives us hope in the promises the Lord has made to those who are obedient to His commandments.

We take these obligations upon ourselves when we are baptized (see D&C 20:37; Mosiah 18:6–10). Thus, when we partake of the sacrament, we renew the covenants we made when we were baptized. Jesus gave us the pattern for partaking of the sacrament (see 3 Nephi 18:1–12) and said that when we follow this pattern, repenting of our sins and believing on His name, we will gain a remission of our sins (see Joseph Smith Translation, Matthew 26:24).

Look particularly at the verses in Mosiah 189:6 - 10. This is the best, most specific passage in the scriptures about our baptismal covenants.

The Lord promises that if we keep our covenants, we will always have His Spirit to be with us. A person guided by the Spirit will have the knowledge, faith, power, and righteousness to gain eternal life.

The purpose of the companionship of the Spirit is to guide us through the process of becoming Christlike in our attitudes and behaviors. The companionship of the Spirit, over time, changes our desires, habits, outlook, and hopes. We begin, little by little to think like Christ, to behave like Christ, to love like Christ. But to do this we have to shed all of our baggage, our sins, our fears, our hangups, our disbelief. This is all part of the cleansing process we go through by staying worthy of the constant companionship of the Holy Ghost.

• What can we do to remember these promises during the week?

It is easy to become a once-a-week Christian. To become a daily Christian we must place habits in our daily routine that remind us of both what we have agreed to do and to become, as well as why we have agreed to do and become. In other words, we need to keep our covenants and their obligations and promises in front of us all the time.

Reminders can come from the habits of daily morning, evening personal and family prayer, the paying of our tithes and offerings, doing our home and visiting teaching faithfully each month, making sure we attend all meetings, both on Sunday and during the week, and that we are praying for the welfare of those over whom we have responsibilities or for those who have responsibilities for us. We can pray for and serve our neighbors, we can seek to deliberately set examples of Christlike attitudes and behaviors to the best of our abilities at this time. Those abilities will improve over time. We can also make sure we are reading and studying our scriptures and the writings and teachings of the prophets, both ancient and modern, both living and the dead. We can be going to the temple and participating in family history work through indexing or genealogy work. We can also be preparing to strengthen subsequent generations by writing in our own journal or writing a family history.

All of these things help us to remember and to keep the promises we make each week during the sacrament.

Our Attitude When Partaking of the Sacrament
• How can we prepare ourselves to partake of the sacrament?

What can we think about during the sacrament to help us remember the Savior's Atonement?

One possibility is to honestly think about a trait you are personally trying to develop. How are you doing? Are you making improvements? What have you done this past week to become better at this trait, and what can you do to work on being better at it in the coming week. It is a time for introspection, for self reflection, and for goal setting. How will this improvement bring you closer to your Father in Heaven and being like Christ?

You don't have much time during the sacrament to do all this, so keep it simple. This is a good time to do a short review of attitudes and weekly behavior, but it is also a good time to quietly contemplate and try to feel the promptings of the Spirit as you begin your Sabbath day meetings.

For teachers: If many of those you teach are parents, you may want to ask them to share ideas about how they can help their children prepare to partake of the sacrament reverently.

Before partaking of the sacrament, we are to prepare ourselves spiritually. The Lord emphasizes that no one should partake of the sacrament unworthily. That means we must repent of our sins before taking the sacrament. The scriptures say, "If any have trespassed, let him not partake until he makes reconciliation" (D&C 46:4). The Lord instructed His twelve Nephite disciples, "Ye shall not suffer any one knowingly to partake of my flesh and blood unworthily, when ye shall minister it; for whoso eateth and drinketh my flesh and blood unworthily eateth and drinketh damnation to his soul" (3 Nephi 18:28–29).

If we know we have knowingly broken commandments and have not repented of them before coming to Church to take the sacrament, it would be better to not take the emblems of the sacrament that week than to take the sacrament knowing that we are unworthy to do so.

This means we need to be aware of our state of worthiness before Sunday arrives. If we are sincerely trying to keep the commandments and do what is right then taking the sacrament should not be a problem. We can be imperfect and still be worthy to take the sacrament. It is only a problem for someone who is willfully being disobedient, but still taking the sacrament. This makes a mockery of Christ's atonement, and God will not be mocked. He has been very clear on that subject. That is why He says that for someone to take the sacrament unworthily is to eat and drink damnation to his/her soul.

During the sacrament service we should dismiss from our minds all worldly thoughts. We should feel prayerful and reverent. We should think of the Atonement of our Savior and be grateful for it. We should examine our lives and look for ways to improve. We should also renew our determination to keep the commandments.

We do not need to be perfect before partaking of the sacrament, but we must have the spirit of repentance in our hearts. The attitude with which we partake of the sacrament influences our experience with it. If we partake of the sacrament with a pure heart, we receive the promised blessings of the Lord.

• Why do you think worthily partaking of the sacrament increases our spiritual strength?

Additional Scriptures
• 1 Corinthians 11:27–29 (partake of the sacrament worthily)
• John 4:5–14 (Jesus is the Living Water)
• John 6:30–35 (Jesus is the Bread of Life)

Chapter 24

The Sabbath Day
Gospel Principles, (2011), 138–43

The Meaning of the Sabbath Day
• What is the Sabbath day?

"Remember the sabbath day, to keep it holy" (Exodus 20:8; see also D&C 68:29).

The word Sabbath comes from a Hebrew word meaning rest. Before the Resurrection of Jesus Christ, the Sabbath day commemorated God's day of rest after He finished the Creation. It was a sign of the covenant between God and His people. We read in the book of Genesis that God created the heavens and the earth in six periods of time, which He called days: "And on the seventh day God ended his work which he had made; and he rested on the seventh day from all his work which he had made. And God blessed the seventh day, and sanctified it" (Genesis 2:2–3). Now the Sabbath also commemorates the Resurrection of Jesus Christ.

The Sabbath day is every seventh day. It is a holy day ordained by God for us to rest from our daily labors and worship Him.

The Purpose of the Sabbath Day
• How would you explain the purpose of the Sabbath day to someone who does not know about the Sabbath?

Jesus taught that the Sabbath day was made for our benefit (see Mark 2:27). The purpose of the Sabbath is to give us a certain day of the week on which to direct our thoughts and actions toward God. It is not a day merely to rest from work. It is a sacred day to be spent in worship and reverence. As we rest from our usual daily activities, our minds are freed to ponder spiritual matters. On this day we should renew our covenants with the Lord and feed our souls on the things of the Spirit.

• Think about what you can do to keep the purpose of the Sabbath in mind as you prepare for the day each week.

This is an important distinction of the Sabbath day. Not only is it to be a day of rest from the cares and the work we associate with the world, but it is also a day to commemorate or celebrate the resurrection of Christ.

Too often the Sabbath is thought of as a "me" day. It is a day for me to do what I want. This is the one day of the week I don't have to answer to a boss or fulfill obligations imposed on me by someone else. It is my time.

This definition of the Sabbath is not correct, nor is it healthy. Notice that the definition of the day, both definitions of the day, refer back to God and His work on our behalf. First in what was created for our eternal progress (to get bodies) then as a celebration for what was done in securing our salvation.

The million dollar question is "What does it mean to worship?"

Short answer is that the Sabbath is the one day out of seven each week when we stop doing our work and do things that bring glory and honor to God. We do His work on that day.

The point of this paragraph is that the Sabbath is not so much about what we do as it is about our attitude. We can go to a family member's home and "party" on Sunday and that would be inappropriate. But we can go to a family member's home and have an enjoyable time and it will be completely appropriate. It depends on how we feel about Christ when we do it. If we have a worshipful spirit and a deep desire to serve Him and love one another then going to visit family becomes a sacred and bonding experience. If we are only going to play then we have missed a special opportunity for worship and growth on the Sabbath. We have also set a poor example for those around us to follow. The Sabbath is all about focusing on spiritual matters, not worldly pursuits.

In what ways can we prepare our homes and ourselves for the Sabbath on Saturday? What shopping needs to be done on Saturday so we don't feel a need to go to the store on Sunday? What do we need to do for the car on Saturday so no gas needs to be purchased on Sunday? Do we need to do the laundry? Should we clean the house so we have a clean environment around us on the day we worship our God? None of these things are major tasks, but all of them contribute to a better experience on the Sabbath.

History of the Sabbath

The seventh day was consecrated by God as a Sabbath in the beginning of the earth (see Genesis 2:2–3). Since earliest times, the tradition of a sacred seventh day has been preserved among various peoples of the earth. God renewed a commandment concerning this day to the Israelites, saying, "Remember the sabbath day, to keep it holy" (Exodus 20:8). Keeping the Sabbath day was also a sign that the Israelites were His covenant people (see Exodus 31:12–13, 16; Isaiah 56:1–8; Jeremiah 17:19–27).

However, some Jewish leaders made many unnecessary rules about the Sabbath. They decided how far people could walk, what kind of knots they could tie, and so forth. When certain Jewish leaders criticized Jesus Christ for healing sick people on the Sabbath, Jesus reminded them that the Sabbath was made for the benefit of man.

We often forget that the Sabbath was made for our benefit, not the other way around. When we do what we can to honor this special day the Lord, in return, sanctifies us and blesses us in ways we cannot receive any other way. These blessings are directly tied to keeping the Sabbath day holy. This is why Satan wants us to violate the spirit of the day. He knows there are special blessings held in reserve for those who keep that day sacred.

The Nephites also observed the Sabbath day according to the commandments of God (see Jarom 1:5).

In modern times the Lord has repeated His commandment that we should remember the Sabbath day and keep it holy (see D&C 68:29).

The Lord's Day

• Why was the Sabbath changed from the seventh day to the first day?

Until His Resurrection, Jesus Christ and His disciples honored the seventh day as the Sabbath. After His Resurrection, Sunday was held sacred as the Lord's day in remembrance of His Resurrection on that day (see Acts 20:7; 1 Corinthians 16:2). From that time on, His followers observed the first day of the week as their Sabbath. In both cases there were six days of labor and one for rest and devotion.

It isn't Sunday in particular that is sacred. It is the 7th day that is sacred. If you live in a land where people worship on Friday then Friday becomes the 7th or Sabbath day. What makes the day sacred is how we keep and honor our covenants with God on that day.

The Lord has given us a direct commandment in these days that we too should honor Sunday, the Lord's day, as our Sabbath (see D&C 59:12).

• How can the remembrance of the Resurrection influence our worship on the Sabbath?

Think of the sacrament service as a memorial service for Christ each week. Will that make any difference in how you see that ordinance?

For teachers: You can help class members or family members think more deeply about a question by giving them time to ponder. After they have had enough time, ask for their responses.

Keeping the Sabbath Day Holy

• What does it mean to keep the Sabbath day holy?

The Lord asks us, first, to sanctify the Sabbath day. In a revelation given to Joseph Smith in 1831, the Lord commanded the Saints to go to the house of prayer and offer up their sacraments, rest from their labors, and pay their devotions to the Most High (see D&C 59:9–12).

Second, He asks us to rest from daily work. This means we should perform no labor that would keep us from giving our full attention to spiritual matters. The Lord told the Israelites, "Thou shalt not do any work, thou, nor thy son, nor thy daughter, thy manservant, nor thy maidservant, nor thy cattle" (Exodus 20:10). Our prophets have told us that we should not shop, hunt, fish, attend sports events, or participate in similar activities on that day.

President Spencer W. Kimball cautioned, however, that if we merely lounge about doing nothing on the Sabbath, we are not keeping the day holy. The Sabbath calls for constructive thoughts and acts. (See Teachings of Presidents of the Church: Spencer W. Kimball [2006], 170.)

Without getting into checklists of do's and don'ts for the Sabbath, what do you think it means to offer up our sacraments to the Lord on Sunday? A sacrament is something that is sacred, like an oath or a covenant. We have all made at least one covenant with the Lord when we were baptized. We go to the house of the Lord and renew this covenant each week when we take the sacrament. We should take time to ponder and consider the power of that covenant and the promises the Lord makes to us for keeping that covenant.

What kinds of things may we do on the Sabbath? The prophet Isaiah suggested that we should turn away from doing our own pleasure and should "call the sabbath a delight, the holy of the Lord, honourable" (Isaiah 58:13).

The spirit of the day is found in our attitude about all the things we do in that day. If we go help roof our neighbor's home on Sunday, but we do it in a spirit of thanksgiving and a desire for that neighbor to feel our love for them, then there isn't really anything wrong with the activity. As long as we are trying to serve the Lord by doing it then we have been faithful to our covenants. If we go help roof out of a sense of obligation or a desire to look good to our neighbor then we have failed in our obligations to worship our Lord on His holy day.

We should consider righteous things we can do on the Sabbath. For example, we can keep the Sabbath day holy by attending Church meetings; reading the scriptures and the words of our Church leaders; visiting the sick, the aged, and our loved ones; listening to uplifting music and singing hymns; praying to our Heavenly Father with praise and thanksgiving; performing Church service; preparing family history records and personal histories; telling faith-promoting stories and bearing our testimony to family members and sharing spiritual experiences with them; writing letters to missionaries and loved ones; fasting with a purpose; and sharing time with children and others in the home.

There are plenty of things we can do on Sunday besides attend church meetings. If we feel resentful of some of the possible activities then perhaps we need to go to the Lord and ask for help in changing our hearts so we find joy in those activities rather than resentment. This takes time, but it really blesses our lives.

In deciding what other activities we could properly engage in on the Sabbath, we could ask ourselves: Will it uplift and inspire me? Does it show respect for the Lord? Does it direct my thoughts to Him?

Notice that deciding if an activity is appropriate requires that we think through the activity and the motivation for the activity. We have to be aware of how we feel about what we do in order for something to be an appropriate activity for the Sabbath day.

There may be times when we are required to work on the Sabbath. We should avoid this whenever possible, but when it is absolutely necessary, we should still maintain the spirit of Sabbath worship in our hearts as much as possible.

This emphasizes again that Sabbath worship is mostly attitude and not practice. We need to participate in the ordinance of the sacrament whenever possible because that is a commandment, but how we are the rest of the day is more about what happens in our hearts and heads than what happens around us.

• Think about something you can do to improve in your efforts to keep the Sabbath day holy. If you are a parent or grandparent, think about something you can do to help your children or grandchildren understand the meaning of the Sabbath.

Blessings for Observing the Sabbath
• What are some blessings we receive when we keep the Sabbath day holy?

If we honor the Sabbath day, we may receive great spiritual and temporal blessings. The Lord has said that if we keep the Sabbath day with thanksgiving and cheerful hearts, we will be full of joy. He has promised:

"The fulness of the earth is yours, … whether for food or for raiment, or for houses, or for barns, or for orchards, or for gardens, or for vineyards;

"Yea, all things which come of the earth, in the season thereof, are made for the benefit and the use of man, both to please the eye and to gladden the heart;

"Yea, for food and for raiment, for taste and for smell, to strengthen the body and to enliven the soul" (D&C 59:16–19).

Have you ever noticed that an attitude of gratitude and thankfulness changes everything that happens in our lives? When we are focused on what we have been blessed with and the opportunities, spiritual and otherwise, the Lord has granted us, then what happens around us isn't nearly so important any more.

Focusing on what we have and how we can use it to be of benefit to others changes our entire outlook on life. The Lord will bless us to find joy in the Sabbath as long as we seek to be a blessing to others on His holy day. This will prosper our studies, our worshiping, our activities, and our relationships with those around us.

Additional Scriptures
• Exodus 31:16–17 (the Sabbath is a perpetual covenant between the Lord and His people)
• Mosiah 13:16–19; 18:23; Exodus 35:1–3; Leviticus 26:2–4, 6, 12 (observe the Sabbath as a holy day)
• Luke 6:1–11 (lawful to do good on the Sabbath)
• Luke 13:11–17; John 5:1–18 (Jesus's example of doing good on the Sabbath)

Chapter 25

Fasting

Gospel Principles, (2011), 144–48

How to Fast Properly

• What can we do to make fasting a joyful experience?

Since the time of Adam, God's people have fasted to help them draw near to Him and to worship Him. Jesus showed the importance of fasting by His own example (see Luke 4:1–4). Through latter-day revelation we learn that the Lord still expects His people to fast and pray often (see D&C 88:76).

Fasting means to go without food and drink. Occasional fasting is good for our bodies and helps our minds become more active.

The Savior taught us that purposeful fasting is more than just going without food and drink. We must also concentrate on spiritual matters.

For teachers: You may want to divide class members or family members into groups of two to four people and give each group an opportunity to discuss ways to make fasting a joyful experience. Then work together to make a list of everyone's ideas—perhaps on the board or on a large piece of paper.

We Should Pray When We Fast

Prayer is a necessary part of fasting. Throughout the scriptures, prayer and fasting are mentioned together. Our fasting should be accompanied by sincere prayer, and we should begin and end our fasting with prayer.

We Should Fast with a Purpose

Fasting can have many purposes. We can overcome weaknesses or problems by fasting and praying. Sometimes we may wish to fast and pray for help or guidance for others, such as a family member who is ill and needs a blessing (see Mosiah 27:22–23). Through fasting we can come to know the truth of things just as did the prophet Alma in the Book of Mormon. He said: "I have fasted and prayed many days that I might know these things of myself. And now I do know of myself that they are true; for the Lord God hath made them manifest unto me by his Holy Spirit" (Alma 5:46).

We can fast to help others embrace the truth. Fasting can help comfort us in times of sorrow and mourning (see

Technically a fast is just going without food for a period of time. But fasting is like prayer. You can recite a prayer that has no meaning or you can pray from the heart and pour your whole soul into those heartfelt emotions and thoughts. How effective your fasting and praying is depends on what you put into it and what you want out of it.

What is it about praying that changes a fast into something special? (And prayer does change a fast into something special.) Adding prayer to a fast is like adding a rudder to a ship. As the rudder allows you to steer the ship where you want it to go, so too does prayer give direction and purpose to going without food. It is purpose that gives fasting its main source of power.

The purpose behind a fast is our reason for fasting in the first place. Do you want to understand something you haven't been able to comprehend up to now? Are you trying to accomplish something in your life? Do you need an answer to a prayer? Does someone you love need extra help from the Lord right now? There are innumerable reasons to fast and pray.

Depriving the body of food and water for a period of time weakens our constitution. This state of weakness helps us be more humble and submissive in our frame of mind

Alma 28:4–6). Fasting can help us become humble and feel closer to our Heavenly Father (see Helaman 3:35).

Our purpose in fasting should not be to impress others. The Lord counseled:

"Moreover when ye fast, be not, as the hypocrites, of a sad countenance: for they disfigure their faces, that they may appear unto men to fast.

"Verily I say unto you, They have their reward.

"But thou, when thou fastest, anoint thine head, and wash thy face; that thou appear not unto men to fast" (Matthew 6:16–18).

We should be cheerful when we fast and not advertise our fasting to others.

• How does our attitude influence our experience when we fast?

The Fast Day

One Sunday each month Latter-day Saints observe a fast day. On this day we neither eat nor drink for two consecutive meals. If we were to eat our evening meal on Saturday, then we would not eat or drink until the evening meal on Sunday.

All members who are physically able should fast. We should encourage our children to fast after they have been baptized, but we should never force them. The fast day is a special day for us to humble ourselves before the Lord in fasting and prayer. It is a day to pray for forgiveness from our sins and for the power to overcome our faults and to forgive others.

On fast Sunday, members of the Church meet together and partake of the sacrament. They strengthen themselves and one another by bearing testimony in fast and testimony meeting.

when we approach the Lord for assistance. Feeling weak helps more easily recognize our own fallibility and dependence on the Lord. It fuels our desire for help and increases our recognition of our own limitations, both physically, and spiritually.

When the Pharisees fasted and made a public show out of their fasting they received exactly what they sought after, public attention. If we want to receive the Lord's attention we need to fast in the way He has told us will work best, and that is to fast and pray privately, in secret. This takes the public part out of the equation. It makes our efforts for answers strictly between us and our God. It creates an intimacy between us and the Lord as we quietly and privately seek out His help.

There is no need for anyone else to know we are fasting. This private struggle is between us and the Lord. So He tells us to dress up, look happy, and appear to be anything but suffering from hunger and spiritual yearnings. His promise to us is that he who does this in private the way the Lord tells us to do it will be publicly rewarded by the Lord. In other words, His blessings to us will be open and obvious to those around us.

Can you think of anything having to do with God where our attitude makes no difference? Our attitude is everything!

The instituted fast Sunday each month serves more than one purpose. Not only does it give us the opportunity to practice the art of fasting, and the opportunity to receive the rewards of fasting and prayer, but it also gives us an opportunity to help others. By giving the money we would have spent on the two meals we skip to feed the poor, we are able to give an offering to the Lord as well.

It is the nature of the Lord to find ways to bless more than one person anytime it is possible. By me fasting and giving the cost of my meals to the Fast Offering fund, I not only get the blessings of fasting and praying, but from giving an offering, and those who receive that money have their lives blessed as well. There is an ever-widening ripple of good that extends from such deeds.

The testimony meeting held each Fast Sunday is meant to strengthen each person's testimony. Testimonies are born and strengthened through the bearing of that testimony. As we listen to others who have had similar experiences to ours, our testimony is strengthened. But if we really want to cement what we have experienced, we need to bear our own testimony, and often. Sometimes in the bearing of a testimony we find that we know something now that we didn't know with this same surety that we know now.

There is something about putting our feelings into words that strengthens our feelings and secures our knowledge.

• How have you benefited from sharing your testimony in fast and testimony meeting? How have you benefited from hearing others share their testimonies?

Fast Offerings

• Why do we contribute fast offerings?

When we fast each month, the Lord asks us to help those in need. One way we do this is by giving through the proper priesthood authority the money we would have spent on food for the two meals. We should give as generously as we are able. Through our fast offerings we become partners with the Lord in administering to the needs of our less-fortunate brothers and sisters.

"We should give as generously as we are able." This is an important principle. Remember the comment earlier that attitude is all important with the Lord? If we are stingy with our substance then the Lord will be stingy with our blessings. When we learn to be generous of heart the Lord will be generous with us. That is an eternal principle.

We Are Blessed When We Fast

• What blessings can we receive when we fast properly?

Isaiah, an Old Testament prophet, wrote of the Lord's rich promises to those who fast and help the needy. We are promised peace, improved health, and spiritual guidance. Isaiah tells us of the blessings that come when we fast: "Then shall thy light break forth as the morning, and thine health shall spring forth speedily: and thy righteousness shall go before thee; the glory of the Lord shall be thy reward. Then shalt thou call, and the Lord shall answer; thou shalt cry, and he shall say, Here I am" (Isaiah 58:8–9).

Do not be guilty of underestimating the power of fasting and prayer. Most of the revelations received by the prophets down through the ages have come because they sought the Lord through fasting and prayer. So often in our lives we will find comfort and peace to our souls during the hard times because we seek out the Lord through fasting and prayer. Small wonder the Lord refers to the process as "rejoicing and prayer." (Doctrine and Covenants 59:14)

Fasting improves our lives and gives us added strength. It helps us live other principles of the gospel because it draws us nearer to the Lord.

It is fasting and prayer that parents use to help bring back their straying children. It is fasting and prayer that brings forgiveness of sins. Fasting and prayer is a powerful combination.

Fasting Teaches Self-Control

Fasting helps us gain strength of character. When we fast properly, we will learn to control our appetites and passions. We are a little stronger by having proved to ourselves that we have self-control. If we teach our children to fast, they will develop the spiritual strength to overcome greater temptations later in their lives.

The process of fasting and praying teaches us that our spiritual side can control our physical side. We cannot get rid of our physical side, but we do need to bring it under control. It is our physical appetites that cause so many of our sins. The more experience we have with fasting and praying the more we learn to control our bodies. This is why it is so important we teach our children not only how to fast and pray, but why it is so important that they learn to find joy in the fast.

Fasting Gives Us Spiritual Power

When we fast wisely and prayerfully, we develop our faith. With that faith we will have greater spiritual power. For example, Alma (a Book of Mormon prophet) tells the story of meeting again with the sons of Mosiah many years after their miraculous conversion. He felt great joy when he learned that they had strengthened their faith and had developed great spiritual power. They had gained this

The important lesson here, besides that fasting and praying can teach us to have greater faith, is that learning how to have greater faith through prayer and fasting is something that takes time. We don't become people of great faith overnight. Development takes time and practice. Be patient with yourself and with others. This growth we are seeking is something that takes time, and we all experience it at a different pace.

power because "they had given themselves to much prayer, and fasting; therefore they had the spirit of prophecy, and the spirit of revelation" (Alma 17:3).

The sons of Mosiah had been preaching for 14 years to the Lamanites. Because the sons of Mosiah had fasted and prayed, the Spirit of the Lord increased the power of their words. This gave them great success in their missionary work. (See Alma 17:4.)

The Savior has said to those who fast properly, "Thy Father, which seeth in secret, shall reward thee openly" (Matthew 6:18).

• How can fasting increase our spiritual power to resist temptations? to receive revelation? to do righteous acts?

Fasting increases our spiritual power because while we fast we are focusing on spiritual things. Most of our spiritual weakness in life comes because we don't think about spiritual things. Spirituality is like any muscle in the body, we need to exercise it or it shrinks and becomes weak.

Additional Scriptures
• Luke 2:37; Alma 45:1 (worshipping God through fasting)
• Isaiah 58:3–11 (proper fasting)
• Mosiah 27:19, 23 (fasting for the sick)
• 3 Nephi 27:1–3; Exodus 34:27–28 (fasting for revelation and testimony)
• Alma 6:6; 17:9 (fasting for those who do not know God)
• Acts 13:2–3 (fasting for selection of Church officers)
• Mosiah 4:26 (retaining a remission of our sins as we help those in need)

Chapter 26

Sacrifice
Gospel Principles, (2011), 149–54

The Meaning of Sacrifice

Sacrifice means giving to the Lord whatever He requires of our time, our earthly possessions, and our energies to further His work. The Lord commanded, "Seek ye first the kingdom of God, and his righteousness" (Matthew 6:33). Our willingness to sacrifice is an indication of our devotion to God. People have always been tried and tested to see if they will put the things of God first in their lives.

For teachers: You do not need to teach everything in each chapter. As you prayerfully prepare to teach, seek the Spirit's guidance to know which portions of the chapter you should cover and which questions you should ask.

• Why is it important to sacrifice as the Lord asks without expecting anything in return?

The Law of Sacrifice Was Practiced Anciently

• What was the significance of the sacrifices performed by the Lord's covenant people anciently?

From the time of Adam and Eve to the time of Jesus Christ, the Lord's people practiced the law of sacrifice. They were commanded to offer as sacrifices the firstlings of their flocks. These animals had to be perfect, without blemish. The ordinance was given to remind the people that Jesus Christ, the Firstborn of the Father, would come into the world. He would be perfect in every way, and He would offer Himself as a sacrifice for our sins. (See Moses 5:5–8.)

In Abraham 3:25 the Lord tells Abraham that His intention is to prove all those who come to earth to see if they will be obedient to Him in all things. The earth was created as a proving ground for us to come to for this very purpose. Our obedience to God, and our willingness to give up anything that is required of us by God is the test of this life. All the blessings we are promised by the Lord are based on our willingness to sacrifice the things of this world to be obedient to His will.

This is an interesting principle. If we always expect something in return for our obedience to the Lord then are we not acting like we are "buying" our way to heaven? Obedience to the Lord must be unconditional and without restriction. We must be willing to give all, without demands or expectations. We have faith that He will only demand what is required of us to be saved. If that is all we have then we must be willing to let Him have it, and gladly.

Learning to gladly give anything to the Lord, be it our substance, our time, our energies, our talents, anything, takes time and experience with the Lord to develop. Don't be deceived, this is one of the most important attributes we can develop in this life.

Sometimes we underestimate what it took to offer up the firstlings of their flocks. They were herders. They lived off the animals their animals birthed once each year. If they did not give birth and increase the size of the flock then the family had to eat their own livestock to survive. The babies born each spring was their livelihood for the next year. The Lord was telling them to take of this precious commodity and kill it as an offering to Him. It is true that it was a symbolic gesture of His sacrifice of His only begotten Son, but it was still a significant sacrifice for those who lived off the animals they could sell each year. And it wasn't just their firstborn, but it had to be the best of their firstborn.

Jesus did come and offer Himself as a sacrifice, just as the people had been taught He would. Because of His sacrifice, everyone will be saved from physical death by the Resurrection and all can be saved from their sins through faith in Jesus Christ (see chapter 12 in this book).

The Lord doesn't ask of us any more than what He has already given Himself. He had to let go of all His children in order for us to come to earth. Many of us will never see His face again. He also gave us His beloved Son as a sacrifice to save us and open the door for us to return to Him. He gave everything He had for us to have this opportunity to become like Him. He requires that we learn to do the same. It is for our own growth and development that we learn this important lesson that we be willing to give up whatever is required of us to attain the blessings of the Celestial kingdom.

Christ's atoning sacrifice marked the end of sacrifices by the shedding of blood. Such outward sacrifice was replaced by the ordinance of the sacrament. The ordinance of the sacrament was given to remind us of the Savior's great sacrifice. We should partake of the sacrament often. The emblems of bread and water remind us of the Savior's body and of His blood, which He shed for us (see chapter 23 in this book).

The law of Sacrifice pointed the people to the great and last sacrifice Jesus would make for us all. Since Jesus fulfilled the purpose of the law of Sacrifice, with His death and resurrection it was no longer needed for us to offer up animal sacrifices that represented His great sacrifice.

• Why is the Atonement considered the great and last sacrifice?

We Still Must Sacrifice
• How do we observe the law of sacrifice today?

Even though sacrifice by the shedding of blood was ended, the Lord still asks us to sacrifice. But now He requires a different kind of offering. He said: "Ye shall offer up unto me no more the shedding of blood, … and your burnt offerings shall be done away. … And ye shall offer for a sacrifice unto me a broken heart and a contrite spirit" (3 Nephi 9:19–20). A "broken heart and a contrite spirit" means that we offer deep sorrow for our sins as we humble ourselves and repent of them.

With the law of Sacrifice fulfilled, the Lord now requires a willing heart. We need to be willing to anything and everything required of us by the Lord. The Lord owns everything in the universe except one thing, our will. Our salvation depends on our ability to surrender our will to His completely, without reservation or condition of any kind. Only then will we discover that by surrendering our will to God's will that we find that His will brings us joy we couldn't even guess at when we followed our own will.

We Must Be Willing to Sacrifice Everything We Have to the Lord
• Why are people willing to make sacrifices?

The Apostle Paul wrote that we should become living sacrifices, holy and acceptable unto God (see Romans 12:1).

If we are to be a living sacrifice, we must be willing to give everything we have for The Church of Jesus Christ of Latter-day Saints—to build the kingdom of God on the earth and labor to bring forth Zion (see 1 Nephi 13:37).

Sacrificing is a matter of faith and testimony. First of all we need to have faith that our sacrifices are for a good reason, even if we don't personally understand what it is. Second, once we have a testimony of the truthfulness of the gospel of Christ, and we have a sense of how great the blessings are to be a part of that gospel, we become more willing to make sacrifices. Our testimonies give us evidence that the sacrifices we are asked to make are worth it.

A rich young ruler asked the Savior, "What shall I do to inherit eternal life?" Jesus answered, "Thou knowest the commandments, Do not commit adultery, Do not kill, Do not steal, Do not bear false witness, Honour thy father and thy mother." And the rich man said, "All these have I kept from my youth." When Jesus heard this, He said, "Yet lackest thou one thing: sell all that thou hast, and distribute unto the poor, and thou shalt have treasure in heaven: and come, follow me." When the young man heard this, he was sorrowful. He was very rich and had his heart set on his riches. (See Luke 18:18–23; see also the picture in this chapter.)

The young ruler was a good man. But when he was put to the test, he was not willing to sacrifice his worldly possessions. On the other hand, the Lord's disciples Peter and Andrew were willing to sacrifice everything for the sake of the kingdom of God. When Jesus said unto them, "Follow me, … they straightway left their nets, and followed him" (Matthew 4:19–20).

Like the disciples, we can offer our daily activities as a sacrifice to the Lord. We can say, "Thy will be done." Abraham did this. He lived on the earth before Christ, in the days when sacrifices and burnt offerings were required. As a test of Abraham's faith, the Lord commanded him to offer up his son Isaac as a sacrifice. Isaac was the only son of Abraham and Sarah. The command to offer him as a sacrifice was extremely painful for Abraham.

Nevertheless, he and Isaac made the long journey to Mount Moriah, where the sacrifice was to be made. They traveled for three days. Imagine Abraham's thoughts and his heartache. His son was to be sacrificed to the Lord. When they reached Mount Moriah, Isaac carried the wood and Abraham carried the fire and the knife to the place where they were to build the altar. Isaac said, "My father … behold the fire and the wood: but where is the lamb for a burnt offering?" Abraham answered, "My son, God will provide himself a lamb." Then Abraham built an altar and arranged the wood on it. He bound Isaac and laid him upon the wood. He then took the knife to kill Isaac. At that moment an angel of the Lord stopped him, saying, "Abraham … lay not thine hand upon the lad, neither do thou any thing unto him: for now I know that thou fearest God, seeing thou hast not withheld thy son, thine only son from me." (See Genesis 22:1–14.)

Abraham must have been overcome with joy when he was no longer required to sacrifice his son. But he loved the Lord so much that he was willing to do anything the Lord asked.

Don't be fooled by this parable. Both the rich young man AND the Lord's disciples had to give everything they had. The rich young man had earthly possessions in abundance, but Peter and Andrew were willing to give all that they had even though what they had was very little. All that they had was still precious to them. The Lord never asks some to give all and others to give only a little. The price is the same for everyone - all that you have, be it little or much. The purpose is not to see how much the Lord can get, physical things all belong to Him anyway. The purpose is to test our attitude, our willingness to subject our will to His so He can bless us as much as He wants to bless us.

What we sacrifice in this life is not just money or material possessions. What we sacrifice includes our time, our energies, our very lives. The part that makes Abraham's test of faith so great is that the Lord demanded Abraham be willing to part with that which was most precious to him, his son. Abraham's hopes for all his posterity rested in Isaac. Isaac was the son God had promised him and had given him in his old age. All Abraham's dreams for the future of his line was tied up in that one son. Then God demanded Abraham offer up Isaac as a blood sacrifice.

This went against everything Abraham ever believed in. This challenged his understanding of everything he knew of God and His ways. He had to rely on his own personal testimony and decide within himself just how far he was willing to go to submit to the Lord's demands. It was only when he was willing to do whatever the Lord required, having full faith that the Lord could give him another son or raise Isaac from the dead if need be, that he was willing to do all that God commanded and offer his son.

The Lord will not ask us to offer our children on an altar, but each of us will be required at some point in our lives to give up something that is more precious to us than life itself. This is the ultimate test of faith and obedience. If we pass this test then the Lord will know that we can be trusted in all things, and His greatest blessings will be ours.

The Lord already knew how far Abraham was willing to go, but Abraham did not. The Lord needed Abraham to know his own limits, and in this case, that Abraham had no limits when it came to his obedience to the Lord. This was part of Abraham's growth and how the Lord helped him to see just how much faith he actually had in God. Sometimes the lessons we need to learn about ourselves, even the good ones, can be painful, but they are the most profitable lessons of all.

• What examples of sacrifice have you observed in the lives of people you know? What examples of sacrifice have you seen in the lives of your ancestors? in the lives of early members of the Church? in the lives of people in the scriptures? What have you learned from these examples?

Sacrifice Helps Us Prepare to Live in the Presence of God

Only through sacrifice can we become worthy to live in the presence of God. Only through sacrifice can we enjoy eternal life. Many who have lived before us have sacrificed all they had. We must be willing to do the same if we would earn the rich reward they enjoy.

This part of the lesson repeats the statement that it isn't what we give up it is our willingness to give up for the Lord that makes all the difference. When we are willing to give whatever is required, and harbor no ill will for the demanded sacrifice we become worthy of the Lord's choicest blessings, those held in reserve for the most faithful.

We may not be asked to sacrifice all things. But like Abraham, we should be willing to sacrifice everything to become worthy to live in the presence of the Lord.

The Lord's people have always sacrificed greatly and in many different ways. Some have suffered hardship and ridicule for the gospel. Some new converts to the Church have been cut off from their families. Lifetime friends have turned away. Some members have lost their jobs; some have lost their lives. But the Lord notices our sacrifices; He promises, "Every one that hath forsaken houses, or brethren, or sisters, or father, or mother, or wife, or children, or lands, for my name's sake, shall receive an hundredfold, and shall inherit everlasting life" (Matthew 19:29).

Different generations are required to sacrifice different things. The early Saints suffered great physical hardships. Once the Church became prosperous and the Saints began to be well accepted in society, their sacrifices changed to remaining faithful despite the pull of the world around them. Now as the world becomes increasingly wicked our sacrifice is demonstrated more and more by our tenacity to be faithful to God, despite the evils that bombard us on a daily basis. Each of us still has to give all we have to give. That doesn't change in any generation.

As our testimonies of the gospel grow, we become able to make greater sacrifices to the Lord. Note the sacrifices made in these true examples:

A member of the Church in Germany saved his tithing for years until someone with priesthood authority could come and accept it.

A Relief Society visiting teacher served for 30 years without missing an assignment.

A group of Saints in South Africa rode for three days, standing up, to be able to hear and see the prophet of the Lord.

At an area conference in Mexico, members of the Church slept on the ground and fasted during the days of the conference. They had used all their money just to get to the conference and had nothing left for food and shelter.

One family sold their car to get the money they wanted to contribute to a temple building fund.

The Lord never will ask someone who is unprepared for it to sacrifice his greatest treasure. To do that the person must be prepared over years of trials and service so the test is fair when it comes. The Lord will never demand more of us than we can be expected to give. But He knows our capacities. Sometimes we feel like He asks too much, but He would not ask it if we were not capable of making the needed sacrifice. In the end, every sacrifice we make for the Lord is rewarded with great spiritual blessings that bring us joy and peace.

Another family sold their home to get money to go to the temple.

Many faithful Latter-day Saints have very little to live on, yet they pay their tithes and offerings.

One brother sacrificed his job because he refused to work on Sunday.

In one branch, the youth gave freely and willingly of their time to care for the young children while their parents helped build the meetinghouse.

Young men and women give up or postpone good job opportunities, education, or sports to serve as missionaries.

Many more examples could be given of those who sacrifice for the Lord. Yet a place in our Heavenly Father's kingdom is worth any sacrifice we have to make of our time, talents, energy, money, and lives. Through sacrifice we can obtain a knowledge from the Lord that we are acceptable to Him (see D&C 97:8).

There is no reward more enviable than that of knowing the Lord has accepted your sacrifices and that you stand approved by Him. This brings a power into our lives that strengthens our faith, gives us greater stamina to be obedient, buoys up our spirits and brings peace to our souls. We should seek to be found acceptable to God. To feel that God is happy with us is a joy without taint.

• Why do you think our willingness to sacrifice is related to our readiness to live in the presence of God?

Additional Scriptures
• Luke 12:16–34 (where the treasure is, there is the heart)
• Luke 9:57–62 (sacrifice to be fit for the kingdom)
• D&C 64:23; 97:12 (today is a day of sacrifice)
• D&C 98:13–15 (those who lose life for the Lord will find it)
• Alma 24 (the people of Ammon sacrifice their lives rather than break their oath to the Lord)

Chapter 27

Work and Personal Responsibility
Gospel Principles, (2011), 155–60

Work Is an Eternal Principle
• What experiences have you had that have shown you the importance of work?

Our Heavenly Father and Jesus Christ have shown us by Their examples and teachings that work is important in heaven and on earth. God worked to create the heavens and the earth. He caused the seas to gather in one place and the dry land to appear. He caused grass, herbs, and trees to grow on the land. He created the sun, the moon, and the stars. He created every living thing in the sea or on the land. Then He placed Adam and Eve on the earth to take care of it and to have dominion over all living things. (See Genesis 1:1–28.)

Jesus said, "My Father worketh hitherto, and I work" (John 5:17). He also said, "I must work the works of him that sent me" (John 9:4).

For teachers: Try to help each class member or family member participate during the lesson. Individuals may help by setting up chairs, offering the opening or closing prayer, writing on the board, reading scriptures aloud, answering questions, sharing testimony, or summarizing the lesson.

We Are Commanded to Work
Work has been the way of life on earth since Adam and Eve left the Garden of Eden. The Lord said to Adam, "In the sweat of thy face shalt thou eat bread" (Genesis 3:19). Adam and Eve worked in the fields so they could provide for their own needs and the needs of their children (see Moses 5:1).

The Lord said to the people of Israel, "Six days shalt thou labour" (Exodus 20:9).

In the early days of the restored Church, the Lord told the Latter-day Saints, "Now, I, the Lord, am not well pleased with the inhabitants of Zion, for there are idlers among them" (D&C 68:31).

A prophet of God has said, "Work is to be reenthroned as the ruling principle of the lives of our Church membership" (Heber J. Grant, Teachings of Presidents of the Church: Heber J. Grant [2002], 115).

To think about work as an eternal principle, try to think of ways that work changes things. Does work change just our surroundings or does it actually change us as well? What does work do for a person's self image? What does work do for a person's maturity level? How is a person's character altered by hard work? Is that a good thing or a bad thing? How does an ethic of working hard effect trust or reliability? How might we view God if He was lazy and did no work?

Can you even imagine how it would be possible to create a world or hold a solar system, let alone a galaxy in order without knowing how to work?

Adam and Eve's directive was to take care of the garden, in other words, to go to work to keep up the beauty of the garden the Lord had already established for them.

The patter is that we are to follow in the footsteps of the Savior and do as He did. He, in turn, followed in the footsteps of His Father and did what He had seen His Father do.

In the garden everything cooperated with Adam and Eve. Once they had to leave the garden they had to fight the elements of the earth to get it to give them of its abundance. It took long hours and long days, with no conveniences, to gain even a subsistence living.

The Lord knows what work does for our souls. He sees that it is work that keeps us sharp, focused, productive, and responsible. Idleness is actually harmful to the soul, so being idle displeases the Lord.

To enthrone something is to put it on the throne or in the ruling position. The people had begun to be lazy and weren't working hard. The prophet was telling them that the virtue of hard work needed to be put back in place as one of the ruling virtues in their lives.

Family Responsibility

• What are some responsibilities that fathers, mothers, and children have to maintain a home? What can family members do to share in the work?

Parents work together to provide for the physical, spiritual, and emotional well-being of their family. They should never expect anyone to take care of this responsibility for them. The Apostle Paul wrote, "If any provide not for his own, and specially for those of his own house, he hath denied the faith" (1 Timothy 5:8).

Couples should seek inspiration from the Lord and follow the counsel of the prophets when establishing individual responsibilities. Creating a home where principles of the gospel are taught daily and where love and order abound is as important as providing the basic necessities of food and clothing.

Children should do their part in the work of the family. It is necessary for children to have work assignments to fit their abilities. They need to be praised for their successes. Good work attitudes, habits, and skills are learned through successful experiences in the home.

Sometimes people encounter hardships when trying to provide for their families. Chronic illness, the loss of a spouse, or the addition of an elderly parent can add to the responsibilities in a home. Our Heavenly Father remembers the families in these situations and gives them the strength to carry out their duties. He will always bless them if they ask Him in faith.

The thought that parents "should never expect anyone to take care of" their family is more difficult to teach in this day and age than it was in times past. Now the government and society teaches us all that it is a good thing for someone else to take care of us, and in many ways those who insist on caring for themselves are financially or socially punished. The governments of the world want people to be dependent on them so they can control their lives.

The Lord is very clear on this subject that we need to be independent in every way possible so we don't have to rely on others if at all possible.

There is no rule book that says this chore belongs only to the man or this chore belongs only to the woman. Division of labor in the family is up to the husband and wife to decide for themselves. There are times in life when the roles may have to alter in order to accommodate current situations. We need to be flexible and willing to do whatever is necessary to keep the family functioning. The most important thing is that all that the family does is based on the gospel of Christ and is centered around our worship of our Father in Heaven.

When we keep our Father in Heaven and the Savior at the center of our marriage and family activities, we will be able to have God's Spirit to guide us in helping us to provide appropriately for our family and in the righteous rearing of our children. We will also have His Spirit to help us in our relationship with our spouse.

As Christ did His Father's work, and we do what we see Christ do, so we need to teach our children that work is a blessing in their lives, and an important part of becoming responsible and trustworthy adults. This may take some thought and effort on the part of the parents. We have so many conveniences these days that the basic work of keeping up a home doesn't take nearly as long to do today as it did a hundred years ago. We may need to be creative in the ways we teach our children to work and expect to work hard on a regular basis.

There are plenty of situations we may find ourselves in that makes it difficult to support ourselves. We may have sick family members that need constant care or we may have problems finding gainful employment that will properly allow us to pay our bills. When we have these difficulties, and they should come to all of us, we need to learn to turn to the Lord for guidance. One of the great lessons of mortality rests in our learning to rely on our

Father in Heaven and His power to bless us beyond our current capacity to do things.

We Can Enjoy Our Work
• How does our attitude affect our work?

To some people work is a drudgery. To others it is an exciting part of life. One way to enjoy life's fullest benefits is to learn to love work.

Great sorrow will be experienced by anyone who finds work to be a punishment and hardship. Work is such an integral and necessary skill and ability for us to learn that to view it as a punishment can not bring anything good into our lives. Our attitude about work, as a principle, is very important. Work is a privilege and a joy. Work brings us independence, self reliance, satisfaction, and prosperity. The sooner we learn this principle, that work is a great blessing, the happier in life we will be.

Sometimes teaching children to enjoy work is difficult. It takes working with them and having a cheerful attitude while working to help them see that work is a blessing and not something to be run away from. If the adults in their lives cherish the ability and privilege to work, the chances are they will learn to see the value in being able to work. If their parents hate work and view it more as a punishment than a blessing, they will likewise look for ways to get out of having to work.

Not all of us can choose the kind of work we do. Some of us labor for long hours for the bare necessities. It is difficult to enjoy such work. Yet the happiest people have learned to enjoy their work, whatever it is.

Happiness doesn't come from the work itself. Happiness is independent of the labor we have to perform. It helps if our work involves something we love to do, but that doesn't mean we can't be happy independent of our labors if we have to work at something we don't naturally want to do. Remember that if we allow the nature of the work to be what determines our happiness then we will be unhappy much of the time. Everyone has things they have to do that are not pleasant. The joy needs to be in being able to work at all. We can often find joy in the company or conversations or activities we enjoy while we work. Even digging ditches or latrines can be enjoyable if you are doing it with friends or discussing the gospel while working.

We can help one another in our work. The heaviest load becomes lighter when someone shares it.

This is a great lesson to teach a child. If we can help them see that work is almost always more fun and productive if we do it with friends then it helps them learn to work with a better attitude.

Our attitude toward work is very important. The following story shows how one man saw beyond his daily labor. A traveler passed a stone quarry and saw three men working. He asked each man what he was doing. Each man's answer revealed a different attitude toward the same job. "I am cutting stone," the first man answered. The second replied, "I am earning three gold pieces per day." The third man smiled and said, "I am helping to build a house of God."

In any honest work we can serve God. King Benjamin, a Nephite prophet, said, "When ye are in the service of your fellow beings ye are only in the service of your God" (Mosiah 2:17). If our work provides only enough for necessities for ourselves or our families, we are still helping some of God's children.

• How can we improve our attitude about work?

God Condemns Idleness
The Lord is not pleased with those who are lazy or idle. He said, "The idler shall not have place in the church, except he repent and mend his ways" (D&C 75:29). He also commanded, "Thou shalt not be idle; for he that is idle shall not eat the bread nor wear the garments of the laborer" (D&C 42:42).

From the earliest days of the Church, the prophets have taught Latter-day Saints to be independent and self-sustaining and to avoid idleness. True Latter-day Saints will not voluntarily shift from themselves the burden of their own support. So long as they are able, they will supply themselves and their families with the necessities of life.

As far as they are able, all Church members should accept the responsibility to care for their relatives who are unable to provide for themselves.

• How does idleness affect an individual? a family? a community?

Work, Recreation, and Rest
• Why is it important to keep a balance in life between work, recreation, and rest?

We should each find the proper balance between work, recreation, and rest. There is an old saying: "Doing nothing is the hardest work of all, because one can never stop to rest." Without work, rest and relaxation have no meaning.

"In any honest work we can serve God." The Lord doesn't expect us to make millions or be classified as failures. He expects us to care for the needs of our family. Period. If we can do more than that then there are added responsibilities laid on us to use that money righteously to help build up His kingdom and bless the lives of more of His children. But honest work is honest work. How much that work pays is not the issue with the Lord. To Him our attitude toward the work and our desire to bless the lives of others is what is important.

Notice that the Lord is not pleased with those who are idle or lazy in the Church as well as those who don't work hard for the upkeep of themselves or their family. It is not the work that is important. It is what happens to us because we work that is important. To the Lord everything we experience is not about the experience, but about what happens to us because of the experiences. He is all about what we are becoming. That is the main focus for the Lord.

We should ask ourselves what happens spiritually, mentally, socially, and physically to those who are idle, as opposed to those who learn to love to work. What is the difference in attitude? What is the difference in reliability and responsibility? Why might He be so upset with those who try to get by without having to work? How are these people hurting themselves with their idleness? What blessings are they cheating themselves out of by not learning to love to work, whether that is through physical work or spiritual development?

Our first responsibility is to care for our family. That starts with our immediate family, but that extends to our relatives as well. The Lord wants us to be a larger family unit. We are going to be in family units in the eternities. We need to start thinking in terms of larger family units here. If a sibling or cousin or niece or nephew have needs, it becomes the responsibility of the whole family to address those needs. Note that I said needs, not wants. The Lord will hold the whole family responsible if we automatically turn to the government or some other source to help care for our own when we, as an extended family could have handled the need ourselves. We are only hurting ourselves.

There are those who know only how to avoid work. There are those who are workaholics and don't understand the need to rest and have a change of venue.

Brigham Young taught that we should work eight hours a day, play eight hours a day, and sleep eight hours a day. I don't know if he was strictly serious about those ratios, because something tells me he probably worked more than eight hours a day, but the point is there needs to be balance in our lives.

Not only is it pleasant and necessary to rest, but we are commanded to rest on the Sabbath day (see Exodus 20:10; D&C 59:9–12). This day of rest after each six days of labor brings refreshment for the days that follow. The Lord also promises the "fulness of the earth" to those who observe the Sabbath day (see D&C 59:16–20; see also chapter 24 in this book).

It is during our times of rest that we can work on our hobbies, our talents, our relationships with others. It is during times of rest we can study scriptures and the words of the prophets and give service to others that is unrelated to our paying jobs.

The most important time spent away from our daily work is on the Sabbath. On this day we are privileged to spend an entire day devoted to the Lord and His work.

On other days of the week, in addition to working, we may spend time to improve our talents and enjoy our hobbies, recreation, or other activities that will refresh us.

• What can we do to keep a good balance between work, recreation, and rest? How can parents help their children maintain this balance?

Parents need to keep involved in the lives of their children to make sure they don't have too much idle time. Most children in American culture today have too much idle time and not enough time devoted to learning to work hard. If more children learned to work hard at a young age, perhaps there would be more children who had their missions and college saved for by the time they were out of high school. This is not only a great blessing to the child, to know that they paid their own way and have a sense of appreciate for the cost of things, but it will also relieve a great financial burden from the shoulders of the parents who would otherwise be expected to pick up the slack and pay their way.

The Blessings of Work
• What are some blessings that come from honest work?

God revealed to Adam, "In the sweat of thy face shalt thou eat bread" (Genesis 3:19). In addition to being a temporal law, this was a law for the salvation of Adam's soul. There is no real division between spiritual, mental, and physical work. Work is essential to each of us for growth, character development, and many satisfactions that the idle never know.

President David O. McKay said, "Let us realize that the privilege to work is a gift, that the power to work is a blessing, that the love of work is success" (Pathways to Happiness [1957], 381).

"The love of work is success." This doesn't say that work that brings in X amount of money a year is success. It is the love of work that constitutes success. A person who loves to work hard will not be idle nor living off others when they could be supporting themselves. One who loves to work will automatically convey the desire to work hard to those around him/her and will set a good example of how to work hard. This is they kind of person the Lord can trust to get a job done.

"Men are, that they might have joy" (2 Nephi 2:25). Work is a key to full joy in the plan of God. If we are righteous, we will return to live with our Heavenly Father, and we will have work to do. As we become like Him, our work will become like His work. His work is "to bring to pass the immortality and eternal life of man" (Moses 1:39).

Additional Scriptures
• Moses 4:23–25 (Adam told that he would work all his life for his food)
• D&C 56:16–17 (God warns the rich and poor against greed, envy, and laziness)
• D&C 58:26–29 (men should be anxiously engaged in a good cause)
• Matthew 25:14–30 (parable of the talents)
• Ephesians 4:28 (steal no more but rather labor)
• 1 Thessalonians 4:11–12 (work with your own hands)
• 2 Nephi 5:17 (Nephi taught his people to work and be industrious)

Chapter 28

Service

Gospel Principles, (2011), 161–66

How We Can Serve

• Think about ways people have served you and your family members.

Jesus said, "I am among you as he that serveth" (Luke 22:27). As true followers of Jesus, we also must serve others.

Service is helping others who need assistance. Christlike service grows out of genuine love for the Savior and of love and concern for those whom He gives us opportunities and direction to help. Love is more than a feeling; when we love others, we want to help them.

All of us must be willing to serve, no matter what our income, age, or social position. Some people believe that only the poor and lowly should serve. Other people think service should be given only by the rich. But Jesus taught otherwise. When the mother of two of His disciples asked Him to honor her sons in His kingdom, Jesus replied, "Whosoever will be great among you, let him be your minister; and whosoever will be chief among you, let him be your servant" (Matthew 20:26–27).

There are many ways to serve. We can help others economically, socially, physically, and spiritually. For example, we can share food or other articles with those who need them. We can help those in need by giving a generous fast offering. We can be a friend to a newcomer. We can plant a garden for an elderly person or care for someone who is sick. We can teach the gospel to someone who needs the truth or comfort someone who grieves.

We can do small and large acts of service. We should never fail to help someone because we are unable to do great things. A widow told of two children who came to her door shortly after she had moved to a new town. The children brought her a lunch basket and a note that read, "If you want anyone to do errands, call us." The widow was gladdened by the small kindness and never forgot it.

Sometimes, however, we must sacrifice greatly to serve someone. The Savior gave up His life in serving us.

• Think about people in your family or community who are in need economically, socially, physically, or spiritually. Ponder things you can do to serve them.

There is more than one motivation to serve others. We can serve out of selfish motivation, hoping to get something for ourselves out of our service, or we can serve because it is a necessity imposed on us from someone else. But Christlike service is an expression of genuine concern for the welfare of others. This type of service has no hope or desire for personal gain attached. The service has only the hope of blessing the life of the one being served. Christlike service cannot be withheld. It is spontaneously urged outward from the heart to the hands in an effort to uplift and care for someone we love.

The concept of the universal need to serve others fits in with all the other commandments. There is no such thing as a commandment that applies only to the wealthy or only to the poor. All of God's commandments are universal and must be experienced by all. The blessing for one commandment is the same for everyone who keeps that commandment. Service is no different in its application or its attending blessings.

Sometimes we feel bad that we can't do more than we want to do. We may feel that service requires money or lots of time or a certain amount of social connections. But service to others can be as simple as a smile to someone who looks lost or lonely. Christlike service is not found in the act, but the love behind the act.

One of the keys to Christlike service is to look for ways to be of help. That means thinking of non-standard ways of being helpful to someone in need. Like the children who offered to run errands for the new widow on the block, we can, with a little effort, think of creative ways to help someone's life be easier or less stressful.

On the other end of the scale is the service that requires our all, all our time, all our efforts, all our love, all our hope. An ailing loved one or a neighbor who has a permanent need, both require giving that goes far beyond the normal volunteering spirit to cut someone's grass for them or to cook them a meal.

Why the Savior Wants Us to Serve Others
• Why does the Lord want us to serve others?

Through the service of men and women and boys and girls, God's work is done. President Spencer W. Kimball explained: "God does notice us, and he watches over us. But it is usually through another person that he meets our needs" (Teachings of Presidents of the Church: Spencer W. Kimball [2006], 82).

One of the basic principles of salvation that we rarely talk about in the church is that salvation is achieved on the scale of the whole human family, not on an individual basis. We have agreed to look out for each other and to lift and support each other, whether in the church organization or outside the church. Our Father in Heaven wants us to learn to think like Christ. He places everyone's needs as a high priority. He sacrificed for all, not just for a few. We need to think along the same lines. There shouldn't be any person or group that lies outside our desire to bless.

Throughout our lives all of us depend on others for help. When we were infants, our parents fed, clothed, and cared for us. Without this care we would have died. When we grew up, other people taught us skills and attitudes. Many of us have needed nursing care during illness or money in a financial crisis. Some of us ask God to bless suffering people and then do nothing for them. We must remember that God works through us.

When we help one another, we serve God. King Benjamin, a great king in Book of Mormon times, taught his people this principle by the way he lived. He served them all his life, earning his own living instead of being supported by the people. In an inspired sermon he explained why he loved service, saying:

In 1 John 4:19 it says, "We love him, because he first loved us." The same holds true for our service. We serve others because that is how we serve Him. We serve Him because he first served us. He said that is we love him we must love one another and keep His commandments. What are those commandments, but to love one another through serving each other. No matter how you slice it, we keep coming back to the need to serve one another in order to show love for God.

"When ye are in the service of your fellow beings ye are only in the service of your God. …

"And if I, whom ye call your king, do labor to serve you, then ought not ye to labor to serve one another?" (Mosiah 2:17–18).

• What can we do to be ready to meet the needs of others?

We Receive Blessings through Service
• What blessings do we receive through service to others?

When we serve others we gain important blessings. Through service we increase our ability to love. We become less selfish. As we think of the problems of others, our own problems seem less serious. We must serve others to gain eternal life. God has said that those who live with Him must love and serve His children (see Matthew 25:34–40).

Aren't the commandments great? We serve because we are commanded to and we learn to overcome our own selfishness. We serve others and we learn to love without reservation. We serve others and our problems seem smaller. We serve others and we gain eternal life. Aren't the commandments great?

When we consider the lives of people who serve unselfishly, we can see that they gain more than they give. One such person was a Latter-day Saint named Paul who lost the use of both legs in an accident. Some men might have become bitter and useless, but Paul chose to think of others instead. He learned a trade and earned enough money to buy a house. There he and his wife made room for many homeless, unwanted children. Some were badly handicapped. Until his death 20 years later, he served these children and others. In return he was greatly loved, and his thoughts turned away from his crippled legs. He grew close to the Lord.

President Spencer W. Kimball said, "We become more substantive as we serve others—indeed, it is easier to 'find' ourselves because there is so much more of us to find!" (Teachings of Presidents of the Church: Spencer W. Kimball, 85–86).

What does it mean to become more substantive as we serve others? Part of that answer might include the fact that service increases our reliability, integrity, responsibility, compassion, empathy, sympathy, appreciation, gratitude, etc. The more we serve the more of all good things there grows in us.

Opportunities to Serve

Some of us serve only those we enjoy being around and avoid all others. However, Jesus commanded us to love and serve everyone. There are many opportunities to serve (see Mosiah 4:15–19).

We can serve members of our families. Husbands and wives should be aware of each other's needs. Parents should serve their children not only by feeding and clothing them but also by teaching and by playing and working with them. Children can serve by helping with household chores and by helping brothers and sisters.

Service should start in the home with serving each other. Even little children can learn to serve others. Sharing is a big part of learning to serve at home. This is more difficult for some children than for others, but learning to give of ourselves and of all our possessions is an important part of learning to serve. Parents can learn to give in a fresh new way when they learn to relax and play with their children in an unstructured way. Relax and let love and play take its course.

Husbands and wives serve and help each other. They can help each other take care of the children, and they can support one another in their individual interests and pursuits. A mother and father may sacrifice to send a child on a mission. An older boy may comfort a little sister who is afraid of the dark or help her learn to read. Our prophets have told us that a family is the most important unit in society. We must serve our families well (see Mosiah 4:14–15).

We are often most cruel to those we are closest to. Learning to be loving and serving to our spouse is a great place to learn how to serve in a selfless way. This will require looking past all the little things that push our buttons, and allowing our spouse to be themselves without judgment. Teaching our children to do the same for their siblings will also bring a measure of peace into the home.

We have many opportunities to serve our neighbors, our friends, and even strangers. If a neighbor is having difficulty harvesting crops before a storm, we can help. If a mother is ill, we can watch her children or help with the housework. If a young man is falling away from the Church, we can lead him back. If a child is ridiculed, we can befriend him and persuade others to be kind. We do not need to know the people we serve. We should look for ways to serve as many of our Heavenly Father's children as we can.

Sometimes service doesn't need to be proposed and accepted beforehand. Some of the best service comes from finding a need then doing what we can to fill that need. It is often the unbidden service that does the most good.

If we have special talents, we should use them to serve others. God blesses us with talents and abilities to help improve the lives of others.

Not all talents are in the performing arts. Some are gifted listeners, some are able to empathize, and some can speak a kind word at the right time. Try not to minimize your abilities to be good to others. It is in the effort to be good that what talents we do possess are strengthened and enlarged. It is in the act and effort of being kind to others that new talents will reveal themselves to us.

We have opportunities to serve in the Church. One purpose of the Church organization is to give us opportunities to help each other. Members of the Church serve by doing missionary work, accepting leadership assignments, visiting other Church members, teaching classes, and doing other Church work. In The Church of Jesus Christ of Latter-day Saints there is no professional clergy, so the lay members must carry on all of the activities of the Church.

• How can we give enough time to our family, even with our many opportunities to give service in the Church and community?

Often it is enough to include our family in our service efforts. By letting our children see and participate in the service we render in the Church that they learn how important service is to us, and happy service can make us.

Jesus Christ Is the Perfect Example of Service
• What are some of your favorite scripture stories in which the Savior sets an example of service?

For teachers: When we share our testimonies of Jesus Christ, we invite the influence of the Holy Ghost. As you prepare and teach, frequently look for ways to testify of the Savior and to invite those you teach to do the same.

The Savior provided the perfect example of service. He explained that He didn't come to earth to be served but to serve and to give His life for us (see Matthew 20:28).

Jesus Christ loves all of us more than we can understand. When He was on earth He served the poor, the ignorant, the sinner, the despised. He taught the gospel to all who would listen, fed crowds of hungry people who came to hear Him, healed the sick, and raised the dead.

He is the Creator of the earth and our Savior, yet He did many humble acts of service. Just before His Crucifixion He met with His disciples. After teaching them, He took a basin of water and a towel and washed their feet (see John 13:4–10; see also the picture in this chapter). In those days washing a visitor's feet was a sign of honor and was usually done by a servant. Jesus did it as an example of love and service. When we willingly serve others in the spirit of love, we become more like Christ.

It is important to recognize that no act of service was beneath or too low for the Savior to perform. He was just as comfortable speaking to kings as he was performing the role of a servant as he washed the feet of the apostles. Jesus was never afraid to get his hands dirty in the service of others.

• What can we learn from the Savior's example of service?

Additional Scriptures
• Mosiah 2 (King Benjamin's discourse on service)
• D&C 81:5 (succor, lift, strengthen)

• Colossians 3:23–24 (serve others as you would serve the Lord)
• Alma 17–18 (Ammon served the king)
• Galatians 5:13 (serve one another by love)

Chapter 29

The Lord's Law of Health

Gospel Principles, (2011), 167–72

Our Bodies Are Temples of God

One of the great blessings we received when we came to earth was a physical body. We need a physical body to become like our Heavenly Father. Our bodies are so important that the Lord calls them temples of God (see 1 Corinthians 3:16–17; 6:19–20). Our bodies are holy.

Because our bodies are important, our Father in Heaven wants us to take good care of them. He knows that we can be happier, better people if we are healthy. The Holy Ghost can be with us if our bodies and minds are clean. Our Father knows that we face temptations to treat our bodies unwisely or to take harmful things into them. For this reason He has told us which things are good for our health and which things are bad. Much of the information God has given us concerning good health is found in Doctrine and Covenants 89. This revelation is called the Word of Wisdom.

We must obey the Word of Wisdom to be worthy to enter the temple. If we do not obey the Word of Wisdom, the Lord's Spirit withdraws from us. If we defile the "temple of God," which is our body, we hurt ourselves physically and spiritually.

We Are Commanded Not to Take Certain Things into Our Bodies

• What has the Lord commanded us not to take into our bodies?

The Lord commands us not to use wine and strong drinks, meaning drinks containing alcohol. The First Presidency has taught that strong drink often brings cruelty, poverty, disease, and plague into the home. It often is a cause of dishonesty, loss of chastity, and loss of good judgment. It is a curse to all who drink it. (See "Message of the First Presidency," Improvement Era, Nov. 1942, 686.) Expectant mothers who drink can cause physical and mental damage to their children. Many automobile accidents are caused each year by people who drink alcohol.

How are our bodies holy, like a temple? We spent the whole first half of eternity without one. We had to prove ourselves worthy to get the body we currently have by "keeping our first estate." In other words, we were faithful to God in the premortal spirit world. Being faithful to Him came with the promise that we would get to have a physical body, similar to his, for eternity. Earth life is the second proving ground that will determine exactly which kind of body we will qualify for, Telestial, Terrestrial, or Celestial. Our obedience to God in our short stay in mortality determines the quality of our body for the other half of eternity. This makes our bodies extremely special, even sacred. Hence the reason they are referred to as temples, which are the most sacred of places. We have literally waited an eternity for this opportunity to get a body like our Father in Heaven.

The healthier our bodies are, the better we feel, and the greater our chances of being happy. Is it any wonder why Satan would have us do things to destroy our chances for happiness by abusing and misusing our bodies? To help us have the best possible experience while in mortality the Lord has given us ways to protect and honor the sacred nature of our bodies.

One of the important lessons we need to learn in mortality is that what we do spiritually affects us physically. What we do physically affects us spiritually. Our spirit is so tightly embedded in our body that you cannot separate the joint effects of all experiences. The Lord's Spirit is a Celestial being. He won't come and spend time with someone who is not making any effort to behave in a manner that invites His presence. When we do things to pollute or mismanage our bodies we offend the Spirit and He leaves us. This hurts us spiritually.

The Word of Wisdom is one of those commandments that causes a lot of confusion in the minds of many. Because the Lord only names a few things we are not to consume, and only names a few things we are to consume, there are those who try to justify why their preferred foods are okay to eat or drink. Others go too far in the opposite direction and try to justify even more strict rules.

It is called the Word of Wisdom because we need to listen to the Spirit and let Him guide and direct us in how to care for our bodies using the Word of Wisdom as a starting point. A good rule of thumb to live by is this: If you haven't heard a prophet teach about eating or drinking certain foods or behaving in a certain way then be careful about adopting it and teaching it as doctrine.

Alcohol, despite the benefits society claims to have from its consumption, is considered to be too risky to drink. The Lord never said there were no benefits from drinking alcohol. What the Lord and his servants have said is that the results of drinking alcohol lead to too many unpleasant affects. It is better to leave it alone and not have to worry about any of the affects of drinking.

For teachers: Writing lists can generate interest and help learners focus their attention. As class members or family members discuss substances that the Lord has commanded us not to take into our bodies, you may want to ask someone to write their answers on the board or on a large piece of paper. You could do the same when they discuss things that are healthful for our bodies.

The Lord has also told us that "tobacco is not for the body" (D&C 89:8). It is harmful to our bodies and our spirits. We should not smoke cigarettes or cigars or use chewing tobacco. Scientists have shown that tobacco causes many diseases and can harm unborn children.

There are no health benefits in smoking tobacco that make it worthy of entering our bodies. Whether it is in smoked form or chewed form, ultimately, tobacco brings nothing but sorrow to those who use it.

The Lord also counsels us against the use of "hot drinks" (D&C 89:9). Church leaders have said that this means coffee and tea, which contain harmful substances. We should avoid all drinks that contain harmful substances.

This is the most hotly contested part of the Word of Wisdom. The prophets have told us that "hot drinks" are defined as coffee and tea (meaning the leaf of the Tea plant). Their definition is pretty simple, and there are substitutes for coffee and tea that are much more healthy for the body if you feel you need to drink them.

We should not use drugs except when they are necessary as medicine. Some drugs are even more harmful than alcohol and tobacco (which are also drugs). Those who misuse drugs need to seek help, pray for strength, and counsel with their bishop so they can fully repent and become clean.

Many drugs are addictive in nature or cause lasting harm to the body. We need to avoid any substance that causes harm or addiction. The Spirit is our guide back to our heavenly home. If we are addicted to any substance it hampers communication with the Spirit, making it more difficult to be taught and led as we ought to be.

We should avoid anything that we know is harmful to our bodies. We should not use any substance that is habit forming. We should also avoid overeating. The Word of Wisdom does not tell us everything to avoid or consume, but it does give us guidelines. It is a valuable temporal law. It is also a great spiritual law. By living the Word of Wisdom, we become stronger spiritually. We purify our bodies so the Spirit of the Lord can dwell with us.

"We should avoid anything that we know is harmful to our bodies." I love this sentence. It is like saying, "It isn't wise to hit yourself over the head with a hammer." Yet how many times do we pick up a drink at the grocery store just loaded with chemicals designed to temporarily stimulate us? How often do we take prescribed meds without even asking if there is a healthier alternative?

The point of the Word of Wisdom is to keep us thinking about what is wise for our bodies. We need to learn to take good care of them so they can provide us with the greatest spiritual benefit in mortality. Once we receive our resurrected bodies we won't have to worry about sickness and degeneration, but we do need to worry about it now. Prayerfully following the counsel in the Word of Wisdom will maximize our chances for a better physical and spiritual experience in mortality.

• What are some things that are not specifically mentioned in the Word of Wisdom that we should avoid?

We Are Taught That Certain Things Are Good for Our Bodies

• According to the Word of Wisdom, what are some things the Lord says are good for us?

Fruits, vegetables, and wholesome herbs are good for us. We should use them with wisdom and thanksgiving.

The flesh of birds and animals is also provided for our food. However, we should eat meat sparingly (see D&C 49:18; 89:12). Fish is also good for us to eat.

Grains are good for us. Wheat is especially good for us.

This portion of the Word of Wisdom tends to cause massive confusion. In the United States, for example, we are a nation that eats massive amounts of red meat, especially beef and pork. We know that lots of meat is not good for us. The only thing the Lord tells us is that we need to eat it "sparingly." The term "sparingly" is not defined. This is something in which we need to seek guidance from the Spirit. He will help us feel good about how we define "sparingly."

Some take the admonition to eat fresh fruits and vegetables in season, and grains regularly, and assume the Lord wants us all to be strict vegans. That is not in the Word of Wisdom. The key to eating most foods, as described in the Word of Wisdom is "moderation."

The Lord is also concerned that we be properly grateful for the food we have to eat. We should be giving thanks over all our meals, and seeking the Spirit constantly. If we are having difficulties feeling the Spirit in our lives, we might want to revisit the Word of Wisdom to see if we are living the best way we know how. This will help us remove some of the obstacles that might be keeping us from experiencing His constant companionship.

• How has the use of these things blessed you?

Work, Rest, and Exercise Are Important

• What do work, rest, and exercise have to do with the Lord's law of health?

In addition to Doctrine and Covenants 89, other scriptures tell us how to be healthy. They tell us that we should "cease to be idle; cease to be unclean; … cease to sleep longer than is needful; retire to thy bed early, that ye may not be weary; arise early, that your bodies and your minds may be invigorated" (D&C 88:124). We are also told, "Six days shalt thou labour, and do all thy work" (Exodus 20:9). The Lord counsels us not to labor more than we have strength for (see D&C 10:4).

Being healthy is more than just what we eat. To experience a full life of energy and vitality we need to get enough sleep, "cease to be idle," bathe regularly, set early bedtimes and early times to arise in the morning. We need exercise to keep our bodies working properly.

Our bodies and our minds are connected. What affects the health of the body also affects the health of the mind and personality. Bodies are highly complex things. We need to become accustomed to searching for and maintaining an overall lifestyle that promotes health and vitality. Ultimately, this is also what is best for us spiritually.

A latter-day prophet has told us that we should keep our bodies healthy. He counseled, "Nutritious meals, regular exercise, and appropriate sleep are necessary for a strong body, just as consistent scripture study and prayer strengthen the mind and spirit" (Thomas S. Monson, in Conference Report, Oct. 1990, 60; or Ensign, Nov. 1990, 46).

Promised Blessings for Living the Lord's Law of Health

• What blessings come to us as we obey the Word of Wisdom?

Our Heavenly Father has given us health laws to teach us how to care for our bodies. The scriptures tell us about God's laws: "No temporal commandment gave I ... , for my commandments are spiritual" (D&C 29:35). This means that His commandments concerning our physical state are for our spiritual good.

This is the most underrated part of the Word of Wisdom. Many mistakenly believe that if we take good care of our bodies we will feel good. That is as far as they understand the Word of Wisdom. The Lord's law of health does much more than help us feel good. Remember that our spirituality is mixed up in here as well. What helps us physically also helps us spiritually.

When we keep the Lord's law of health and obey His other commandments, the Lord promises to bless us physically and spiritually.

Physically we have been promised good health. As a result of this good health we "shall run and not be weary, and shall walk and not faint" (D&C 89:20). This is a great blessing, but the spiritual blessings He has promised us are even greater than the physical ones.

The Lord promises us that we "shall find wisdom and great treasures of knowledge, even hidden treasures" (D&C 89:19). We will be taught important truths by the Holy Ghost through revelation. President Boyd K. Packer taught: "Our physical body is the instrument of our spirit. In that marvelous revelation the Word of Wisdom, we are told how to keep our bodies free from impurities which might dull, even destroy, those delicate physical senses which have to do with spiritual communication. The Word of Wisdom is a key to individual revelation" (in Conference Report, Oct. 1989, 16; or Ensign, Nov. 1989, 14).

A mystery is something that is unknown. Once we know a thing it is no longer a mystery. Most things of the Spirit are heavenly mysteries until we learn them. When the Lord promises us "treasures of knowledge, even hidden treasures" we are being promised that not only will our thinking be more clear and sharp, but because of the added companionship of the Holy Ghost we will learn of the things of heaven, the mysteries. These are the "hidden treasures." Keeping the Word of Wisdom helps us keep our sensitivity to the Spirit sharp so we can follow His promptings more easily. This means we also receive answers to our prayers more easily.

The Lord also promises that the destroying angel shall pass us by. President Heber J. Grant said, "If you and I desire the blessings of life, of health, of vigor of body and mind; if we desire the destroying angel to pass us by, as he did in the days of the children of Israel, we must obey the Word of Wisdom; then God is bound, and the blessing shall come to us" (Teachings of Presidents of the Church: Heber J. Grant [2002], 192).

Some of the blessings of keeping the Lord's law of health we have to take on faith. The Lord has promised us that those who obey this law, in addition to all the other promised blessings, will also be protected from things that will kill others. Whether that refers to spiritually dying or physically dying is a matter of opinion, but either way will answer the promise.

• How can we help children and youth understand the eternal significance of the Word of Wisdom?

• What can we do to help family members or friends who have difficulty obeying the Word of Wisdom?

Additional Scriptures

• Judges 13:13–14; Proverbs 20:1; Isaiah 5:11–12; Daniel 1 (avoid strong drink)

• D&C 59:16–20 (things of the earth for the benefit of man)

• Proverbs 23:20–21 (warning against drunkenness, gluttony, laziness)

• D&C 136:24 (cease drunkenness)

Chapter 30

Charity

Gospel Principles, (2011), 173–78

What Is Charity?

• How would you define charity?

The life of the Savior reflects His pure love for all people. He even gave His life for us. Charity is that pure love which our Savior Jesus Christ has. He has commanded us to love one another as He loves us. The scriptures tell us that charity comes from a pure heart (see 1 Timothy 1:5). We have pure love when, from the heart, we show genuine concern and compassion for all our brothers and sisters.

Charity Is the Greatest of All Virtues

The prophet Mormon tells us, "Wherefore, cleave unto charity, which is the greatest of all, for all things must fail—but charity is the pure love of Christ, and it endureth forever" (Moroni 7:46–47; see also 1 Corinthians 13; 2 Nephi 26:30; Moroni 7:44–45, 48).

The Savior gave us the example of His life to follow. He was the Son of God. He had perfect love, and He showed us how to love. By His example, He showed us that the spiritual and physical needs of our fellowmen are as important as our own. Before He gave His life for us, He said:

"This is my commandment, That ye love one another, as I have loved you.

"Greater love hath no man than this, that a man lay down his life for his friends" (John 15:12–13).

Speaking to the Lord, Moroni said:

"I remember that thou hast said that thou hast loved the world, even unto the laying down of thy life for the world.
…

"And now I know that this love which thou hast had for the children of men is charity; wherefore, except men shall have charity they cannot inherit that place which thou hast prepared in the mansions of thy Father" (Ether 12:33–34).

It may not be necessary for us to give our lives as the Savior did. But we can have charity if we make Him the center of our lives and follow His example and teachings.

Charity is the most mature form of love. Trying to describe charity to most people is like trying to describe adult marital love to a child. We can give examples and lists till we are blue in the face, but it really has to be experienced to be understood.

Despite our difficulty in understanding and comprehending this godly form of love, we still need to work toward experiencing it. Our greatest joy will come from developing the character needed to experience charity.

Consider that a pure heart and pure love refers to love that is untainted by ulterior motives. There is nothing selfish in pure love. The only concern is the safety and happiness of the object of that love. This kind of love is completely unselfish in nature. A person feeling this kind of love is not concerned about personal inconvenience or personal sacrifices that might be required. The only thing that truly matters is the welfare of the other person.

God's love for us is undying, and never ending. It implies a level of devotion to the cause of our happiness that never flags or tires, and a belief in our capacity to do and be better than we are today. This kind of love gives its holder the ability to continue loving despite rejection, and demonstrations of disdain for efforts made on their behalf.

The closest examples of this kind of love we have is a mother's love. Even mothers cannot explain how they can continue to love an ungrateful and spiteful child. A mother's love becomes true charity when it is able to be felt in equal force for a family member as it is for a perfect stranger.

The purpose of the second of the two great commandments is to love our neighbor (one another) as Christ has loved us. This is that spreading of concern for someone's welfare from just a family member to the population as a whole.

This is the beginning of charity, to "bless the lives of our brother and sisters here on earth." When we center our lives around Christ and his teachings the Holy Ghost will

Like the Savior, we too can bless the lives of our brothers and sisters here on earth.

• Why is charity the greatest of all virtues?

Charity Includes Giving to the Sick, Afflicted, and Poor
The Savior gave us many teachings in the form of stories or parables. The parable of the good Samaritan teaches us that we should give to those in need, regardless of whether they are our friends or not (see Luke 10:30–37; see also James E. Talmage, Jesus the Christ, 3rd ed. [1916], 430–32). In the parable, the Savior said that a man was traveling to another city. On the road he was attacked by bandits. They stole his clothes and money and beat him, leaving him half dead. A priest came along, saw him, and passed him by. Then a temple attendant walked over, looked at him, and went on. However, a Samaritan, who was despised by the Jews, came along, and when he saw the man he felt compassion (see the picture in this chapter). Kneeling beside him, the good Samaritan bandaged his wounds and took him on a donkey to an inn. He paid the innkeeper to take care of the man until he recovered.

Jesus taught that we should give food to the hungry, shelter to those who have none, and clothes to the poor. When we visit the sick and those who are in prison, it is as if we were doing these things for Him instead. He promises that as we do these things, we will inherit His kingdom. (See Matthew 25:34–46.)

We should not try to decide whether someone really deserves our help or not (see Mosiah 4:16–24). If we have taken care of our own family's needs first, then we should help all who need help. In this way we will be like our Father in Heaven, who causes rain to fall on the just and on the unjust alike (see Matthew 5:44–45).

President Thomas S. Monson reminded us that there are those who need more than material goods:

teach us how to begin to feel true compassion for others, and to forget ourselves in the process of serving others.

Charity and pride are opposites. Pride is enmity or hatred towards others, and is completely focused on self. Charity is love and concern for the welfare of others. To experience charity we have to turn our attention outward and focus on a concern for the happiness of someone other than ourselves. A charitable person knows that focusing on others brings joy to self. A truly charitable person never needs to worry about finding happiness for self because happiness is generated automatically as a result of caring for others.

Part of the power behind the story of the good Samaritan is that the Samaritan, who was hated and treated as an inferior to the Jews, was the one who willingly cared for an injured Jew, placing himself in possible danger to care for him out on the open road where the man had already been attacked. He also gave of himself by paying for his time in the inn, giving the man a chance to recover before he had to move on. He also gave of himself by personally seeing to the injured man's wounds.

We may not run across injured people in the road that need our assistance, but there is still plenty to be done to relieve suffering among our brothers and sister here in mortality. The goal is to get us to see our neighbor in the same light we should be viewing our immediate siblings. Are we just as forgiving and patient with a stranger as we are with our own family member or our own child? Would we stand by and watch a family member suffer day in and day out for want of food, clothing, work, or anything else for that matter, or would we step in and see what we could do to help a person we care deeply about? Are we doing this for our neighbors?

We are all beggars before the Lord. We are all undeserving of the rich blessings we receive at His hands. It is for this reason that we are told in the scriptures that if we turn away those who beg for help from us it is we who will be punished for our ingratitude to God. It is because we become hypocrites when we beg the Lord for blessings, but turn away the beggar when we get up off our knees. King Benjamin's sermon in the first four chapters of Mosiah in the Book of Mormon is the best description of this doctrine to be found anywhere in the scriptures.

An important lesson about doing good is that the opportunity to do good doesn't always last forever. Sometimes, as President Monson says, our opportunities

"Let us ask ourselves the questions: 'Have I done any good in the world today? Have I helped anyone in need?' [Hymns, no. 223]. What a formula for happiness! What a prescription for contentment, for inner peace—to have inspired gratitude in another human being.

"Our opportunities to give of ourselves are indeed limitless, but they are also perishable. There are hearts to gladden. There are kind words to say. There are gifts to be given. There are deeds to be done. There are souls to be saved" (in Conference Report, Oct. 2001, 72; or Ensign, Nov. 2001, 60).

to give of ourselves are limitless, "but they are also perishable." Life changes quickly. An opportunity to change a life today may no longer be there tomorrow. We need to learn to seize those opportunities as soon as we see them. If we pause and consider too long we may just have "considered" ourselves right out of a blessing of possibly eternal duration. We just never know how much a small act of kindness will affect another person. Nor can we tell for how long it will affect them. And we aren't doing good for the personal glory of being able to say, "Yes, I did that!" We are doing good because we are concerned about the happiness of the other person. Our happiness flows out of our efforts to secure their happiness.

• In the parable of the good Samaritan, how would you describe those who passed the injured man? How would you describe the Samaritan? In what ways can we apply the message of this parable in our lives?

Charity Comes from the Heart
• How can we love people in spite of their sins and faults?

Even when we give to those in need, unless we feel compassion for them we do not have charity (see 1 John 3:16–17). The Apostle Paul taught that when we have charity we are filled with good feelings for all people. We are patient and kind. We are not boastful or proud, selfish or rude. When we have charity we do not remember or rejoice in the evil others have done. Neither do we do good things just because it is to our advantage. Instead, we share the joy of those who live by truth. When we have charity we are loyal, we believe the best of others, and we are kind to them. The scriptures teach that "charity never faileth." (See 1 Corinthians 13:4–8.)

Charity is not an action, but the intent behind the action. It is the reason for why we do good, not the good that we do. This is why charity is the most mature spiritual virtue we can develop. It goes beyond just habits of doing good. Charity is what creates the inner need for us to do good. It propels us and pushes us, inspires us to bless the lives of others. Charity won't let us rest when there is good we could be doing.

The Savior was our example of how to feel toward and treat others. He despised wickedness, but He loved sinners in spite of their sins. He had compassion for children, the elderly, the poor, and the needy. He had such great love that He could beg our Heavenly Father to forgive the soldiers who drove the nails into His hands and feet (see Luke 23:34). He taught us that if we do not forgive others, our Father in Heaven will not forgive us (see Matthew 18:33–35). He said: "I say unto you, Love your enemies, bless them that curse you, do good to them that hate you, and pray for them which despitefully use you, and persecute you. … For if ye love them which love you, what reward have ye?" (Matthew 5:44, 46). We must learn to feel toward others as Jesus did.

To learn how to love someone who does not love you back is hard to do. To pray for someone who despitefully uses you is painful to do. To find it within yourself to bless someone who has cursed you is almost unimaginable, unless of course, you have developed a degree of charity. Charity sees the potential of a person, not their behavior. Charity sees the value of the redeemed person, even when they are behaving in an unredeemable way. Charity is the optimistic voice of hope for every person who is hurting themselves through disobedience. Charity sees the person for who they could be, not who they are acting like now. Charity is that fixed ability to see beyond the now and see the potential for greatness and joy within each soul. It is that driving desire to help bring that person to their potential that motivates us to love them and want to help them.

Page 143

Developing the Virtue of Charity

• How can we become more charitable?

For teachers: Under the heading "Developing the Virtue of Charity," each of the first four paragraphs teaches one way we can become more charitable. If the setting allows for small group discussion, consider dividing class members or family members into groups of four. Assign one of the four paragraphs to each member of each group. Invite participants to study their assigned paragraphs individually. Ask them to think of examples, from the lives of people they know or people in the scriptures, that represent this way of becoming charitable. Then ask them to share their examples with each other in their groups.

One way we can become charitable is by studying the life of Jesus Christ and keeping His commandments. We can study what He did in certain situations and do the same things when we are in the same kinds of situations.

As they say, "imitation is the sincerest form of flattery." If we want to become Christlike then acting like Christ in every situation we can think of is a great way to start.

Second, when we have uncharitable feelings, we can pray to have greater charity. Mormon urges us, "Pray unto the Father with all the energy of heart, that ye may be filled with this love [charity], which he hath bestowed upon all who are true followers of his Son, Jesus Christ" (Moroni 7:48).

Remember always that the changing of our hearts from where we are now to where we want to be is a gift from God. Only He has the ability to change the very desires of our hearts. But fortunately, God wants us to seek for these changes, and wants to grant this blessing to us. He knows that it is only through these changes of heart that we will find the joy He has to offer us in greater measure. So by all means, pray for a change of heart. Beg and plead to have a softer, more manageable heart. Plead to become more like Christ and the Lord will lead you to that destiny one experience at a time. As long as you continue to follow the promptings to do good and to forgive and are willing to think well of others then you are on the right road.

Third, we can learn to love ourselves, which means that we understand our true worth as children of our Heavenly Father. The Savior taught that we must love others as we love ourselves (see Matthew 22:39). To love ourselves, we must respect and trust ourselves. This means that we must be obedient to the principles of the gospel. We must repent of any wrongdoings. We must forgive ourselves when we have repented. We will come to love ourselves better when we can feel the deep, comforting assurance that the Savior truly loves us.

While we are already praying for others, it wouldn't hurt to pray that we can learn to see ourselves as God sees us. If we are going to learn to see others as God sees them, we will need to be able to comprehend our own worth as well. That part may be more difficult than praying for someone else, for we must repent of our own wrongs and try to see what God sees in us. This, when it comes, will fill us with unspeakable gratitude for His kindness and charity toward us. It will make loving others who are behaving in unlovable ways so much easier when we realize just how unlovable we have been in the past. Our love for others will be grounded in our love for Christ and our God.

Fourth, we can avoid thinking we are better than other people. We can have patience with their faults. Joseph Smith said, "The nearer we get to our heavenly Father, the more we are disposed to look with compassion on perishing souls; we feel that we want to take them upon our shoulders, and cast their sins behind our backs" (Teachings of Presidents of the Church: Joseph Smith [2007], 428–29).

Part of having deep and abiding gratitude for the forgiveness and love shown to us from the Lord is recognizing that others are in the same boat we are. Realizing how dependent we are on the Lord's love and mercy to find and realize any true joy in this life helps us to find the patience we need to bear with the faults of others.

In the Book of Mormon we read of Enos, a young man who wanted to know that his sins had been forgiven. He tells us:

"My soul hungered; and I kneeled down before my Maker, and I cried unto him in mighty prayer and supplication for mine own soul; and all the day long did I cry unto him; yea, and when the night came I did still raise my voice high that it reached the heavens.

"And there came a voice unto me, saying: Enos, thy sins are forgiven thee, and thou shalt be blessed" (Enos 1:4–5).

The Lord explained to Enos that because of his faith in Christ his sins had been forgiven. When Enos heard these words he no longer was concerned about himself. He knew the Lord loved him and would bless him. He began instead to feel concern for the welfare of his friends and relatives, the Nephites. He poured out his whole soul unto God for them. The Lord answered and said they would be blessed according to their faithfulness in keeping the commandments they had already been given. Enos's love increased even further after these words, and he prayed with many long strugglings for the Lamanites, who were the enemies of the Nephites. The Lord granted his desires, and he spent the rest of his life trying to save the souls of the Nephites and the Lamanites. (See Enos 1:6–26.)

Enos was so grateful for the Lord's love and forgiveness that he willingly spent the rest of his life helping others receive this same gift. Enos had become truly charitable. We too can do so. In fact, we must do so to inherit the place that has been prepared for us in our Father's kingdom.

Additional Scriptures
• Colossians 3:12–14 (charity is the bond of perfectness)
• Alma 34:28–29 (our prayers are vain if we do not act charitably)
• 1 Corinthians 12:29–13:3 (definition of charity)
• D&C 121:45–46 (let us be full of charity toward all people)

Love comes to us in layers. The beauty of the story of Enos is that when the story starts he can only think of himself. It isn't until he is sure he has been forgiven, and has felt the redeeming love and acceptance of God that he begins to feel for his own people. Only after having that same experience for his own people does he begin to feel after the Lamanites, the Nephite's mortal enemy. Each time he experienced the Love of God enter into his life in a new and deeper way, he was able to expand who he was able to love in return. This even included, eventually, his enemies, those who would have killed him as soon as look at him.

Enos is a good example of someone who discovered the power of charity in his life. He is unusual in that he discovered it initially all in one night. For the majority of us this process takes years of self discovery and practice. We learn it step by step, a bit here and a bit there, but it comes as long as we keep trying.

Chapter 31

Honesty

Gospel Principles, (2011), 179–83

Honesty Is a Principle of Salvation

• What would society be like if everyone were perfectly honest?

The 13th article of faith says, "We believe in being honest." The Book of Mormon tells us about a group of people who were "distinguished for their zeal towards God, and also towards men; for they were perfectly honest and upright in all things; and they were firm in the faith of Christ, even unto the end" (Alma 27:27). Because of their honesty, these people were noted by their fellowmen and by God. It is important to learn what honesty is, how we are tempted to be dishonest, and how we can overcome this temptation.

Complete honesty is necessary for our salvation. President Brigham Young said, "If we accept salvation on the terms it is offered to us, we have got to be honest in every thought, in our reflections, in our meditations, in our private circles, in our deals, in our declarations, and in every act of our lives" (Teachings of Presidents of the Church: Brigham Young [1997], 293).

God is honest and just in all things (see Alma 7:20). We too must be honest in all things to become like Him. The brother of Jared testified, "Yea, Lord, I know that thou … art a God of truth, and canst not lie" (Ether 3:12). In contrast, the devil is a liar. In fact, he is the father of lies (see 2 Nephi 9:9). "Those who choose to cheat and lie and deceive and misrepresent become his slaves" (Mark E. Petersen, in Conference Report, Oct. 1971, 65; or Ensign, Dec. 1971, 73).

Honest people love truth and justice. They are honest in their words and actions. They do not lie, steal, or cheat.

To Lie Is Dishonest

For teachers: This chapter contains three sections that describe forms of dishonesty: lying, stealing, and cheating. You might consider dividing class members or family members into three groups. Assign each group one of these three sections. Ask the individuals in each group to silently read their assigned section and consider the forms of dishonesty described in that section. Then discuss the sections as a class or as a family. Ask how we can be honest in each of the situations described.

Lying is intentionally deceiving others. Bearing false witness is one form of lying. The Lord gave this

The main questions for consideration in this lesson have to do with what honesty means to our soul. How does honesty affect us and our behavior? How does honesty affect our relationships with others? How does honesty affect our faith in God? Does honest affect God's ability to be a God? If it affects his ability to be divine, what does that mean for us who want to become like our Father in Heaven? There must be reasons for the prophets to point out the honesty of these people and for emphasizing to us that they were so honest in all things.

Why do you think our salvation depends on our honesty? What is it that makes being completely honest a necessary part of salvation? Can we be pure in heart if we are not honest? Can we truly love our neighbor if we are dishonest with them? Can we really love God and still lie or cheat others?

One the most treasured attributes of God is his dependability. If we couldn't trust that he was telling us the truth or that he would keep his end of a deal, could we ever exercise faith in him sufficient to become like him? It is his very honesty that makes him the rock of reliability we depend on when all others fail us. It is the fact that when he gives His word we can stake our lives on the truthfulness of his declarations that makes him what He is.

Just as our Father in Heaven is always honest with us and is completely truthful in all things, so too is Satan dishonest with us. He will cheat us in any way he can. He will deceive and short us in any way that he can connive to do so.

There are almost infinite ways to be dishonest, but very few ways to be completely honest. Either we are honest or we are not. Either we are misrepresenting the truth or we are not. Life is much easier for those who choose honesty.

Our modern society has found many ways to mask lying. We call it misinformation, mis-speaking, speaking commandment to the children of Israel: "Thou shalt not bear false witness against thy neighbour" (Exodus 20:16). Jesus also taught this when He was on earth (see Matthew 19:18). There are many other forms of lying. When we speak untruths, we are guilty of lying. We can also intentionally deceive others by a gesture or a look, by silence, or by telling only part of the truth. Whenever we lead people in any way to believe something that is not true, we are not being honest.

The Lord is not pleased with such dishonesty, and we will have to account for our lies. Satan would have us believe it is all right to lie. He says, "Yea, lie a little; … there is no harm in this" (2 Nephi 28:8). Satan encourages us to justify our lies to ourselves. Honest people will recognize Satan's temptations and will speak the whole truth, even if it seems to be to their disadvantage.

To Steal Is Dishonest

Jesus taught, "Thou shalt not steal" (Matthew 19:18). Stealing is taking something that does not belong to us. When we take what belongs to someone else or to a store or to the community without permission, we are stealing. Taking merchandise or supplies from an employer is stealing. Copying music, movies, pictures, or written text without the permission of the copyright owners is dishonest and is a form of theft. Accepting more change or goods than one should is dishonest. Taking more than our share of anything is stealing.

To Cheat Is Dishonest

We cheat when we give less than we owe, or when we get something we do not deserve. Some employees cheat their employers by not working their full time; yet they accept full pay. Some employers are not fair to their employees; they pay them less than they should. Satan says, "Take the advantage of one because of his words, dig a pit for thy neighbor" (2 Nephi 28:8). Taking unfair advantage is a form of dishonesty. Providing inferior service or merchandise is cheating.

untruths, etc. Any way you slice it it is deception, which is lying.

When we make claims falsely, whether we know them to be false or even suspect they may be false, we are bearing false witness. Misdirection and deception can happen with a movement of a finger, a nod, a glancing of the eye, or any one of a thousand other ways to make someone assume something you know is not true. All of these things are dishonest and hurtful to one's character.

Sometimes it seems like such a small inconvenience to deceive someone else because it would be so much more difficult to have to deal with the honest truth. Such times are a test of our character. Would God be dishonest with us for his own convenience? Would Jesus lie to us to make his own life easier?

One of the greatest signs of a noble character is when someone is willing to be completely honest even when it will hurt them personally. This shows that truth matters to them. It shows that they care about being respectful of others and that they are not willing to deceive those around them, especially for personal comfort or gain.

If stealing is taking that which does not belong to us then there are a thousand ways to steal. We steal when we take more than our share of something. We steal when we don't deliver what is owed to someone, be it in time, effort, work, etc. We steal when we take credit for someone else's work or thoughts. We steal when we assume we have the right to something that is not ours to dispose of. This could include taking office supplies from work that we say we are only "borrowing." It could include opening a bag of fruit in a grocery store and handpicking the best fruit to make a custom bag for yourself, leaving the worst for others to have to take home. Dishonesty even includes "little" things like eating a grape from the fruit bin without paying for it. If we have to make excuses for our behavior then our behavior is probably dishonest. There are many ways to be dishonest.

Can you imagine your Father in Heaven cheating you on blessings you are owed? I can't. When He gives his word on something that word is as good as an iron clad contract. It cannot be broken by him. Why? Because He is honest. When we don't receive the promised blessings of covenants we have made with God it is because we have broken the covenant, not because He has. Shorting someone happens anytime we feel we deserve more than we are actually owed. When we convince ourselves that we deserve or are owed something that we haven't earned or been rightfully given we wind up cheating someone else.

Unfortunately, sometimes to get what we want we have to cause someone else to hurt themselves so we gain the advantage. This is what happens when Satan says to "dig a pit for they neighbor." We set them up to hurt themselves so we get what we want dishonestly. If we were supporting and loving our neighbor we would never consider taking advantage of them in such a way. We would do without rather than hurt another to get something we wanted.

We Must Not Excuse Our Dishonesty

• What happens to us spiritually when we excuse our dishonesty?

People use many excuses for being dishonest. People lie to protect themselves and to have others think well of them. Some excuse themselves for stealing, thinking they deserve what they took, intend to return it, or need it more than the owner. Some cheat to get better grades in school or because "everyone else does it" or to get even.

Excusing our dishonesty numbs us to our own weaknesses. Excusing our own dishonesty blinds us over time to what we are doing. We actually begin to believe our own lies. Self deception is the worst form of lying. It is more difficult to see the ways we deceive ourselves than it is to see how we are deceiving others. Satan uses our own blindness and spiritually numbed thinking to his advantage. As long as we are not listening to the Spirit, which always tells us to do the right thing, then Satan can whisper in the Spirit's place and he becomes our guide. This is why learning to be completely honest is so important. The only protection we have against the lies of Satan is the Spirit of God, and that requires honesty, the more the better.

These excuses and many more are given as reasons for dishonesty. To the Lord, there are no acceptable reasons. When we excuse ourselves, we cheat ourselves and the Spirit of God ceases to be with us. We become more and more unrighteous.

We Can Be Completely Honest

• What does it mean to be completely honest?

To become completely honest, we must look carefully at our lives. If there are ways in which we are being even the least bit dishonest, we should repent of them immediately.

Someone told me once that it was hard to have to think about everything they said so as not to offend anyone. And they were correct. It is hard. It is difficult, at least it is difficult until it becomes a way of life. Once being honest is just the way we are then we don't have to think about it, we just do the right thing. But at first we have to make the commitment to monitor everything we do and say to make sure we are being as honest as we know how to be.

Like anything else in life, we begin with the little things and over time we learn how to incorporate the harder ones. We need to start somewhere, and today is as good a time as any.

When we are completely honest, we cannot be corrupted. We are true to every trust, duty, agreement, or covenant, even if it costs us money, friends, or our lives. Then we can face the Lord, ourselves, and others without shame.

This is a wonderful concept that those who are completely honest cannot be corrupted. It is also very true. How can someone blackmail you if you haven't done anything

President Joseph F. Smith counseled, "Let every man's life be so that his character will bear the closest inspection, and that it may be seen as an open book, so that he will have nothing to shrink from or be ashamed of" (Gospel Doctrine, 5th ed. [1939], 252).

• In what ways does our honesty or dishonesty affect how we feel about ourselves?

Additional Scriptures
• D&C 50:17 (speak only by the spirit of truth)
• D&C 76:103–6 (destination of liars)
• D&C 42:27 (commandment not to speak evil of neighbors)
• Exodus 20:15–16 (commandments not to steal and not to bear false witness)
• D&C 42:20, 84–85; 59:6 (forbidden to steal)
• D&C 3:2 (God is honest)
• D&C 10:25–28 (Satan deceives)

wrong? How can someone play on your weaknesses if you don't have any?

I am talking about those who work in the business world. If you don't have a drinking problem, you don't sleep around, do drugs, cheat on your spouse, you do pay your taxes and all your debts in a timely manner, etc. Then what is there to hold over your head and control you with? The wicked use the wickedness of others to control them. A person who is above reproach because of their complete honesty in all things cannot be controlled or corrupted.

Tithes and Offerings

Chapter 32

Gospel Principles, (2011), 184–88

Paying Tithes and Offerings

• How does our willingness to pay tithes and offerings show gratitude to our Heavenly Father for all His blessings to us?

We have been given commandments to help us prepare in every way to live in the presence of our Heavenly Father. He has given us a way to thank Him for our blessings. Willingly paying tithes and offerings is one way we thank Him. As we pay these offerings, we show that we love Him and will obey His counsel.

• In what ways does the payment of tithes and offerings help us thank our Heavenly Father?

Obeying the Law of Tithing

• What is an honest tithe?

For teachers: Use questions at the beginning of a section to start a discussion and send class members or family members to the text to find more information. Use questions at the end of a section to help class members or family members ponder and discuss the meaning of what they have read and apply it in their lives.

Anciently, Abraham and Jacob obeyed the commandment to pay a tithe of one-tenth of their increase (see Hebrews 7:1–10; Genesis 14:19–20; 28:20–22).

In modern times the Prophet Joseph Smith prayed, "O Lord, show unto thy servants how much thou requirest of the properties of thy people for a tithing" (D&C 119, section introduction). The Lord answered: "This shall be the beginning of the tithing of my people. And after that, those who have thus been tithed shall pay one-tenth of all their interest annually; and this shall be a standing law unto them forever" (D&C 119:3–4). The First Presidency has explained that "one-tenth of all their interest annually" refers to our income (see First Presidency letter, Mar. 19, 1970).

Offerings are sometimes referred to in the Christian world as free will offerings. This means they are gifts, and not required by the church. Tithing is also an offering, but it is a commandment. The difference is that it isn't the church who requires our tithing, it is the Lord. Tithing has been a commandment since the very beginning, and will be a law to the Lord's people until the end of the earth.

We give offerings because of gratitude to the Lord for his blessings. We give them to the church because His priesthood servants are in charge of putting His offerings to good use.

One of the ways we prepare to be like God is to learn to be giving and generous like Christ. Our Tithes pay for temples and chapels, and our other offerings help the poor and the needy. When we give to the Church we can always be assured our entire donation goes toward what we give it to rather than to pay someone's salary.

We need to be willing to give all that we have for the building up of the kingdom of God. Our willingness to sacrifice for the furtherance of the Lord's work says a lot about our belief in and our commitment to the cause we have espoused.

The Lord said we are to "pay one-tenth of all their interest annually." What is meant by the word interest? Interest is what is added above the money we already had. When we work we earn money we did not have. This, to us, is like interest. Gifts are things we did not have before, so we tithe our gifts. Anything that is new or above and beyond what we already possessed is an increase, and therefore subject to being tithed.

How we choose to count what is increase and what is not is where the honesty comes into play. If we are making excuses as to why something doesn't count or we are minimizing our sources of income then chances are we are

When we pay tithing we show our faithfulness to the Lord. We also teach our children the value of this law. They will want to follow our example and pay tithing on any money they receive.

not being completely honest in our tithes. Offerings is a whole different subject.

All things in mortality belong to God. They are His creation and His property. The rule is, if you can take it with you into the afterlife then you can claim it as your own. In other words, nothing here belongs to us.

The Lord has told us that we can use the full bounty of the earth. We can earn or create as much wealth as we want to, but for our sakes He wants us to return one-tenth of what we have amassed to Him to be used for His purposes. That's its. We can use anything God has put on the earth to create wealth for ourselves, and we can keep 90 percent of it for our own use. We are only required to give back to Him one-tenth of our increase. With that money He will build up His kingdom and prepare His people for His return.

• In what ways is tithing a principle of faith more than a principle of finances?

The bounties of the earth are already the Lord's. He doesn't need our money. He could tell the prophet where to buy property to go dig out diamonds or gold if that was all that was needed. Tithing, like all commandments is all about what paying it does to us

Paying tithes and offerings helps us by demonstrating our gratitude to the Lord for His blessings. It reminds us where our livelihoods come from. Paying tithes and offerings helps us exercise our faith in the Lord. He has promised to pour blessings from heaven down on our heads if we pay our tithing and give offerings generously. As we do this we show the Lord that we believe in his promises and that we want his blessings. We show him we will sacrifice anything we need to in order to obey Him and keep his commandments. He, in return enriches our lives in all the ways that are most beneficial to us, whether that is in spiritual ways, physical ways, or financial ways. We leave the blessings up to Him because he is our Father and knows best what we need.

• What can parents do to teach their children to pay tithing and understand its importance?

One of the best ways for a parent to teach tithes and offerings to a child is to show them that they pay tithes and offerings, and to bear testimony of the blessings they receive because of it. Example is always one of the best teachers.

We Should Give Willingly
• Why is our attitude important as we pay tithing?

It is important to give willingly. "When one pays his tithing without enjoyment he is robbed of a part of the blessing. He must learn to give cheerfully, willingly and joyfully, and his gift will be blessed" (Stephen L Richards, The Law of Tithing [pamphlet, 1983], 8).

The point of the offering is that it is given out of gratitude. If we aren't grateful for what we have received and we aren't pleased to be able to contribute our little amount to the Lord's cause, then why are we parting with our money, except to be hypocritical?

Page 151

There is a genuine joy in being able to express gratitude to someone who has done great things for you. Expressing gratitude brings peace and satisfaction to the soul. Sometimes we have to give until we learn to be properly grateful, but it is still important that we obey the law of the Tithe until we have grown to be grateful for the blessings that come from living the law. How long that lesson takes is pretty much up to us.

The Apostle Paul taught that how we give is as important as what we give. He said, "Let him give; not grudgingly, or of necessity: for God loveth a cheerful giver" (2 Corinthians 9:7).

• What does it mean to you to be a "cheerful giver"?

A cheerful giver is someone whose heart is in the right place. A cheerful giver finds joy in the act of giving, just like Christ does. Don't we all tend to love like-minded people?

Tithing and Other Offerings

• In what ways does the Church use tithing funds and other offerings?

As members of the Church, we give tithing and other offerings to the Lord.

Tithing

Tithing is used by the Church for many purposes. Some of these are to:
1. Build, maintain, and operate temples, meetinghouses, and other buildings.
2. Provide operating funds for stakes, wards, and other units of the Church. (These units use the funds to carry out the ecclesiastical programs of the Church, which include teaching the gospel and conducting social activities.)
3. Help the missionary program.
4. Educate young people in Church schools, seminaries, and institutes.
5. Print and distribute lesson materials.
6. Help in family history and temple work.
Other Offerings

A generous tithe is one that is fully compliant with the law of Tithing we have been given, and then some. If we find that we strictly owe $52.25 cents, a generous tithe would be anything above and beyond what fulfills the letter of the law.

A generous fast offering is anything that is strictly more than just the money we would have spent on those two meals we fasted through. If we would have spent $25.00 per person on each meal, a generous fast might mean we pay the equivalent of $50.00 per person for each meal instead. If we are able to, we might move it up to a much higher figure. The Lord only gives minimums. It is up to us as to how generous we want to be with the Lord and his other children. One thing is certain, there is never a lack of need in the world. The Lord will be as generous in blessing us as we are generous in our desire to bless the lives of our brothers and sisters.

Fast Offerings.

Church members fast each month by going without food and drink for two consecutive meals. They contribute at least the amount of money they would have spent for the meals. They may give as generously as they are able. This offering is called the fast offering. Bishops use these fast offerings to provide food, shelter, clothing, and medical care for the needy. (See chapter 25 in this book.)

As part of the fast day, members attend a meeting called the fast and testimony meeting, where they share with each other their testimonies of Christ and His gospel.

Other Donations. Church members may donate to other efforts of the Church, such as missionary work, the Perpetual Education Fund, temple construction, and humanitarian aid.

Service.
Members also offer their time, skills, and goods to help others. This service allows the Church to help needy members and nonmembers around the world at community, national, and international levels, especially when disasters occur.

We Are Blessed When We Give Tithes and Offerings
The Lord promises to bless us as we faithfully pay our tithes and offerings. He said, "Bring ye all the tithes into the storehouse, that there may be meat in mine house, and prove me now herewith … if I will not open you the windows of heaven, and pour you out a blessing, that there shall not be room enough to receive it" (Malachi 3:10).

Latter-day revelation tells of another blessing for those who tithe: "Verily it is a day of sacrifice, and a day for the tithing of my people; for he that is tithed shall not be burned at his coming" (D&C 64:23).

The blessings we have been promised are both material and spiritual. If we give willingly, Heavenly Father will help us provide for our daily needs of food, clothes, and shelter. Speaking to Latter-day Saints in the Philippines, President Gordon B. Hinckley said that if people "will accept the gospel and live it, pay their tithes and offerings, even though those be meager, the Lord will keep His ancient promise in their behalf, and they will have rice in their bowls and clothing on their backs and shelter over their heads. I do not see any other solution. They need a power greater than any earthly power to lift them and help them" ("Inspirational Thoughts," Ensign, Aug. 1997, 7). The Lord will also help us grow "in a knowledge of God, and in a testimony, and in the power to live the gospel and

One of the blessings of paying our tithes and offerings on fast Sunday is that the Spirit, which should be in greater abundance on that day, helps us to feel greater love for and gratitude for God's blessings on that day. This makes us more generous because our gratitude to God is greater. When we pay our tithes and offerings generously we will never be sorry.

Opening our wallets is only one very limited way for us to give back to our Father in Heaven and Jesus Christ for what they have done for us. There are innumerable ways for us to physically be of assistance to other around us in our wards and in our communities. We don't need to wait until a disaster strikes for us to get into the habit of serving others.

Every effort we make to live outside of ourselves, and bless the lives of those around us, will be recognized and blessed by the Lord. The law of tithing is a simple law and one that anyone who wants to be faithful to the Lord can learn to live. But in return the Lord has made great promises to us that He will care for us and bless us in all the ways we need to be blessed.

Sometimes member of the church mistakenly think that because we are normally paying in money our blessings will come back to us in money. This is not true. The Lord only says He will open the windows of heaven for us and pour a blessing upon us that is so great we will not have room enough to receive it. That doesn't sound like money to me. Money is the least of the Lord's worries.

Read the paragraph with President Hinckley's quote in it again. The blessings of paying our tithes and offerings are physical in that the Lord will help us take care of our families. But God also promises us that we will grow in knowledge and testimony. Just like all of God's commandments, the commandment isn't about the physical observance, it is about how the honoring of the commandment changes us into something better than what we currently are.

God does not give just physical commandments. All commandments are meant to grow us spiritually, first and foremost. Any physical benefit is secondary in nature. We are eternal beings living in the midst of eternity. Any to inspire our families to do the same" (Teachings of Presidents of the Church: Heber J. Grant [2002], 124).

blessings we receive of a physical nature while living in mortality is of fleeting value. The real virtue of keeping the commandments is the growth we experience to our immortal souls.

Those who pay their tithes and offerings are greatly blessed. They have a good feeling that they are helping to build the kingdom of God on earth.

• What are some blessings you, your family members, or your friends have received through the payment of tithing and other offerings?

Additional Scriptures
• D&C 119:1–4 (the law of tithing)
• Genesis 14:18–20; Alma 13:13–16 (Abraham paid tithes)

Chapter 33

Missionary Work
Gospel Principles, (2011), 189–95

Here is an interesting companion question to the one that starts this lesson: How is God's plan supposed to save His children if none of His children know about the plan?

The Lord's Church Is a Missionary Church
• In what ways is missionary work part of God's plan for His children?

The Lord revealed the gospel plan to Adam: "And thus the Gospel began to be preached, from the beginning" (Moses 5:58). Later, Adam's righteous descendants were sent to preach the gospel: "They … called upon all men, everywhere, to repent; and faith was taught unto the children of men" (Moses 6:23).

For teachers: Sharing experiences with gospel principles can invite the Spirit. You may want to contact a few class members or family members in advance, asking them to prepare to share experiences that are meaningful to them and that may help others.

All the prophets have been missionaries. Each in his day was commanded to preach the gospel message. Whenever the priesthood has been on the earth, the Lord has needed missionaries to preach the eternal principles of the gospel to His children.

The Lord's Church has always been a missionary church. When the Savior lived on the earth, He ordained Apostles and Seventies and gave them the authority and responsibility to preach the gospel. Most of their preaching was to their own people, the Jews (see Matthew 10:5–6). After Jesus was resurrected, He sent Apostles to preach the gospel to the Gentiles. He commanded the Apostles, "Go ye into all the world, and preach the gospel to every creature" (Mark 16:15).

The Apostle Paul was a great missionary sent to the Gentiles. After he was converted to the Church, he spent the remainder of his life preaching the gospel to them. At different times during his mission he was whipped, stoned, and imprisoned. Yet he continued to preach the gospel (see Acts 23:10–12; 26).

Missionary work began again when the Lord's Church was restored through the Prophet Joseph Smith. Today the Apostles and Seventies have been given the chief responsibility for preaching the gospel and seeing that it is preached in all the world. The Lord told Joseph Smith:

Missionary work, i.e. teaching people about God's plan for their happiness, is as old as the human family. Even Adam had to teach his descendants who had fallen away in unbelief.

Missionary work is a priesthood responsibility. Whenever there has been the priesthood power on the earth missionary work was a requirement of those who held the priesthood. What good is the priesthood if it isn't saving the souls of God's children? How are they to be saved if no one tells them about His gospel plan?

When Christ came to earth His mission was to the house of Israel, the Jews. Since the Jew rejected His message and they killed their Messiah, after His resurrection the gospel was sent to the gentile nations.

The teaching of God's plan has always had its special challenges. Historically, the prophets were stoned, killed, driven out of the cities, and mistreated for their message. But for those who accept the message of salvation, those who bear the message hold a sacred place in the people's hearts. To the converts, prophets and missionaries are revered and reverenced, and treated like angels. They are greatly loved for the message of salvation they bring.

"Proclaim my gospel from land to land, and from city to city. … Bear testimony in every place, unto every people" (D&C 66:5, 7). In June 1830, Samuel Harrison Smith, the Prophet's brother, began the first missionary journey for the Church.

Since that time, over one million missionaries have been called and sent forth to preach the gospel. The message they take to the world is that Jesus Christ is the Son of God and our Savior. They testify that the gospel has been restored to the earth through a prophet of God. The missionaries are given the responsibility to preach the gospel to all people, to baptize them, and to teach them to do all things that the Lord has commanded (see Matthew 28:19–20). Latter-day Saint missionaries go at their own expense to all parts of the world to preach the gospel message.

The message the missionaries take to the world does not change in any major details from one generation to another. They are all sent out to teach about the reality of a living Christ. They all teach that God's message and salvation, along with His priesthood power is on the earth and has the power to save anyone who is willing to have faith in Christ. The missionary message includes everything we need to do to conform to God's will and obey the commandments.

The Gospel Will Be Preached to All the World

• What are some different ways the Lord has prepared for us to share the gospel?

We have been told in latter-day revelation that we must take the restored gospel to every nation and people (see D&C 133:37). The Lord never gives us a commandment without preparing a way for us to accomplish it (see 1 Nephi 3:7). The Lord has prepared ways for us to teach the gospel in nations that were once closed to us. As we continue to pray and exercise faith, the Lord will open other nations to missionary work.

The Lord is also "inspiring the minds of great people to create inventions that further the work of the Lord in ways this world has never known" (Russell M. Nelson, in "Computerized Scriptures Now Available," Ensign, Apr. 1988, 73). Newspapers, magazines, television, radio, satellites, computers, the Internet, and related technology help give the gospel message to millions of people. We who have the fulness of the gospel need to use these inventions to fulfill the Lord's commandment: "For, verily, the sound must go forth from this place into all the world, and unto the uttermost parts of the earth—the gospel must be preached unto every [person]" (D&C 58:64).

One of the many blessings of being alive in the last days is the many ways in which we are able to share the gospel message with others. There have been times in centuries past when word of mouth was the only way to tell someone about the gospel. If a person did not personally meet a member of the church then they lived their whole life without any knowledge of the gospel plan for their salvation.

In the latter days we have word of mouth, but we also have a wide variety of printed material that has not been available to such a degree in any other time in the history of the world. We have video and movies that can help to teach the gospel message. We have social media that allows us to reach vast audiences who otherwise wouldn't ever meet a member of the church.

There are technologies, like the Internet, satellites, cell phones, faxes, etc. that aid in the transfer of information over vast distances to large audiences. When General Conference airs in April and October, it is broadcast simultaneously to more than a hundred countries around the world in many dozen's of languages.

The Lord still requires that at some point every person speak with one of His representatives, a missionary, but the basic message can be transmitted over many avenues for people to hear about and start thinking about. Using these technologies the Lord begins to prepare people to accept the gospel message, in many cases, long before they ever meet a missionary.

• In what ways have you seen technology used effectively to share the gospel?

Missionary Work Is Important
• Why is it important for each person to hear and understand the gospel?

"This is our first interest as a Church—to save and exalt the souls of the children of men" (Ezra Taft Benson, in Conference Report, Apr. 1974, 151; or Ensign, May 1974, 104). Missionary work is necessary in order to give the people of the world an opportunity to hear and accept the gospel. They need to learn the truth, turn to God, and receive forgiveness from their sins.

Many of our brothers and sisters on earth are blinded by false teachings and "are only kept from the truth because they know not where to find it" (D&C 123:12). Through missionary work we can bring them the truth.

The Lord has commanded, "Labor ye in my vineyard for the last time—for the last time call upon the inhabitants of the earth" (D&C 43:28). As we teach the gospel to our brothers and sisters, we are preparing the way for the Second Coming of the Savior (see D&C 34:6).

No one can be forgiven of their sins and become perfected in Christ if they never hear His gospel message. Missionaries are required so the people can hear the message. That missionary can be in the form of an officially called missionary, a ward missionary, or any member of the church who is willing to share what he/she knows about the gospel.

The gospel of Christ is a liberating influence in our lives. We become free from the effects of sin and the bondage sin brings into our lives. There are many who would love to be free of these things, if they only knew where to go to find that freedom. That freedom is only available in the gospel of Christ.

In every dispensation since the days of Adam missionaries have labored to spread the message of the plan of salvation. This is the very last dispensation, the last time the Lord will restore his church on the earth before his second coming. Because this is the last time it will be restored, we have a limited amount of time before the Savior returns to reign personally on the earth. That means we need to push to get to all the nations of the earth and to make sure that as many as possible hear the message before the Savior's second coming.

We Should All Be Missionaries
• In what ways can we actively seek opportunities to share the gospel with others? In what ways can we prepare ourselves for such opportunities?

Every member of the Church is a missionary. We should be missionaries even if we are not formally called and set apart. We are responsible to teach the gospel by word and deed to all of our Heavenly Father's children. The Lord has told us, "It becometh every man who hath been warned to warn his neighbor" (D&C 88:81). We have been told by a prophet that we should show our neighbors that we love them before we warn them (see Teachings of Presidents of the Church: Spencer W. Kimball [2006], 262). They need to experience our friendship and fellowship.

The sons of Mosiah willingly accepted their responsibility to teach the gospel. When they were converted to the Church, their hearts were filled with compassion for others. They wanted to preach the gospel to their enemies the Lamanites, "for they could not bear that any human soul should perish; yea, even the very thoughts that any soul should endure endless torment did cause them to quake and

Sometimes we forget that part of our baptismal covenant is to
"stand as witnesses of God at all times and in all things, and in all places that ye may be in, even until death, that ye may be redeemed of God, and be numbered with those of the first resurrection, that ye may have eternal life."
We are all called to be missionaries and to teach anyone we meet about Christ's gospel. When did Jesus ever shy away from teaching about His Father? When did He ever withhold any information about the joy that comes from repenting and keeping the commandments? If we are to stand as witnesses then we must become as willing to share with others as the Lord was willing to share with us.

As missionaries, we are not being asked to go door to door. What we are expected to do is to not be ashamed of what we have been given, and to be willing to share it joyfully in any manner we can, be that by way of example, upholding the teachings of Christ or speaking up about the principles of righteousness found in the gospel. Just tremble" (Mosiah 28:3). As the gospel fills our lives with joy, we will feel this kind of love and compassion for our brothers and sisters. We will want to share the message of the gospel with everyone who desires to listen.

There are many ways we can share the gospel. Following are some suggestions:
1. We can show friends and others the joy we experience from living the truths of the gospel. In this way we will be a light to the world (see Matthew 5:16).
2. We can overcome our natural shyness by being friendly to others and doing kind things for them. We can help them see that we are sincerely interested in them and are not seeking personal gain.
3. We can explain the gospel to nonmember friends and others.
4. We can invite friends who are interested in learning more about the gospel into our homes to be taught by the missionaries. If our nonmember friends live too far away, we can request that missionaries in their areas visit them.
5. We can teach our children the importance of sharing the gospel, and we can prepare them spiritually and financially to go on missions. We can also prepare ourselves to serve full-time missions in our senior years.
6. We can pay our tithing and contribute to the missionary fund. These donations are used for furthering missionary work.
7. We can contribute to the ward, branch, or general missionary fund to give financial support to missionaries whose families are unable to support them.
8. We can do family history research and temple work to help our ancestors receive the full blessings of the gospel.
9. We can invite nonmembers to activities such as family home evenings and Church socials, conferences, and meetings.
10. We can give copies of Church magazines. We can also share gospel messages by using features available on the Church's official Internet sites, LDS.org and Mormon.org. Our Heavenly Father will help us be effective missionaries when we have the desire to share the gospel and pray for guidance. He will help us find ways to share the gospel with those around us.

• Think about people you can share the gospel with. Decide how you will do so. Consider setting a goal to share the gospel with these people by a certain date.

The Lord Promises Us Blessings for Doing Missionary Work
The Lord told the Prophet Joseph Smith that missionaries would receive great blessings. Speaking to elders who were returning from their missions, the Lord said, "Ye are blessed, for the testimony which ye have borne is recorded

living a life of Christian virtues offers us many ways to share what Jesus taught, both in word and especially in deed.

Just doing good is a wonderful way to "preach" the gospel. The example of good deeds is a powerful testimony. If we can help people in financial ways, whether to go on missions themselves or by contributing to missionary funds is a way to show our support to the missionary effort.

Sometimes we forget that the work of saving our dead is just as important as our work to save the living. Our mistake is in thinking the dead aren't living. They are, just on the other side of the veil.

Sometimes people don't realize that what they are looking for in life is already what we have in our hands. By inviting our friends from other faiths to ward activities or family activities we set a great example of love for them.

A great set of meetings to invite people to sit in on are the General Conference sessions. Those who speak at Conference are always well prepared, uplifting, and kind in their remarks.

If you exercise your faith in Christ and in his promises, and set a date by which you will do certain missionary activities, He will bless you with the opportunities to fulfill your goal. You are doing his work, so expect doors to open and unexplainable things to take place to enable you to accomplish what you have promised the Lord you will do. That is the nature of faith in missionary work.

When we think of the scriptural principle about "do unto others" we don't usually think that applies to our own salvation. It does. These verses (D&C 4:4, 31:5, 84:61) tell us that we guarantee our own salvation and forgiveness of sin when we help take the gospel of salvation to others. Jesus really does believe in the Golden Rule.

in heaven for the angels to look upon; and they rejoice over you" (D&C 62:3). He has also said that those who work for the salvation of others will have their sins forgiven and will bring salvation to their own souls (see D&C 4:4; 31:5; 84:61).

The Lord has told us:

"If it so be that you should labor all your days in crying repentance unto this people, and bring, save it be one soul unto me, how great shall be your joy with him in the kingdom of my Father!

"And now, if your joy will be great with one soul that you have brought unto me into the kingdom of my Father, how great will be your joy if you should bring many souls unto me!" (D&C 18:15–16).

• When have you experienced the joy of missionary work?

The joy that comes from missionary work doesn't generally come at the time we are frightened because we are expected to open our mouths when we are scared and tell someone about the church. The joy generally comes when we have served someone, when we have helped someone, when we have uplifted someone who needed a kindness shown to them. The gospel isn't just doctrines and rules, it is all about bringing joy into the lives of others. When we spend our lives serving others and bringing joy into their lives, we are doing the missionary work the Lord needs us to do, and we, in turn, find that our lives are full of joy as well.

Additional Scriptures
• D&C 1:17–23 (Joseph Smith commanded to preach)
• D&C 24:12 (Lord strengthens those who always seek to declare His gospel)
• D&C 38:41 (share the gospel in mildness and meekness)
• D&C 34:4–6; Acts 5:42 (gospel to be preached)
• D&C 60:1–2 (Lord warns those who are afraid to preach the gospel)
• D&C 75:2–5 (those who declare the gospel and are faithful will be blessed with eternal life)
• D&C 88:81–82 (all those who have been warned should warn their neighbors)
• Matthew 24:14 (gospel to be preached before the end shall come)
• Abraham 2:9–11 (gospel and priesthood to be given to all nations)

Chapter 34

Developing Our Talents

Gospel Principles, (2011), 196–99

We All Have Different Talents and Abilities

We all have special gifts, talents, and abilities given to us by our Heavenly Father. When we were born, we brought these gifts, talents, and abilities with us (see chapter 2 in this book).

The prophet Moses was a great leader, but he needed Aaron, his brother, to help as a spokesman (see Exodus 4:14–16). Some of us are leaders like Moses or good speakers like Aaron. Some of us can sing well or play an instrument. Others of us may be good in sports or able to work well with our hands. Other talents we might have are understanding others, patience, cheerfulness, or the ability to teach others.

• How have you benefited from the talents of others?

For teachers: One way to show class members that you care about them individually is to call them by name. Learn their names. When new class members attend the class, introduce them to the others.

We Should Use and Improve Our Talents

• How can we develop our talents?

We have a responsibility to develop the talents we have been given. Sometimes we think we do not have many talents or that other people have been blessed with more abilities than we possess. Sometimes we do not use our talents because we are afraid that we might fail or be criticized by others. We should not hide our talents. We should use them. Then others can see our good works and glorify our Heavenly Father (see Matthew 5:16).

There are certain things we must do to develop our talents. First, we must discover our talents. We should evaluate

Our talents work together with the talents of others to do two things for us. First, we are able to do some things well that others struggle with. In this way we are able to bless the lives of others with abilities we have been able to learn well. Second, because we are not gifted in all things, our lack of talent in certain areas of our lives prompts us to rely on others who do have talents in those areas. This combination of ability and lack of ability is designed by the Lord to encourage us to rely on each other and work together to bless each other.

When we think of Moses we don't think of his weakness in not being able to speak well in public. What we think of is his leadership and what he accomplished. We should all be as generous with ourselves as we are when we think of Moses. We all have weaknesses that other's talents help us with. We should focus on the good we can do with what talents we have. And when we discover a new ability we should do all we can to develop it well so we can help bless others with that talent or ability.

When it comes to talents we all need to stretch our imaginations a bit. We tend to think of talents being only those things that are great for public display, like an artist or a dancer or a musician. But what about those people who have the ability to lend a listening ear (without judgment). What is the worth of such a talent to someone who is alone or feels neglected? What about the talent to have a compassionate heart or a sensitivity to the Spirit? There are so many talents and abilities people have that are huge blessings to those around them, but they are not public in nature. These are just as precious to the well being of others as any music or dance performance is, and sometimes are actually life savers.

Talents (abilities) are just like muscles. If you want to make a muscle strong you have to stretch it and work it. Talents are no different. Learning to have tact, the ability to not offend, takes a lot of practice, and hopefully some natural skill in that area. Learning to have consideration for others take a lot of practice. We have to become aware of everything around us and be thinking about how and where we can use that ability.

Some talents are natural to us. We all know of people who can draw or sing, dance or cook, all with relative ease, and ourselves to find our strengths and abilities. Our family and friends can help us do this. We should also ask our Heavenly Father to help us learn about our talents.

Second, we must be willing to spend the time and effort to develop the talent we are seeking.

Third, we must have faith that our Heavenly Father will help us, and we must have faith in ourselves.

Fourth, we must learn the skills necessary for us to develop our talents. We might do this by taking a class, asking a friend to teach us, or reading a book.

Fifth, we must practice using our talent. Every talent takes effort and work to develop. The mastery of a talent must be earned.

Sixth, we must share our talent with others. It is by our using our talents that they grow (see Matthew 25:29).

All of these steps are easier if we pray and seek the Lord's help. He wants us to develop our talents, and He will help us.

We Can Develop Our Talents in Spite of Our Weaknesses

• How can we develop our talents in spite of our weaknesses?

Because we are mortal and fallen, we have weaknesses. With the Lord's help, our weakness and fallen nature can be overcome (see Ether 12:27, 37). Beethoven composed his greatest music after he was deaf. Enoch overcame his slowness of speech to become a powerful teacher (see Moses 6:26–47).

seemingly without effort. But there are also people who have decided to develop certain abilities, and they have spent years practicing and working on those abilities so they feel like they can contribute in that area.

Not all talents are visible to us right off the bat. We need to seek out abilities we think we might be able to learn and practice them and work at them. This increases our ability to bless the lives of others. We can use our family members or friends to help us identify areas in our lives where we might already have natural strengths, and we can decide for ourselves which abilities we would like to spend the time to develop. Though sometimes using friends and family as a sounding board will help us identify areas in our lives where we are weak or lacking. Family is really good at pointing out where we are lacking. Hopefully they will do it in a kind-spirited way.

Some talents require actual study, other talents can be learned by listening or watching others. Any ability we want to develop will have its own requirements for us to learn it.

Talents is the word used in the Bible for an ability. In the Bible the talents were actually large sums of money, and not abilities at all. But the principle behind the story has come to mean any endowment or gift or ability that we are given from God we can call a talent. The important thing to remember is that all of us have potential talents within us that the Lord expects us to discover for ourselves and enlarge them through hard work and learning. We will be held just as accountable for improving on these abilities as we are the naturally obvious talents that come easily to us. This is all part of our personal development in the Lord's kingdom.

An ability kept to oneself is of no use to anyone. All abilities are meant to be shared and used for the benefit of others. This is how we enlarge or increase our abilities, by using them to bless the lives of others.

The Lord gave us both abilities and weaknesses. The abilities so we could go and bless the lives of others, and the weaknesses so we can learn to turn to Him for help in overcoming them so they become strengths to us. They are not meant to remain as weaknesses, the Lord wants us to use our weaknesses as stepping stones to greatness.

Some great athletes have had to overcome handicaps before they have succeeded in developing their talents. Shelly Mann was such an example. "At the age of five she had polio. … Her parents took her daily to a swimming pool where they hoped the water would help hold her arms up as she tried to use them again. When she could lift her arm out of the water with her own power, she cried for joy. Then her goal was to swim the width of the pool, then the length, then several lengths. She kept on trying, swimming, enduring, day after day after day, until she won the [Olympic] gold medal for the butterfly stroke—one of the most difficult of all swimming strokes" (Marvin J. Ashton, in Conference Report, Apr. 1975, 127; or Ensign, May 1975, 86).

Heber J. Grant overcame many of his weaknesses and turned them into talents. He had as a motto these words: "That which we persist in doing becomes easier for us to do; not that the nature of the thing is changed, but that our power to do is increased" (in Teachings of Presidents of the Church: Heber J. Grant [2002], 35).

The Lord Will Bless Us If We Use Our Talents Wisely

President Joseph F. Smith said, "Every son and every daughter of God has received some talent, and each will be held to strict account for the use or misuse to which it is put" (Gospel Doctrine, 5th ed. [1939], 370). A talent is one kind of stewardship (responsibility in the kingdom of God). The parable of the talents tells us that when we serve well in our stewardship, we will be given greater responsibilities. If we do not serve well, our stewardship will eventually be taken from us. (See Matthew 25:14–30.)

We are also told in the scriptures that we will be judged according to our works (see Matthew 16:27). By developing and using our talents for other people, we perform good works.

The Lord is pleased when we use our talents wisely. He will bless us if we use our talents to benefit other people and to build up His kingdom here on earth. Some of the blessings we gain are joy and love from serving our brothers and sisters here on earth. We also learn self-control. All these things are necessary if we are going to be worthy to live with our Heavenly Father again.

• What are some examples of people whose talents have been magnified because they used them wisely? (Consider people you know or people in the scriptures or Church history.)

Heber J. Grant knew what he was talking about. He had terrible handwriting, but through persistence and practice in later years became famous for his beautiful handwriting. He was held up as the example for others to emulate.

This quote from President Smith shows us that the Lord does not take our abilities lightly. We were given specific abilities for a reason known only to the Lord, but the purpose behind our individual abilities is our own improvement and advancement. God has given us our abilities because he knows us and knows that these particular abilities will be what will bless us the most. For this reason we will be held accountable for the talents we have been given, and for those abilities we are expected to seek out and develop.

Additional Scriptures
• James 1:17 (gifts come from God)

• D&C 46:8–11; 1 Timothy 4:14 (seek and develop gifts)
• 2 Corinthians 12:9 (weak things made strong)
• Revelation 20:13; 1 Nephi 15:33; D&C 19:3 (judged by our works)
• Hebrews 13:21 (show good works)

Chapter 35

Obedience
Gospel Principles, (2011), 200–206

We Should Obey God Willingly
• What difference does it make to obey willingly rather than unwillingly?

For teachers: You can help class members or family members think more deeply about a question by giving them time to ponder. After they have had enough time, ask for their responses.

When Jesus was on the earth, a lawyer asked Him a question:

"Master, which is the great commandment in the law?

"Jesus said unto him, Thou shalt love the Lord thy God with all thy heart, and with all thy soul, and with all thy mind.

"This is the first and great commandment.

"And the second is like unto it, Thou shalt love thy neighbour as thyself.

"On these two commandments hang all the law and the prophets" (Matthew 22:36–40).

From these scriptures we learn how important it is for us to love the Lord and our neighbors. But how do we show our love for the Lord?

Jesus answered this question when He said, "He that hath my commandments, and keepeth them, he it is that loveth me: and he that loveth me shall be loved of my Father" (John 14:21).

Each of us should ask ourselves why we obey God's commandments. Is it because we fear punishment? Is it because we desire the rewards for living a good life? Is it

The point of using the story about which is the greatest of the commandments is that in order to obey either of the two greatest commandments we need to love someone other than ourselves. The Lord can tell if we love him by whether or not we keep either of these commandments. His love is turned outward to other people. If we display the same kind of love He has for us then we are trying to be like Him. This kind of behavior is demonstrated by a willingness to be obedient and to demonstrate Christlike love.

If we are unwilling to demonstrate our love for others unless forced into a corner or made to by social pressure (etc., etc.) what does that say about our feelings for God and his commandments?

This statement by Jesus that "he that loveth me shall be loved of my Father" is deceptive in that it isn't clear what it means in this context. This verse isn't saying that God only loves those who love him. But we need to understand that God is bound by his own laws. He wants to bless us. He wants to exalt us. But His ability to fully demonstrate his generosity to his children is hampered by their own disobedience. He is not able to bless someone who breaks the law, instead he has to withhold his blessings from them. It is those who keep the commandments and seek to bless the lives of others, like God blesses us, that He is able to shower with his blessings. He is anxious for us to be obedient so he can show us just how generous He can be. But the first step is always ours.

There are levels of obedience. Out of fear of punishment is the lowest level, out of selfish desire for personal reward is another level then out of love for God and love for others is the highest level.

because we love God and Jesus Christ and want to serve Them?

It is better to obey the commandments because we fear punishment than not to obey them at all. But we will be much happier if we obey God because we love Him and want to obey Him. When we obey Him freely, He can bless us freely. He said, "I, the Lord, … delight to honor those who serve me in righteousness and in truth unto the end" (D&C 76:5). Obedience also helps us progress and become more like our Heavenly Father. But those who do nothing until they are commanded and then keep the commandments unwillingly lose their reward (see D&C 58:26–29).

Doing good always has its own reward, but doing good isn't what "doing good" is all about. We do good because of what doing good does to us. It changes us and enlarges our capacity to love. Doing good increases our ability to have and show empathy, to feel sympathy. Doing good helps us see things from other people's perspectives more clearly. Basically, doing good enlarges our souls and makes us more like Christ.

In the end, those who do good only for the fear of punishment or for the desire for personal gain will fail to make the needed changes in their hearts and will lose the rewards that doing good has the ability to bestow on all of us.

• How can we increase our desire to obey?

Asking in prayer on a consistent basis for the Lord to change our hearts will help us achieve an increased desire. Only the Lord can change the desires of our hearts, but we can ask for that change, and if we act upon the commandments that increase those desires to do good then He will certainly give us what we have asked for. This is one of those things we don't have to wonder if it is okay to ask for. He wants us to undergo this change. He wants us to experience the joys of a loving heart and generous soul. This is one prayer you are guaranteed to have answered with a big "Yes!"

We Can Obey without Understanding Why
• Why do we not always need to understand the Lord's purposes in order to be obedient?

By keeping God's commandments, we prepare for eternal life and exaltation. Sometimes we do not know the reason for a particular commandment. However, we show our faith and trust in God when we obey Him without knowing why.

I will speak plainly on this question. We do not always need to know or understand the reasons for keeping a particular commandment. To expect the Lord to explain Himself before we grant Him our faith is the height of arrogance. We should never assume that He is required to explain his actions to his children. We should never be so presumptuous as to think He should have to give us a reason for why we should be happy. That is what all the commandments lead to, our happiness.

Adam and Eve were commanded to offer sacrifices to God. One day an angel appeared to Adam and asked why he offered sacrifices. Adam replied that he did not know the reason. He did it because the Lord commanded him. (See Moses 5:5–6 and the picture in this chapter.)

It is in the times we don't understand a commandment we need to learn humility and exercise our faith in God's love for us. We tell him we love him by keeping the commandment, even though we don't understand it. That is how we demonstrate our willingness to be obedient in all things.

We have been told clearly in the scriptures that we will never receive the confirmation of our faith until after the trial of that faith. The requirement to prove onself is always on us first, then God second. He wants us to prove

Page 165

The angel then taught Adam the gospel and told him of the Savior who was to come. The Holy Ghost fell upon Adam, and Adam prophesied concerning the inhabitants of the earth down to the last generation. (See Moses 5:7–10; D&C 107:56.) This knowledge and great blessings came to Adam because he was obedient.

God Will Prepare a Way

The Book of Mormon tells us that Nephi and his older brothers received a very difficult assignment from the Lord (see 1 Nephi 3:1–6). Nephi's brothers complained, saying that the Lord required a hard thing of them. But Nephi said, "I will go and do the things which the Lord hath commanded, for I know that the Lord giveth no commandments unto the children of men, save he shall prepare a way for them that they may accomplish the thing which he commandeth them" (1 Nephi 3:7). When we find it difficult to obey a commandment of the Lord, we should remember Nephi's words.

• When has the Lord prepared a way for you to obey Him?

No Commandment Is Too Small or Too Great to Obey

Sometimes we may think a commandment is not very important. The scriptures tell of a man named Naaman who thought that way. Naaman had a dreadful disease and traveled from Syria to Israel to ask the prophet Elisha to heal him. Naaman was an important man in his own country, so he was offended when Elisha did not greet him in person but sent his servant instead. Naaman was even more offended when he received Elisha's message: wash seven times in the river Jordan. "Are not [the] rivers of Damascus better than all the waters of Israel? may I not wash in them, and be clean?" he demanded. He went away in a rage. But his servants asked him: "If the prophet had bid thee do some great thing, wouldest thou not have done it? how much rather then, when he saith to thee, Wash, and be clean?" Naaman was wise enough to understand that it was important to obey the prophet of God, even if it seemed a small matter. So he washed in the Jordan and was healed. (See 2 Kings 5:1–14.)

him in all things, but we have to prove ourselves to Him first by exercising our faith in Him.

Adam makes this example. He didn't understand why he had been commanded to offer sacrifices, but he exercised his faith in God by being obedient. Once he had demonstrated his faith was sincere the Lord revealed the reasons behind the commandment. This was proof to Adam that the Lord would always keep his promises, and it showed Adam that God was worthy of his faith.

The notion that "God will prepare a way" is sort of a logical no brainer. Think about it this way - if God knows the end of time from the beginning of time, and He knows our faithfulness and our capacities, then why would he ever give us a commandment we could not keep? We assume He loves us, so why would he place us in an impossible position?

The answer is, he doesn't. We are never given any instruction from our Father in Heaven that is not possible to accomplish. There is always a way prepared for us to accomplish what he wants us to do. Now that does not mean it will always be easy. On the contrary. It normally means we will have to work very hard and exercise a lot of faith in order to accomplish what the Lord has designed for us. But He never gives us something to do that will not ultimately benefit us and make us more fit to return home to Him.

Just as we have no right to expect God to explain himself to us, so we have no right to decide which commandments are worth our time and attention and which are not.

The only reason commandments are given is to bring us happiness in some way. It may be in the form of a protection from physical or spiritual dangers or it may create in us a greater love for others, or it may just show the Lord that we trust Him. All commandments are spiritual in nature to the Lord. They may have physical benefits as well, but the most important reason for any commandment is for the spiritual growth that comes from obedience to that commandment.

Does it matter if the commandment is a small thing or a large thing, especially if the result is that we will be spiritually blessed and will grow from keeping that commandment? There is no such thing as a commandment that is unworthy of our attention.

Sometimes we may think a commandment is too difficult for us to obey. Like Nephi's brothers, we may say, "It is a hard thing God requires of us." Yet, like Nephi, we can be sure that God will give us no commandment unless He prepares a way for us to obey Him.

Many commandments, especially the ones with the biggest payoffs are the ones that require the greatest amount of faith and sacrifice to obey. These are the ones that most significantly affect our testimonies and our commitment levels to the Lord. But we always have the knowledge to fall back on that there is no commandment given to men but what a way has been provided for them to keep that commandment. God will never ask us to do what is impossible. The way to obey has always been prepared ahead of time. We just have to find it. Therein lies the trial of our faith.

It was a "hard thing" when the Lord commanded Abraham to offer his beloved son Isaac as a sacrifice (see Genesis 22:1–13; see also chapter 26 in this book). Abraham had waited many years for the birth of Isaac, the son God had promised him. How could he lose his son in such a way? This commandment must have been exceedingly difficult for Abraham. Yet he chose to obey God.

We too should be willing to do anything God requires. The Prophet Joseph Smith said, "I made this my rule: When the Lord commands, do it" (Teachings of Presidents of the Church: Joseph Smith [2007], 160). This can be our rule also.

This rule Joseph Smith lived by may seem simple and pragmatic, but it makes sens. Once you understand and fully believe that the Lord will not ask us to do frivolous things, and especially without good reason, then choosing to obey is always a good choice.

• When have you received blessings as a result of your obedience to commandments that seemed small?

Jesus Christ Obeyed His Father
• What examples come to mind when you think of Jesus Christ obeying His Father?

Jesus Christ was the sublime example of obedience to our Heavenly Father. He said, "I came down from heaven, not to do mine own will, but the will of him that sent me" (John 6:38). His whole life was devoted to obeying His Father; yet it was not always easy for him. He was tempted in all ways as other mortals (see Hebrews 4:15). In the Garden of Gethsemane He prayed, saying, "O my Father, if it be possible, let this cup pass from me: nevertheless not as I will, but as thou wilt" (Matthew 26:39).

Jesus was tempted, taunted, and challenged every hour of every day of his life. He allowed himself to be brutalized on our behalf because of his love for God and for us. His determination was to always do the will of his Father, no matter what the outcome was. It was because of this absolute devotion to the Father's will that he was able to come off the conqueror of sin and death.

We will not see the same kind of spectacular accomplishments as Jesus had, but the principle is no different. He has commanded us to do as He did and obey the Father in all things. If we really want to conquer the trials of mortality, obedience to God is the only path available to us. Any other path will lead us to places we don't want to be when all is said and done. The path back to God is strait (confined) and narrow. If we want the broad path, where we can do what we want, well, that leads to hell. That's not a great option.

Because Jesus obeyed the Father's will in all things, He made salvation possible for all of us.

• How can remembering the Savior's example help us be obedient?

Results of Obedience and Disobedience
• What are the consequences of obeying or disobeying the Lord's commandments?

The kingdom of heaven is governed by law, and when we receive any blessing, it is by obedience to the law upon which that blessing is based (see D&C 130:20–21; 132:5). The Lord has told us that through our obedience and diligence we may gain knowledge and intelligence (see D&C 130:18–19). We may also grow spiritually (see Jeremiah 7:23–24). On the other hand, disobedience brings disappointment and results in a loss of blessings. "Who am I, saith the Lord, that have promised and have not fulfilled? I command and men obey not; I revoke and they receive not the blessing. Then they say in their hearts: This is not the work of the Lord, for his promises are not fulfilled" (D&C 58:31–33).

When we keep the commandments of God, He fulfills His promises, as King Benjamin told his people: "He doth require that ye should do as he hath commanded you; for which if ye do, he doth immediately bless you" (Mosiah 2:24).

Obedience has always been the key to everything. If you want spiritual power, obedience is the answer. If you want revelation, obedience is the prerequisite. If you want answers to prayers obedience is the basis for your answers. If you want more knowledge, obedience to the knowledge you already possess is required.

We are quick, at times, to blame the Lord for not answering our prayers, or for giving us answers that do not please us. If we were more obedient to what we have already received we would be more grateful for what we have and more apt to refrain from criticizing the Lord for what we don't currently have.

The Lord always, always, always keeps His promises, but the ability to fulfill those promises is always, always, always based on our obedience to the commandments that produce those promises.

The Obedient Gain Eternal Life
The Lord counsels us, "If you keep my commandments and endure to the end you shall have eternal life, which gift is the greatest of all the gifts of God" (D&C 14:7).

The Lord has described other blessings that will come to those who obey Him in righteousness and truth until the end:

"Thus saith the Lord—I, the Lord, am merciful and gracious unto those who fear me, and delight to honor those who serve me in righteousness and in truth unto the end.

"Great shall be their reward and eternal shall be their glory.

"And to them will I reveal all mysteries, yea, all the hidden mysteries of my kingdom from days of old, and for ages to come, will I make known unto them the good pleasure of my will concerning all things pertaining to my kingdom.

"Yea, even the wonders of eternity shall they know, and things to come will I show them, even the things of many generations.

If we are obedient enough there is nothing that will be withheld from us. We will have all that the Father has. He has promised this to those who keep the commandments. All that He has includes having the mysteries of heaven revealed to us, visions, visitations, receiving hidden treasures of knowledge, and being changed by the Holy Ghost into someone who thinks and acts like Christ.

The Lord is so anxious to bless us with everything He has, but He is patient and waits for us to decide that this is what we really want. He will never force His happiness upon us, this is something we must actively seek out for ourselves.

It is important to remember that obedience is not a one-time behavior. Obedience must become our mantra, our guiding principle. There are so many tests we need to be given to prove our love and devotion to wanting to live the life our Father in Heaven lives. Obedience must be a part of who we are, how we define ourselves. We must

"And their wisdom shall be great, and their understanding reach to heaven. …

"For by my Spirit will I enlighten them, and by my power will I make known unto them the secrets of my will—yea, even those things which eye has not seen, nor ear heard, nor yet entered into the heart of man" (D&C 76:5–10).

• What does the phrase "endure to the end" mean to you?

• What can we do to stay true to gospel principles even when it is unpopular to do so? How can we help children and youth stay true to gospel principles?

Additional Scriptures
• Abraham 3:25 (we came to earth to prove our obedience)
• 1 Samuel 15:22 (obedience is better than sacrifice)
• Ecclesiastes 12:13; John 14:15; Romans 6:16; D&C 78:7; 132:36; Deuteronomy 4:1–40 (we should obey God)
• 2 Nephi 31:7 (Jesus Christ was obedient)
• Proverbs 3:1–4; 6:20–22; 7:1–3; Ephesians 6:1–3; Colossians 3:20 (children should obey their parents)
• D&C 21:4–6 (obey the prophet)
• John 8:29–32; Mosiah 2:22, 41; D&C 82:10; 1 Nephi 2:20 (blessings for obedience)
• D&C 58:21–22; 98:4–6; 134:5–7 (obey the laws of the land)
• Isaiah 60:12; D&C 1:14; 93:39; 132:6, 39 (consequences of disobedience)
• 2 Nephi 31:16; D&C 53:7; Matthew 24:13; Luke 9:62 (endure to the end)

become like the Savior who lived only to do His Father's will.

Chapter 36

The Family Can Be Eternal

Gospel Principles, (2011), 207–11

The Importance of Families

• Why did our Heavenly Father send us to earth as members of families?

"Marriage between a man and a woman is ordained of God. ... The family is central to the Creator's plan for the eternal destiny of His children" ("The Family: A Proclamation to the World," Ensign, Nov. 1995, 102).

For teachers: As you teach this chapter and the next two chapters about families, be sensitive to the feelings of those who do not have ideal situations at home.

After Heavenly Father brought Adam and Eve together in marriage, He commanded them to have children (see Genesis 1:28). He has revealed that one of the purposes of marriage is to provide mortal bodies for His spirit children. Parents are partners with our Heavenly Father. He wants each of His spirit children to receive a physical body and to experience earth life. When a man and a woman bring children into this world, they help our Heavenly Father carry out His plan.

Every new child should be welcomed into the family with gladness. Each is a child of God. We should take time to enjoy our children, to play with them, and to teach them.

President David O. McKay said, "With all my heart I believe that the best place to prepare for ... eternal life is in the home" ("Blueprint for Family Living," Improvement Era, Apr. 1963, 252). At home, with our families, we can learn self-control, sacrifice, loyalty, and the value of work. We can learn to love, to share, and to serve one another.

Fathers and mothers are responsible to teach their children about Heavenly Father. They should show by example that they love Him because they keep His commandments. Parents should also teach their children to pray and to obey the commandments (see Proverbs 22:6).

• Why is the home the best place to prepare for eternal life?

• How can we help the youth of the Church understand the sacredness of the family and the marriage covenant?

Heaven is organized by families. The family is the basic unit of all societies. Earth was patterned after where we used to live when we were home with our heavenly parents. Family relationships are what is natural to us, for we have been in a family since we have been spirit children of our Father in Heaven.

Gender and the relationship between men and women is patterned on earth as it is in heaven. This is how we will be living for eternity.

The most basic blessing of being able to come to earth is to receive a mortal body. This is what we all wanted in the spirit world, to have a body like our parents. Only those who honored the laws of God were able to come to earth and receive a body. Those who rebelled against God were cast out of heaven and denied the ability to ever have their own body. This is why having children is such a sacred responsibility. It is through this means that our brother and sisters come to earth and receive their reward of getting a body so they can prove themselves to God.

Children are our brothers and sisters from the premortal world. It is a privilege for us to bring them into this world and to teach them right from wrong and to help them become responsible and obedient adults. This should be something we look forward to and enjoy doing.

The power of living in families is that it is the perfect unit for teaching children to be honest, respectful, loving, etc. When parents work closely with their children they build a bond of trust that will support and be a source of encouragement to those children the rest of their lives.

Our Father in Heaven has given us, as parents, the responsibility of teaching our children about Him. If we don't teach them the difference between right and wrong, and to be obedient to His commandments by the time they are accountable for their own behavior (age 8) then the sins of that child will be on our heads.

The Eternal Family

Families can be together forever. To enjoy this blessing we must be married in the temple. When people are married outside the temple, the marriage ends when one of the partners dies. When we are married in the temple by the authority of the Melchizedek Priesthood, we are married for time and eternity. If we keep our covenants with the Lord, our families will be united eternally as husband, wife, and children. Death cannot separate us.

We will always be part of our Father in Heaven's family, even if we don't live with Him. But if we want to start and keep our own eternal family unit we will have to be married in the temple for eternity then be obedient to all our covenants until we leave mortality. Only then can death have no effect on our marriage.

Loving Family Relationships

• How can we develop greater harmony in our homes?

Husbands and wives should be thoughtful and kind to each other. They should never do or say anything to hurt each other's feelings. They should also try to do everything possible to make each other happy.

For those who are sealed for eternity in the temple, our relationship with our spouse should be of the utmost importance. He or she is not just someone we will ride out our journey through life with, but we will have them by our side forever.

As parents come to know God and strive to be like Him, they will teach children to love one another. In the Book of Mormon, King Benjamin explained:

"Ye will not suffer your children ... [to] fight and quarrel one with another. ...

"But ye will teach them to walk in the ways of truth and soberness; ye will teach them to love one another, and to serve one another" (Mosiah 4:14–15).

As King Benjamin taught that parents should teach children how to behave to one another, it is noteworthy that it is almost impossible to teach a behavior you have not already mastered. How is a parent supposed to teach a child how to serve others if they have never learned how to do it themselves?

As family members we can help each other feel confident by giving encouragement and sincere praise. Each child should feel important. Parents need to show they are interested in what their children do and express love and concern for their children. Children should likewise show their love for their parents. They should be obedient and try to live the kind of life that will bring honor to their parents and to their family name.

Children have a natural trust in their parents. It is only when they learn from sad experience that their parent are not really interested in them that they begin to mistrust what their parents say and mistrust their actions and promises. It is very important that we demonstrate our love and concern for each child on a constant basis.

• What can parents do to encourage their sons and daughters to be good friends with one another? What can brothers and sisters do to nurture their friendship with one another?

Serving each other is a good way to build unity among siblings.

• What can husbands and wives do to help each other be happy?

Putting each other's needs ahead of our own is a good way to help our spouse be happy in the marriage.

How to Have a Successful Family

• What are you doing to help strengthen your family and make it successful?

President Harold B. Lee taught, "The most important of the Lord's work you will ever do will be within the walls of your own homes" (Teachings of Presidents of the Church: Harold B. Lee [2000], 134).

We may feel that the influence we exert within the walls of our home is smaller than what we might be able to accomplish out in the business world or in the community at large. But the changes we make in the perceptions and understandings of our children carry on for generations to come. The customs and traditions we instill in our children will still be felt several generations down the road. The cumulative influence of what we teach in our home will eventually be felt by many thousands of people.

Satan knows how important families are to our Heavenly Father's plan. He seeks to destroy them by keeping us from drawing near to the Lord. He will tempt us to do things that will draw our families apart.

It is because the family is the basic unit of society, and the unit God has ordained for us to teach His other children about him that Satan focuses so intently on destroying the family. He works to get us so involved in activities that pull away from spending time together that it becomes difficult for us to teach and be the examples we need to be as parents.

The First Presidency and Quorum of the Twelve Apostles declared, "Successful marriages and families are established and maintained on principles of faith, prayer, repentance, forgiveness, respect, love, compassion, work, and wholesome recreational activities" (Ensign, Nov. 1995, 102).

All of us want to have happy, successful families. The following things will help us achieve this:
1. Have family prayer every night and morning (see 3 Nephi 18:21). Pray together as husband and wife.
2. Teach children the gospel every week in family home evening.
3. Study the scriptures regularly as a family.
4. Do things together as a family, such as work projects, outings, and decision making.
5. Learn to be kind, patient, long-suffering, and charitable (see Moroni 7:45–48).
6. Attend Church meetings regularly (see D&C 59:9–10).
7. Follow the counsel of the Lord in D&C 88:119: "Organize yourselves; prepare every needful thing; and establish a house, even a house of prayer, a house of fasting, a house of faith, a house of learning, a house of glory, a house of order, a house of God."
8. Keep a family history, perform temple work together, and receive the sealing ordinances of the temple.

As you go through this list notice that everything in the list includes spending time together as a family. If our children are spending time away from the family you can be sure that it is not healthy or productive for the child or the family. Raising children should be and needs to be a family affair, not an individual affair.

The family is the most important unit in The Church of Jesus Christ of Latter-day Saints. The Church exists to help families gain eternal blessings and exaltation. The organizations and programs within the Church are designed to strengthen us individually and help us live as families forever.

The Church is not designed to take over for the family in the teaching of the children. Church is only supposed to remind and emphasis to the children the points and principles that are already being taught in the home. The home is where the bulk of all spiritual learning is supposed to take place.

• What can families do to work through difficult times?

How can unity in the home help families work through difficult times? What does it take for us to develop unity among ourselves as a family?

• What evidence have you seen that efforts such as family prayer, family scripture study, family councils, family meal times, and family home evening make a difference?

Additional Scriptures and Other Sources

• Moses 2:27–28 (man and woman created and blessed)
• Genesis 2:24 (man to cleave unto his wife)
• D&C 49:15–16 (God ordained marriage)
• Ephesians 6:4 (train children in righteousness)
• D&C 132:15–21 (eternal marriage)
• D&C 88:119–26 (instructions for a successful family)
• D&C 93:40–50 (the Lord commands parents to bring up their children in light and truth)
• "The Family: A Proclamation to the World" (available on LDS.org and in many Church publications, including Ensign, Nov. 1995, page 102; For the Strength of Youth: Fulfilling Our Duty to God [item number 36550], page 44; and True to the Faith: A Gospel Reference [item number 36863], pages 59–61)

Chapter 37

Family Responsibilities

Gospel Principles, (2011), 212–17

Is there a valid reason why either parent should be excused from any responsibility when it comes to raising their own children?

Responsibilities of the Parents

• What responsibilities do husbands and wives share in raising their children?

Each person has an important place in his or her family. Through prophets the Lord has explained how fathers, mothers, and children should behave and feel toward one another. As husbands, wives, and children, we need to learn what the Lord expects us to do to fulfill our purpose as a family. If we all do our part, we will be united eternally.

For teachers: As with chapter 36, be sensitive to the feelings of those who do not have ideal situations at home. Emphasize that with guidance from the Lord and help from family members and the Church, single parents can successfully raise their children.

In the sacred responsibilities of parenthood, "fathers and mothers are obligated to help one another as equal partners" ("The Family: A Proclamation to the World," Ensign, Nov. 1995, 102). They should work together to provide for the spiritual, emotional, intellectual, and physical needs of the family.

The belief that each person in a marriage or family has a "place" in the marriage and family is very unpopular in today's society. People don't like to hear that the Lord intends for us to fulfill certain roles in this life. It is not politically correct to make such claims. In a society where people are being allowed to change their gender based on how they feel or wish to be identified that day, declaring that we have God-given roles to play is saying a lot!

For anyone who is married, the definition of being in an equal partnership does NOT mean you are equal as long as your partner recognizes you as the final authority in all things. Equal partners means that whatever has to be done both people are willing and ready to do it. If there is something to be discussed then both people discuss it until a respectful solution has been found that satisfies both people. If you have already come home from a long day away from the family, you don't get to retire from the family to rest yourself if your spouse is still cooking, cleaning, and caring for the children. An equal partner will continue to work and help out around the house until all the work is done, the children are cared for, and the spouse feels like his or her spouse has recognized what kind of day they have had.

Some responsibilities must be shared by the husband and the wife. Parents should teach their children the gospel. The Lord warned that if parents do not teach their children about faith, repentance, baptism, and the gift of the Holy Ghost, the sin will be upon the heads of the parents. Parents should also teach their children to pray and to obey the Lord's commandments. (See D&C 68:25, 28.)

It is good for the parents to teach the children to take on the responsibilities of helping out in the family. Children are ready to start accepting responsibilities when they start to show interest in it at an early age. They can teach lessons in family home evening when taught how to by the parents. They can conduct meetings, handle workloads around the house, all kinds of things. They won't learn any of these things if the parents don't explicitly teach them about how to read the scriptures, how to mop a floor, or how to pray in the family and in private.

One of the best ways parents can teach their children is by example. Husbands and wives should show love and respect for each other and for their children by both actions

Parents do not own their children. Children are on loan to them from their Heavenly Father. We do not own our and words. It is important to remember that each member of the family is a child of God. Parents should treat their children with love and respect, being firm but kind to them.

Parents should understand that sometimes children will make wrong choices even after they have been taught the truth. When this happens, parents should not give up. They should continue to teach their children, to express love for them, to be good examples to them, and to fast and pray for them.

The Book of Mormon tells us how the prayers of a father helped a rebellious son return to the ways of the Lord. Alma the Younger had fallen away from the teachings of his righteous father, Alma, and had gone about seeking to destroy the Church. The father prayed with faith for his son. Alma the Younger was visited by an angel and repented of his evil way of living. He became a great leader of the Church. (See Mosiah 27:8–32.)

Parents can provide an atmosphere of reverence and respect in the home if they teach and guide their children with love. Parents should also provide happy experiences for their children.

• How can husbands and wives support each other in their roles? Where can single parents turn for support?

Responsibilities of the Father
• What positive examples have you seen of fathers raising their children?

"By divine design, fathers are to preside over their families in love and righteousness and are responsible to provide the necessities of life and protection for their families" (Ensign, Nov. 1995, 102). A worthy father who is a member of the Church has the opportunity to hold the priesthood, making him the priesthood leader of his family. He should guide his family with humility and kindness rather than with force or cruelty. The scriptures teach that those who hold the priesthood should lead others by persuasion, gentleness, love, and kindness (see D&C 121:41–44; Ephesians 6:4).

The father shares the blessings of the priesthood with the members of his family. When a man holds the

spouse, not do we have the right to think we can or should be able to control our spouse. We are equals in God's sight and should be humble enough to admit when we need their help or when we are wrong about something.

Parents have a difficult job when it comes to teaching right and wrong to their children. We can teach, and teach, and teach, but when they are old enough to make their own decisions, we cannot control them. All we can do at that point is love them and be there for them to help them pick up the pieces. Some of the best lessons our children will ever learn will require the parents to help them put their lives back together when they have made a major mistake. We do all we can to help them avoid mistakes, but it is ultimately up the individual as to the choice they make. Then they have to learn to live with the consequences.

Some children wander off or willfully rebel. The parent is left with little choice but to daily pray for their child. The Lord wants us to lean on Him and come to Him with our prayers in behalf of our children or spouse. These prayers give us personal strength to carry on in the face of difficult situations. The hard part is to have the kind of faith that Alma had for his son. Faith means that we believe that if we ask we will be answered or that something will happen. The Lord will stretch our capacity and our faith. Oh the blessings of children.

It doesn't take money to create happy experiences. Children are simple people at heart. Time and attention is the best gift you can give them.

This is a difficult assignment for the men. Learning how to guide and direct one's family, without becoming a dictator is a real balancing act. A father must learn how to honor and respect his wife as his equal, while recognizing that he cannot pass on her the responsibility for what happens in the home. As a priesthood holder he will have to answer to the Lord for how well he lead his family in righteousness. To do this requires he learn patience, long suffering, meekness, and still have a dedication to the Lord that will not accept slacking in spiritual matters. He must lead out in all things spiritual in the home.

The priesthood is a blessing to the members of the family. Every member of the family should be able to ask for a

Melchizedek Priesthood, he can share these blessings by administering to the sick and giving special priesthood blessings. Under the direction of a presiding priesthood leader, he can bless babies, baptize, confirm, and perform priesthood ordinations. He should set a good example for his family by keeping the commandments. He should also make sure the family prays together twice daily and holds family home evening.

The father should spend time with each child individually. He should teach his children correct principles, talk with them about their problems and concerns, and counsel them lovingly. Some good examples are found in the Book of Mormon (see 2 Nephi 1:14–3:25; Alma 36–42).

blessing whenever they are sick or feel the need for a blessing. The priesthood leader should also be blessing his children before important events. Often priesthood holders will give each child a blessing before the first day of school or before going off to college or other important events. Prayers, the paying of tithes and offerings, and family home evening are also under his responsibilities.

Some fathers have personal priesthood interviews (PPIs) with each child once a month to see how they are doing in life. Some fathers just make sure they have enough alone time on a regular basis with each child that they come to know what is going on in that child's life. This requires that the father has built an intimate enough relationship with each child that they will share with him how they feel about what is going on in their life at that time.

It is also the father's duty to provide for the physical needs of his family, making sure they have the necessary food, housing, clothing, and education. Even if he is unable to provide all the support himself, he does not give up the responsibility of the care of his family.

Responsibilities of the Mother
• What positive examples have you seen of mothers raising their children?

President David O. McKay said that motherhood is the noblest calling (see Teachings of Presidents of the Church: David O. McKay [2003], 156). It is a sacred calling, a partnership with God in bringing His spirit children into the world. Bearing children is one of the greatest of all blessings. If there is no father in the home, the mother presides over the family.

The mother works alongside the father in the home to watch over the spiritual and physical welfare of the children. She also has to balance her need to honor the presiding authority in the home while still speaking up and helping to steer the course of the family. If the father is the backbone of the family, the mother is the heart of the family.

President Boyd K. Packer praised women who were unable to have children of their own yet sought to care for others. He said: "When I speak of mothers, I speak not only of those women who have borne children, but also of those who have fostered children born to others, and of the many women who, without children of their own, have mothered the children of others" (Mothers [1977], 8).

Latter-day prophets have taught, "Mothers are primarily responsible for the nurture of their children" (Ensign, Nov. 1995, 102). A mother needs to spend time with her children and teach them the gospel. She should play and work with them so they can discover the world around them. She also needs to help her family know how to make the home a pleasant place to be. If she is warm and loving, she helps her children feel good about themselves.

Just because mothers are "primarily" responsible for the nurture of the children, it doesn't mean the father is off the hook. He needs to be actively involved in the care of each child.

The Book of Mormon describes a group of 2,000 young men who rose to greatness because of the teachings of their mothers (see Alma 53:16–23). Led by the prophet Helaman, they went into battle against their enemies. They

Children naturally have a great trust in what their mothers teach them, especially if she teaches them the same principles repeatedly so they don't forget them. Children had learned to be honest, brave, and trustworthy from their mothers. Their mothers also taught them that if they did not doubt, God would deliver them (see Alma 56:47). They all survived the battle. They expressed faith in the teachings of their mothers, saying, "We do not doubt our mothers knew it" (Alma 56:48). Every mother who has a testimony can have a profound effect on her children.

do not naturally know how to identify the influence of the Holy Ghost. It is the teachings from their parents that they learn to tell when they are being lead by the Spirit.

Responsibilities of the Children
• How do children help their parents build a happy home?

Children share with their parents the responsibilities of building a happy home. They should obey the commandments and cooperate with other family members. The Lord is not pleased when children quarrel (see Mosiah 4:14).

Children are sponges in one sense in that they soak up whatever their parents expose them to. But they should also be taught that it is their responsibility to contribute to the welfare of the family. Having a happy home is not just the responsibility of the mother and father. All members of the family contribute to the spirit that is in the home. Children can be taught to safeguard the home from bad influences and to promote good influences. This has to become a priority of the parents. The children will only focus on whatever the parents make a priority in the home.

The Lord has commanded children to honor their parents. He said, "Honour thy father and thy mother: that thy days may be long upon the land" (Exodus 20:12). To honor parents means to love and respect them. It also means to obey them. The scriptures tell children to "obey your parents in the Lord: for this is right" (Ephesians 6:1).

Fathers need to make sure the children show respect to their mother, and that they respect each other. The mother needs to make sure she only speaks well of the children's father so they respect him.

President Spencer W. Kimball said that children should learn to work and to share responsibilities in the home and yard. They should be given assignments to keep the house neat and clean. (See Teachings of Presidents of the Church: Spencer W. Kimball [2006], 120.)

Teaching children to work, especially when living in town is difficult. There are so many conveniences that we often have more time on our hands than chores to fill the hours. But the parents need to teach the children that work is not only required to live, but can be an enjoyable part of living. Working with them is the best way to teach this. Remember that specific lessons have to be spelled out or the children will miss them. If we want them to learn how to love work, we must share stories about great times we had when working, as well as providing good experiences with the children that involve work.

• What should children do to honor and respect their parents?

• What did your parents do that led you to honor and respect them?

Accepting Responsibilities Brings Blessings
• What can each member of the family do to make home a happy place?

A loving and happy family does not happen by accident. Each person in the family must do his or her part. The Lord has given responsibilities to both parents and children. The scriptures teach that we must be thoughtful,

Just as success is not accidental, so a happy home is not an accident. It requires a focused application of work, attention, and lots of love and discipline. Children may take an exhaustive amount of work and energy to raise, cheerful, and considerate of others. When we speak, pray, sing, or work together, we can enjoy the blessings of harmony in our families. (See Colossians 3.)

• What are some traditions and practices that can make home a happy place?

Additional Scriptures and Other Sources
• Proverbs 22:6 (train up a child)
• Ephesians 6:1–3 (children are to obey parents)
• D&C 68:25–28; Ephesians 6:4 (responsibilities of parents)
• "The Family: A Proclamation to the World," (available on LDS.org and in many Church publications, including Ensign, Nov. 1995, page 102; For the Strength of Youth [item number 36550], page 44; and True to the Faith [item number 36863], pages 59–61)
• Family Guidebook (item number 31180)

but there is nothing more important we can accomplish in mortality. Nothing outside the home is more important than what happens inside the home.

Chapter 38

Eternal Marriage
Gospel Principles, (2011), 218–23

Marriage Is Ordained of God
Marriage between a man and a woman is a vital part of God's plan. The Lord has said, "Whoso forbiddeth to marry is not ordained of God, for marriage is ordained of God unto man" (D&C 49:15). Since the beginning, marriage has been a law of the gospel. Marriages are intended to last forever, not just for our mortal lives.

Adam and Eve were married by God before there was any death in the world. They had an eternal marriage. They taught the law of eternal marriage to their children and their children's children. As the years passed, wickedness entered the hearts of the people and the authority to perform this sacred ordinance was taken from the earth. Through the Restoration of the gospel, eternal marriage has been restored to earth.

• Why is it important to know that marriage between a man and a woman is ordained of God?

Eternal Marriage Is Essential for Exaltation
• What is the Lord's doctrine of marriage, and how does it differ from the views of the world?

Many people in the world consider marriage to be only a social custom, a legal agreement between a man and a woman to live together. But to Latter-day Saints, marriage is much more. Our exaltation depends on marriage, along with other principles and ordinances, such as faith, repentance, baptism, and receiving the gift of the Holy Ghost. We believe that marriage is the most sacred relationship that can exist between a man and a woman. This sacred relationship affects our happiness now and in the eternities.

Heavenly Father has given us the law of eternal marriage so we can become like Him. The Lord has said:

"In the celestial glory there are three heavens or degrees;

"And in order to obtain the highest, a man must enter into this order of the priesthood [meaning the new and everlasting covenant of marriage];

"And if he does not, he cannot obtain it" (D&C 131:1–3).

For teachers: All members, whether married or single, need to understand the doctrine of eternal marriage. However, you should be sensitive to the feelings of adults who are not married. As needed, help class members or

The Lord does not think in terms of mortality and temporary arrangements. When commandments are given they are meant to affect the eternal soul forever. In something as important as marriage, He would never encourage us to start a family that was only meant to be temporary. This is why Adam and Eve began their mortal experience as eternal companions, married by God. This is the same type of union they taught their children.

When the world was much more religious, even marriages by the church were considered most sacred. As the world has become far less religious, marriage has lost its status as something ordained of God and viewed by many to be not much more than a social contract for convenience or with tax benefits. To those in The Church of Jesus Christ of Latter-day Saints marriage is the highest of all the covenants or sacraments we make with our God. It is the last thing done in the temple ceremony, the pinnacle of the temple experience.

We cannot walk into the Celestial kingdom as a single person. Gods are all married. To be single in the eternities is to be only half a person, for you cannot have children if you are alone. Eternal progression depends on our ability to have family relations.

We often speak in absolute terms of having a spouse and needing a spouse to progress throughout eternity, and that is all true. But it is also important to remember that there are those in mortality who won't receive the *family members know that all Heavenly Father's children who are faithful to their covenants in this life will have the opportunity to receive all the blessings of the gospel in the eternities, including the opportunity to have an eternal family.*

opportunity to marry until after this life. That doesn't change the requirement for entering the Celestial kingdom, but we do need to remember that not everyone will marry in the here and now. They will receive an opportunity for a spouse later. As long as they are worthy of the blessing, no one will be deprived of any blessing they are worthy to receive.

Eternal Marriage Must Be Performed by Proper Authority in the Temple

• Why must a marriage be performed by proper authority in the temple to be eternal?

An eternal marriage must be performed by one who holds the sealing power. The Lord promised, "If a man marry a wife by … the new and everlasting covenant … by him who is anointed, … and if [they] abide in [the Lord's] covenant, … it … shall be of full force when they are out of the world" (D&C 132:19).

There are very few people on earth who possess the sealing power that can bind husbands, wives, and children into eternal families. There are probably less than a thousand sealers living today. Each temple only has a few men who possess the sealing power, and sealings are only done within the walls of the temples. This should give you an idea of how sacred and special it is to be sealed to your spouse.

Not only must an eternal marriage be performed by the proper priesthood authority, but it must also be done in one of the holy temples of our Lord. The temple is the only place this holy ordinance can be performed.

In the temple, Latter-day Saint couples kneel at one of the sacred altars in the presence of their family and friends who have received the temple endowment. They make their marriage covenants before God. They are pronounced husband and wife for time and all eternity. This is done by one who holds the holy priesthood of God and has been given the authority to perform this sacred ordinance. He acts under the direction of the Lord and promises the couple the blessings of exaltation. He instructs them in the things they must do to receive these blessings. He reminds them that all blessings depend on obedience to the laws of God.

All the covenants of the temple we make from the time we enter and begin the ceremonies lead up to the covenants and promises of the eternal marriage. The greatest blessing pronounced on any couple is done over the marriage altar of the temple.

If we are married by any authority other than by the priesthood in a temple, the marriage is for this life only. After death, the marriage partners have no claim on each other or on their children. An eternal marriage gives us the opportunity to continue as families after this life.

Sometimes people in the Church think of marriage as a casual thing. They think to themselves that it is okay to marry civilly first then, when they get around to it, they will marry in the temple. Unfortunately, there are far too many who never make it to the temple because they did not insist on being worthy to go there the first time. In some countries it is not possible to marry in the temple the first time, because the laws of the land require a government wedding first.

Benefits of an Eternal Marriage

• What are the blessings of an eternal marriage in this life and in eternity?

As Latter-day Saints, we are living with an eternal perspective, not just for the moment. However, we can

Having an eternal perspective about our marriage can really change our level of commitment. When we think of receive blessings in this life as a result of being married for eternity. Some of those blessings are as follows:

1. We know that our marriage can last forever. Death can part us from one another only temporarily. Nothing can part us forever except our own disobedience. This knowledge helps us work harder to have a happy, successful marriage.

2. We know that our family relationships can continue throughout eternity. This knowledge helps us be careful in teaching and training our children. It also helps us show them greater patience and love. As a result, we should have a happier home.

3. Because we have been married in God's ordained way, we are entitled to an outpouring of the Spirit on our marriage as we remain worthy.

our union with our spouse as one that is meant to last for eternity, that comes with the understanding that we are going to have to work hard for that relationship to be good enough to be sustained through all the hardships of mortal life and to last into the eternities. With this perspective it is more difficult to throw in the towel when things get rough and we begin to question why we are in the marriage.

Having an eternal perspective about our marriage also helps us raise our children as those who will be with us forever. Raising children to have an eternal perspective about life requires more work, but produces more obedient children. It also helps us, as parents, to become more like what we need to be in the way of righteous people. We have to be close to the Spirit to teach our children how to identify the Spirit in their lives. We need to be close to the Spirit in order to give them blessings and to be more keenly in tune with their needs as they grow up.

Some of the blessings we can enjoy for eternity are as follows:

1. We can live in the highest degree of the celestial kingdom of God.

2. We can be exalted as God is and receive a fulness of joy.

• How can an eternal perspective influence the way we feel about marriage and families?

We Must Prepare for an Eternal Marriage

• What can we do to help youth prepare for eternal marriage?

President Spencer W. Kimball taught: "Marriage is perhaps the most vital of all the decisions and has the most far-reaching effects, for it has to do not only with immediate happiness, but also with eternal joys. It affects not only the two people involved, but also their families and particularly their children and their children's children down through the many generations. In selecting a companion for life and for eternity, certainly the most careful planning and thinking and praying and fasting should be done to be sure that of all the decisions, this one must not be wrong" (Teachings of Presidents of the Church: Spencer W. Kimball [2006], 193).

According to President Kimball there is no such thing as "the one and only." Any two people who are willing to keep all the commandments can live together in harmony. But that opens a wide door for possible matches in marriage. In selecting a suitable spouse we need to be aware that this person will be helping us raise our children and will be our best friend forever. This really is a big decision.

An eternal marriage should be the goal of every Latter-day Saint. This is true even for those already married by civil law. To prepare for an eternal marriage takes much thought and prayer. Only members of the Church who live righteously are permitted to enter the temple (see D&C 97:15–17). We do not suddenly decide one day that we want to be married in the temple, then enter the temple that

Are you aware of the temple recommend interview questions? If not then keep reading this lesson to see the kinds of questions you will be asked in your recommend interview. To be worthy to enter the temple to be married there we must be keeping all the basic commandments we made at baptism. We should be attending our church meetings, paying our tithes and offerings, and living the Word of Wisdom.

day and get married. We must first meet certain requirements.

Before we can go to the temple, we must be active, worthy members of the Church for at least one year. Men must hold the Melchizedek Priesthood. We must be interviewed by the branch president or bishop. If he finds us worthy, he will give us a temple recommend. If we are not worthy, he will counsel with us and help us set goals to become worthy to go to the temple.

After we receive a recommend from our bishop or branch president, we must be interviewed by the stake president or the mission president. We are asked questions like the following in interviews for a temple recommend:
1. Do you have faith in and a testimony of God, the Eternal Father; His Son, Jesus Christ; and the Holy Ghost? Do you have a firm testimony of the restored gospel?
2. Do you sustain the President of The Church of Jesus Christ of Latter-day Saints as the prophet, seer, and revelator? Do you recognize him as the only person on earth authorized to exercise all priesthood keys?
3. Do you live the law of chastity?
4. Are you a full-tithe payer?
5. Do you keep the Word of Wisdom?
6. Are you honest in your dealings with others?
7. Do you strive to keep the covenants you have made, to attend your sacrament and priesthood meetings, and to keep your life in harmony with the laws and commandments of the gospel?
When you ask for a temple recommend, you should remember that entering the temple is a sacred privilege. It is a serious act, not something to be taken lightly.

These are personal statements of worthiness. For example, when asked if you are honest, if you feel you have problems with certain aspects of honesty then this is a good time to discuss it with your Branch President or Bishop. Otherwise these are basic yes/no questions.

We must seek earnestly to obey every covenant that we make in the temple. The Lord has said that if we are true and faithful, we will enter into our exaltation. We will become like our Heavenly Father. (See D&C 132:19–20.) Temple marriage is worth any sacrifice. It is a way of obtaining eternal blessings beyond measure.

Being sealed as an eternal family in the temple does not guarantee that we will be an eternal family. The blessing is pronounced on our heads contingent on our obedience to the commandments of the Lord. Only if we are faithful until death will we receive the promised blessings.

• What can we do to encourage young people to set a goal to be married in the temple? How can we help them prepare for this?

Additional Scriptures
• Genesis 1:26–28 (we should multiply and replenish the earth)
• Genesis 2:21–24 (the first marriage was performed by God)
• Matthew 19:3–8 (what God has joined)
• D&C 132 (the eternal nature of the marriage law)
• D&C 42:22–26 (marriage vows should be kept)
• Jacob 3:5–7 (husbands and wives should be true to each other)

Chapter 39

The Law of Chastity

Gospel Principles, (2011), 224–32

A Note to Parents

This chapter includes some parts that are beyond the maturity of young children. It is best to wait until children are old enough to understand sexual relations and procreation before teaching them these parts of the chapter. Our Church leaders have told us that parents are responsible to teach their children about procreation (the process of conceiving and bearing children). Parents must also teach them the law of chastity, which is explained in this chapter.

Parents can begin teaching children to have proper attitudes toward their bodies when children are very young. Talking to children frankly but reverently and using the correct names for the parts and functions of their bodies will help them grow up without unnecessary embarrassment about their bodies.

Children are naturally curious. They want to know how their bodies work. They want to know where babies come from. If parents answer all such questions immediately and clearly so children can understand, children will continue to take their questions to their parents. However, if parents answer questions so that children feel embarrassed, rejected, or dissatisfied, they will probably go to someone else with their questions and perhaps get incorrect ideas and improper attitudes.

It is not wise or necessary, however, to tell children everything at once. Parents need only give them the information they have asked for and can understand. While answering these questions, parents can teach children the importance of respecting their bodies and the bodies of others. Parents should teach children to dress modestly. They should correct the false ideas and vulgar language that children learn from others.

By the time children reach maturity, parents should have frankly discussed procreation with them. Children should understand that these powers are good and were given to us by the Lord. He expects us to use them within the bounds He has given us.

When teaching children about their bodies it is important to remember that little children cannot comprehend everything about the making of babies. We can tell them just enough to answer their questions at their level of understanding so they are satisfied. As they get older, and can comprehend more, they will ask other questions that we can answer more clearly and directly. The key is keeping our answers at their current level of understanding.

Whether we are talking about children or adults, we need to remember that the subject of chastity is just as much about our attitudes about our bodies as it is about how we treat our bodies or how we behave with our bodies.

Our children will learn inappropriate terminology and concepts about their bodies at an early age. Do not assume your child is innocent. Innocence in today's society is a rarity and far more difficult to keep these days. As you plan on talking to your children about their bodies, look for the words they use in response. This will indicate if they have already been exposed to the topic from other sources.

People make jokes about having "the talk" with their children, but if the children don't have that talk with a trustworthy parent then where are they getting their information? That should scare a parent more than having to personally have "the talk."

Our children need to learn from us how sacred the procreative power is. They need to learn from us, their parents that this power is built into every body, and everyone has to learn how to control it and use it properly so they receive the blessings of the Lord. Much of the happiness we experience in this life will be connected to the proper use of this natural power.

Little children come to earth pure and innocent from Heavenly Father. As parents pray for guidance, the Lord will inspire them to teach children at the right time and in the right way.

The Power of Procreation
• Why should parents teach their children about procreation and chastity? How can they appropriately do this?

God commanded each living thing to reproduce after its own kind (see Genesis 1:22). Reproduction was part of His plan so that all forms of life could continue to exist upon the earth.

Then He placed Adam and Eve on the earth. They were different from His other creations because they were His spirit children. In the Garden of Eden, He brought Adam and Eve together in marriage and commanded them to multiply and replenish the earth (see Genesis 1:28). However, their lives were to be governed by moral laws rather than by instinct.

The first commandment given to Adam and Eve was to have children. When we are sealed in the temple that is also the first commandment we are given. This is because this is the method God has ordained for bringing His children to earth. As spirit children we wanted to have a body like our heavenly parents. Now that we are on earth, we do, and we are expected to use these bodies just like our heavenly parents do, to create families and to do much good.

God wanted His spirit children to be born into families so they could be properly cared for and taught. We, like Adam and Eve, are to provide physical bodies for these spirit children. The First Presidency and Quorum of the Twelve Apostles have stated, "We declare the means by which mortal life is created to be divinely appointed" ("The Family: A Proclamation to the World," Ensign, Nov. 1995, 102). God has commanded us that only in marriage between a man and a woman are we to have sexual relations. This commandment is called the law of chastity.

The big difference between us and the animals is that God has given them instincts so they behave in a certain predictable way. They don't have control over their instincts. We, on the other hand, do have control over our behavior, so He has given us commandments that teach us how to behave so we are free from sin and spiritual bondage and can experience the maximum amount of joy. These commandments centering around how we treat and think about our bodies is what the law of chastity is all about. By honoring this law as it is intended for us, we experience lasting joy.

The Law of Chastity
• What is the law of chastity?

We are to have sexual relations only with our spouse to whom we are legally married. No one, male or female, is to have sexual relations before marriage. After marriage, sexual relations are permitted only with our spouse.

To the Israelites the Lord said, "Thou shalt not commit adultery" (Exodus 20:14). Those Israelites who broke this commandment were subject to severe penalties. The Lord has repeated this commandment in the latter days (see D&C 42:24).

Page 184

We have been taught that the law of chastity encompasses more than sexual intercourse. The First Presidency warned young people of other sexual sins:

"Before marriage, do not do anything to arouse the powerful emotions that must be expressed only in marriage. Do not participate in passionate kissing, lie on top of another person, or touch the private, sacred parts of another person's body, with or without clothing. Do not allow anyone to do that with you. Do not arouse those emotions in your own body" (For the Strength of Youth [pamphlet, 2001], 27).

Like other violations of the law of chastity, homosexual behavior is a serious sin. Latter-day prophets have spoken about the dangers of homosexual behavior and about the Church's concern for people who may have such inclinations. President Gordon B. Hinckley said:

"In the first place, we believe that marriage between a man and a woman is ordained of God. We believe that marriage may be eternal through exercise of the power of the everlasting priesthood in the house of the Lord.

"People inquire about our position on those who consider themselves so-called gays and lesbians. My response is that we love them as sons and daughters of God. They may have certain inclinations which are powerful and which may be difficult to control. Most people have inclinations of one kind or another at various times. If they do not act upon these inclinations, then they can go forward as do all other members of the Church. If they violate the law of chastity and the moral standards of the Church, then they are subject to the discipline of the Church, just as others are.

"We want to help these people, to strengthen them, to assist them with their problems and to help them with their difficulties. But we cannot stand idle if they indulge in immoral activity, if they try to uphold and defend and live in a so-called same-sex marriage situation. To permit such would be to make light of the very serious and sacred foundation of God-sanctioned marriage and its very purpose, the rearing of families" (in Conference Report, Oct. 1998, 91; or Ensign, Nov. 1998, 71).

Satan Wants Us to Break the Law of Chastity
• What are some ways Satan tempts people to break the law of chastity?

Satan's plan is to deceive as many of us as he can to prevent us from returning to live with our Heavenly Father. One of the most damaging things he can do is entice us to break the law of chastity. He is cunning and powerful. He would like us to believe it is no sin to break this law. Many people have been deceived. We must guard ourselves against evil influences.

If you have a standing rule that says: "Thou shalt not burn thyself," then wouldn't the next most reasonable rule be: "Thou shalt not play with fire?" Anyone knows that the more you play with fire, the more likely you are to burn yourself.

This is why we teach children not to do anything that even arouses "the powerful emotions" that are meant to be expressed only in marriage. Anything that gets the mind dwelling and lingering on the topic of physical pleasure only creates opportunities for sin to enter in through the front door.

Pornography and homosexuality are the two major sins plaguing our society in the last days. In 1995 the Brethren wrote a proclamation on the family that details the Church's position on marriage, homosexuality, and the responsibilities of each family member.

Satan's channels of temptation to break the law of chastity come through advertising, television, movies, games, popular clothing, and social customs. He will do anything he can to get us to break this commandment. Sexual purity is one of the most desirable of all virtues, so he wants us to feel less than worthy, and will do anything in his power to get us to do something that will compromise ourselves before the Lord. We don't have to do anything big, like fornication or adultery, he just needs to get us to become casual about our bodies and what we are willing to do with them and what we are willing to watch others do with their bodies.

How many of us wouldn't commit adultery, yet we will pay to see a movie where we can watch someone else do it? How often is infidelity a casual and acceptable behavior in the TV shows we watch or in the videos we see?

Satan attacks the standards of modesty. He wants us to believe that because the human body is beautiful, it is something to flaunt and expose. Our Heavenly Father wants us to keep our bodies covered so that we do not encourage improper thoughts in the minds of others.

Satan not only encourages us to dress immodestly, but he also encourages us to think immoral or improper thoughts. He does this with pictures, movies, stories, jokes, music, and dances that suggest immoral acts. The law of chastity requires that our thoughts as well as our actions be pure. The prophet Alma taught that when we are judged by God, "our thoughts will also condemn us; and in this awful state we shall not dare to look up to our God" (Alma 12:14).

Jesus taught, "Ye have heard that it was said by them of old time, Thou shalt not commit adultery:

"But I say unto you, That whosoever looketh on a woman to lust after her hath committed adultery with her already in his heart" (Matthew 5:27–28).

President Gordon B. Hinckley warned: "You live in a world of terrible temptations. Pornography, with its sleazy filth, sweeps over the earth like a horrible, engulfing tide. It is poison. Do not watch it or read it. It will destroy you if you do. It will take from you your self-respect. It will rob you of a sense of the beauties of life. It will tear you down and pull you into a slough of evil thoughts and possibly of evil actions. Stay away from it. Shun it as you would a foul disease, for it is just as deadly. Be virtuous in thought and in deed. God has planted in you, for a purpose, a divine urge which may be easily subverted to evil and destructive ends. When you are young, do not get involved in steady dating. When you reach an age where you think of marriage, then is the time to become so involved. But you boys who are in high school don't need this, and neither do the girls" (in Conference Report, Oct. 1997, 71–72; or Ensign, Nov. 1997, 51).

Satan sometimes tempts us through our emotions. He knows when we are lonely, confused, or depressed. He chooses this time of weakness to tempt us to break the law

Our thoughts are difficult to control. We must be aware of what we are thinking from moment to moment if we are to ever have any hope of keeping our thoughts clean. We can help this process along by filling our days with good works, hymns, and clean music and thoughts. This does take effort. It won't happen spontaneously.

The Savior taught that even thinking about committing adultery is to have already done the deed in our heart. Our thoughts form and shape our actions. They also inspire our desires. We will never have to worry about improper desires if we don't have improper thoughts. Learning to control what enters AND STAYS in our minds is what it is all about. Even the Lord had improper thoughts placed in his head. Satan tempted Jesus all the time. But Jesus kept his mind pure by only allowing himself to think and entertain clean thoughts.

The thoughts that become dangerous to us are not the inappropriate thoughts that enter our mind, but the inappropriate thoughts we embrace and nurture, making them part of us. The only way to change our thinking is to learn to shun such thoughts and replace them with more virtuous thoughts and behaviors.

Something we need to teach to our children is that Satan will use our weakest points, when we are feeling lonely or depressed, ugly, or not as strong as others to tempt us to of chastity. Our Heavenly Father can give us the strength to pass through these trials unharmed.

do things that will lead to sin. We need to learn how to combat these temptations, and how to help our children combat them. It is possible.

The scriptures tell about a righteous young man named Joseph who was greatly trusted by his master, Potiphar. Potiphar had given Joseph command over everything he had. Potiphar's wife lusted after Joseph and tempted him to commit adultery with her. But Joseph resisted her and fled from her. (See Genesis 39:1–18.)

Paul taught, "There hath no temptation taken you but such as is common to man: but God is faithful, who will not suffer you to be tempted above that ye are able; but will with the temptation also make a way to escape, that ye may be able to bear it" (1 Corinthians 10:13). Alma emphasized that we will "not be tempted above that which [we] can bear" as we "humble [ourselves] before the Lord, and call on his holy name, and watch and pray continually" (Alma 13:28).

Some temptations are private and you are the only one aware of that particular temptation. Others come in very public places so there is an element of social pressure applied to get us to give in and commit sin. The prophets have long taught that if we think of these types of situations and decide how we will react ahead of time then when it happens we will have greater strength to resist the temptation because the decision was made long ago. We just have to honor our previous decision. This really works.

For teachers: For help with questions about modesty and chastity, you may want to refer to the pamphlet titled For the Strength of Youth (item number 36550), which is available at distribution centers and at LDS.org and which may be available at your meetinghouse library.

• How are modesty and chastity related? How can parents teach their children to be modest in dress, language, and behavior?

Generally speaking, modesty is how we feel about and how we treat our bodies, and chastity is how we behave with our bodies. There is a lot of overlap between the two, but in both cases our behavior is based on our attitudes about our bodies and the commandments of the Lord. Modesty, for example, prevents us from dressing, speaking, or acting in such a way as to compromise our state of chastity. A modest individual will always behave, dress, and speak in pure ways.

• How can we fight the spread and influence of pornography?

• What promises has the Lord given us to help us overcome Satan's temptations?

Breaking the Law of Chastity Is Extremely Serious

The prophet Alma grieved because one of his sons had broken the law of chastity. Alma said to his son Corianton, "Know ye not, my son, that these things are an abomination in the sight of the Lord; yea, most abominable above all sins save it be the shedding of innocent blood or denying the Holy Ghost?" (Alma 39:5). Unchastity is next to murder in seriousness.

Sexual sin in the form of adultery or fornication is the third most serious of all sins. Yet it is such a common sin because Satan has been so successful in luring people to break the commandments.

If a man and a woman break the law of chastity and conceive a child, they may be tempted to commit another abominable sin: abortion. There is seldom any justifiable reason for abortion. Church leaders have said that some exceptional circumstances may justify an abortion, such as when pregnancy is the result of incest or rape, when the life or health of the mother is judged by competent medical authority to be in serious jeopardy, or when the fetus is known by competent medical authority to have severe defects that will not allow the baby to survive beyond birth. But even these circumstances do not automatically justify an abortion. Those who face such circumstances should consider abortion only after consulting with their local Church leaders and receiving a confirmation through earnest prayer.

"When a man and woman conceive a child out of wedlock, every effort should be made to encourage them to marry. When the probability of a successful marriage is unlikely due to age or other circumstances, unwed parents should be counseled to place the child for adoption through LDS Family Services to ensure that the baby will be sealed to temple-worthy parents" (First Presidency letter, June 26, 2002, and July 19, 2002).

It is extremely important to our Heavenly Father that His children obey the law of chastity. Members of the Church who break this law or influence others to do so are subject to Church discipline.

Those Who Break the Law of Chastity Can Be Forgiven

Peace can come to those who have broken the law of chastity. The Lord tells us, "If the wicked will turn from all his sins that he hath committed, and keep all my statutes, ... all his transgressions that he hath committed, they shall not be mentioned unto him" (Ezekiel 18:21–22). Peace comes only through forgiveness.

President Kimball said: "To every forgiveness there is a condition. ... The fasting, the prayers, the humility must be equal to or greater than the sin. There must be a broken heart and a contrite spirit. ... There must be tears and genuine change of heart. There must be conviction of the sin, abandonment of the evil, confession of the error to properly constituted authorities of the Lord" (The Miracle of Forgiveness [1969], 353).

For many people, confession is the most difficult part of repentance. We must confess not only to the Lord but also to the person we have offended, such as a husband or wife, and to the proper priesthood authority. The priesthood leader (bishop or stake president) will judge our standing in the Church. The Lord told Alma, "Whosoever transgresseth against me ... if he confess his sins before thee and me, and repenteth in the sincerity of his heart, him shall ye forgive, and I will forgive him also" (Mosiah 26:29).

Violating the law of chastity is one of those laws that requires a visit to the Bishop or Branch President. It is up to the Bishop to counsel and decide what needs to be done to be properly forgiven of the sin.

When it comes to sexual purity there is a social stigma that is attached to impurity that is hard to get rid of. What we need to do is focus on what the Lord and His servants think of us, and not dwell on what other may think of us. The lord is not only able, but anxious to forgive us of sins we commit. We need to make sure we repent completely so we feel forgiven. Once forgiven it doesn't matter what others may think. The Lord is the one who sets the commandments and who is our judge, and no one else.

But President Kimball warned: "Even though forgiveness is so abundantly promised there is no promise nor indication of forgiveness to any soul who does not totally repent. … We can hardly be too forceful in reminding people that they cannot sin and be forgiven and then sin again and again and expect repeated forgiveness" (The Miracle of Forgiveness, 353, 360). Those who receive forgiveness and then repeat the sin are held accountable for their former sins (see D&C 82:7; Ether 2:15).

This last comment means that repeated sinning, after having received forgiveness, creates a compounding of the sin that makes it more difficult to be forgiven the next time. When we repent we need to guard ourselves to make sure we never return to the sin that we worked so hard to overcome.

Those Who Keep the Law of Chastity Are Greatly Blessed

• What blessings do we receive as we keep the law of chastity?

When we obey the law of chastity, we can live without guilt or shame. Our lives and our children's lives are blessed when we keep ourselves pure and spotless before the Lord. Children can look to our example and follow in our footsteps.

To live without guilt and shame is the real payoff for keeping the law of chastity. Satan uses shame and guilt to control us any way he can. To rid our lives of those tools of the devil is a great blessing indeed!

Additional Scriptures

• Matthew 19:5–9; Genesis 2:24 (marriage relationship is sacred)
• Titus 2:4–12 (instructions for chastity)
• 1 Corinthians 7:2–5; Ephesians 5:28 (loyalty to spouse)
• Revelation 14:4–5 (blessings for obedience to the law of chastity)
• Proverbs 31:10 (virtue praised)
• Alma 39:9 (do not go after the lusts of your eyes)
• D&C 121:45 (let virtue garnish thy thoughts unceasingly)
• Alma 42:16 (repentance does not come without punishment)
• Alma 42:30 (do not excuse yourself for sinning)
• D&C 58:42–43 (the repentant confess and forsake their sins)

Chapter 40

Temple Work and Family History

Gospel Principles, (2011), 233–39

Heavenly Father Wants His Children to Return to Him

The Atonement of Jesus Christ assures each of us that we will be resurrected and live forever. But if we are to live forever with our families in Heavenly Father's presence, we must do all that the Savior commands us to do. This includes being baptized and confirmed and receiving the ordinances of the temple.

As members of The Church of Jesus Christ of Latter-day Saints, we have each been baptized and confirmed by one having the proper priesthood authority. Each of us may also go to the temple to receive the saving priesthood ordinances performed there. But many of God's children have not had these same opportunities. They lived at a time or place when the gospel was not available to them.

Heavenly Father wants all of His children to return and live with Him. For those who died without baptism or the temple ordinances, He has provided a way for this to happen. He has asked us to perform ordinances for our ancestors in the temples.

Temples of the Lord

• Why are temples important in our lives?

For teachers: Pictures can generate interest and help learners increase their understanding. Consider asking class members or family members to ponder their feelings about temple work as they look at the picture of a temple in this chapter.

Temples of The Church of Jesus Christ of Latter-day Saints are special buildings dedicated to the Lord. Worthy Church members may go there to receive sacred ordinances and make covenants with God. Like baptism, these ordinances and covenants are necessary for our salvation. They must be performed in the temples of the Lord.

We also go to the temple to learn more about Heavenly Father and His Son, Jesus Christ. We gain a better understanding of our purpose in life and our relationship with Heavenly Father and Jesus Christ. We are taught about our premortal existence, the meaning of earth life, and life after death.

It should be a comfort to us all that the requirements for salvation are the same for every age and generation. No one is exempt from the need for baptism and the temple ordinances. The fortunate ones are those who are able to receive these ordinances during mortality. This allows them to not only enjoy the blessings of the eternal gospel while still in mortality, but to offer those same blessings to their relatives who have already passed on. This opens the door for uniting all the generations of one's own kindred dead for many generations past. This is the least we can do for those who came before us and gave us our legacy in life.

This process of doing the saving ordinance in behalf of our ancestors makes us partners with Christ in being saviors on mount Zion. We are helping our Father in Heaven and Jesus Christ save all God's children. What a privilege!

The temple ceremonies are like living scriptures we can go to listen and watch as often as we like. Each time we go, after the first time, we are performing those same ordinances in behalf of another person.

Temple Ordinances Seal Families Together Forever

• What does it mean to be sealed?

All temple ordinances are performed by the power of the priesthood. Through this power, ordinances performed on earth are sealed, or bound, in heaven. The Savior taught His Apostles, "Whatsoever thou shalt bind on earth shall be bound in heaven" (Matthew 16:19; see also D&C 132:7).

Only in the temple can we be sealed together forever as families. Marriage in the temple joins a man and woman as husband and wife eternally if they honor their covenants. Baptism and all other ordinances prepare us for this sacred event.

When a man and woman are married in the temple, their children who are born thereafter also become part of their eternal family. Couples who have been married civilly can receive these blessings by preparing themselves and their children to go to the temple and be sealed to each other. Parents who adopt children legally may have those children sealed to them.

• What must a couple do to make the sealing power effective in their marriage?

Nothing of an eternal nature takes place outside of the Lord's temples. All sealings that unite families together, and baptisms for the dead, as well as all endowments of blessings on the living and the dead take place only in the temple.

The temples are all about family. The object of going to the temple is not to remain single forever. The goal of the temple ceremonies is to create eternal families, connecting one generation of families to the next generation of families. The goal is to connect all the generations of mankind from Adam to the end of the earth with the priesthood ordinances of salvation. The Savior's work will not be finished until this is done.

No ordinance is a guaranty of salvation. In order for the ordinance to be in force in the eternities we have to be obedient to the commandments. Only then will the Spirit ratify that ordinance in our behalf. In order for a couple to remain sealed for eternity, both people must be obedient to the commandments of the gospel to the end of their mortal lives.

Our Ancestors Need Our Help

• What responsibilities do we have toward our ancestors who have died without receiving priesthood ordinances?

Notice the wording of this question. We do indeed have responsibilities toward our ancestors. That is part of our current blessing. We must love our brothers and sisters enough to help them receive what we have been blessed to receive. If we are selfish with our blessings then those blessings will ultimately be taken from us.

Mario Cannamela married Maria Vitta in 1882. They lived in Tripani, Italy, where they raised a family and shared many wonderful years together. Mario and Maria did not hear the message of the restored gospel of Jesus Christ during their lifetimes. They were not baptized. They did not have the opportunity to go to the temple and be sealed together as an eternal family. At death, their marriage ended.

Over a century later a great reunion took place. Descendants of Mario and Maria went to the Los Angeles Temple, where a great-grandson and his wife knelt at an altar and served as proxies for the sealing of Mario and Maria. Tears filled their eyes as they shared in Mario and Maria's joy.

It is true that we don't know who will accept the work we do for them in the temple. Our responsibility is to do the work and hope they accept our offering. It is sort of like Jesus performed the atonement, is just waiting to see if we accept the work He did for us. All we can do is what we can do. We cannot take away another person's

Many of our ancestors are among those who died without hearing about the gospel while on the earth. They now live in the spirit world (see chapter 41 in this book). There they are taught the gospel of Jesus Christ. Those who have accepted the gospel are waiting for the temple ordinances to be performed for them. As we perform these ordinances in the temple for our ancestors, we can share their joy.

• How does the doctrine of salvation for the dead show God's justice, compassion, and mercy?

agency. But we need to make sure they cannot point the finger at us and rightfully accuse us of denying them the opportunity to have these blessings.

Our Father in Heaven has not condemned any of His children, since all of them will ultimately have the opportunity to hear and accept Christ's atoning sacrifice for them. One of the blessings of the gospel plan is that all of God's family has to pull together as a family in order to provide salvation for each other. This is a family requirement. Fulfilling this requirement will be part of how we will be judged in the end.

• What experiences have you had doing temple work for your ancestors?

Family History—How We Begin Helping Our Ancestors

• What are the basic steps of doing family history work?

Latter-day Saints are encouraged to participate in family history activities. Through these activities we learn about our ancestors so that we can perform ordinances for them. Family history involves three basic steps:
1. Identify our ancestors.
2. Find out which ancestors need temple ordinances performed.
3. Make certain that the ordinances are performed for them.

While the basic step in this lesson are correct, since this lesson was first written the ability to perform these three steps has been vastly improved and made easier. There are several advancements in technologies and programs that make information and the ability to find ancestors so much easier than it ever was when we, who are older than 25, were young.

Most wards and branches have family history consultants who can answer questions and direct us to the resources we need. If a ward or branch does not have a family history consultant, the bishop or branch president can provide direction.

Identify Our Ancestors

To perform temple ordinances for our ancestors, we need to know their names. Many wonderful resources are available today to help us identify our ancestors' names.

A good way to begin gathering information about our ancestors is to see what we have in our own homes. We may have birth, marriage, or death certificates. We may also find family Bibles, obituaries, family histories, or diaries and journals. In addition, we can ask relatives for information they have. After gathering information in our homes and from our ancestors, we can search other resources, such as FamilySearch.org. We may also visit one of the Church's local family history centers.

How much we learn will depend on what information is available to us. We may have only a little family information and may be able to do no more than identify our parents and grandparents. If we already have a large collection of family records, we may be able to identify ancestors from generations further back in time.

We can keep track of the information we gather on family group records and pedigree charts.

Find Out Which Ancestors Need Temple Ordinances Performed

Temple ordinances have been performed for the dead since the early days of the Church. Consequently, some ordinances for our ancestors may have already been done. To find out which ancestors need temple ordinances, we can look in two places. Our own family records might have information about what has been done. If not, the Church has a record of all ordinances that have been performed in the temple. Your ward or branch family history consultant can help you in this effort.

Make Certain the Ordinances Are Performed

Many of our ancestors in the spirit world may be anxious to receive their temple ordinances. As soon as we identify these ancestors, we should arrange for this work to be done for them.

One of the blessings of family history work comes from going to the temple and performing ordinances in behalf of our ancestors. We should prepare ourselves to receive a temple recommend so that, when possible, we can do this work. If our children are 12 years old or older, they can share in these blessings by being baptized and confirmed for their ancestors.

If it is not possible for us to go to the temple to participate in the ordinances, the temple will arrange to have the ordinances performed by other Church members.

• How has the Lord helped you or members of your family find information about your ancestors?

It is important to remember that some cultures have been more careful to preserve records of their people than other cultures. In some societies war and governments have destroyed many records. But the good news is that new records are being brought to light all the time. If you can't find anything on your relatives now, don't be too discouraged, you may have more than you can handle in five more years. Keep digging and you will eventually hit pay dirt. (Pay dirt is a mining term meaning you will find that vein of ore that will make you rich. In this case, you will find a family line that will open the doors of salvation for your family.)

Check out www.ancestry.com and www.lds.org to see more possibilities. Chances are you will be amazed at the resources available to you today.

If you find more names, which is likely, than you are able to perform the ordinance for, you can get the work done for them in a variety of ways. The youth go to the temples on a regular basis. If you have a temple in your area you can give a long list of names to the youth and they can do the baptisms and confirmations for you. You can share names with your ward for ward temple night. You can also submit names to the temple and they will be shared with other temples around the world and other members of the Church will help get the work done for your ancestors. You literally have millions of latter-day Saints who are willing to help you perform the ordinances for your ancestors.

Additional Family History Opportunities

• What are some simple ways for someone with many other responsibilities to participate in family history work?

In addition to providing temple ordinances for the ancestors we know about, we can help those in the spirit world in many other ways. We should seek the guidance of the Spirit as we prayerfully consider what we might do. Depending on our circumstances, we can do the following things:

1. Attend the temple as often as possible. After we have gone to the temple for ourselves, we can perform the saving ordinances for others waiting in the spirit world.

2. Do research to identify ancestors who are more difficult to find. Family history consultants can guide us to helpful resources.

3. Help with the Church's indexing program. Through this program, members prepare genealogical information for use in the Church's family history computer programs. These programs make it easier for us to identify our ancestors.

4. Contribute family history information to the Church's current computer programs for family history. These programs contain genealogies contributed by people all over the world. They allow people to share their family information. Family history consultants can provide more information about the Church's computer programs.

5. Participate in family organizations. We can accomplish much more for our ancestors as we work together with other family members.

• Think about what you can do to increase your participation in temple and family history work.

Additional Scriptures

• 1 Peter 4:6 (gospel was preached to the dead)
• Malachi 4:5–6; D&C 2:2; 3 Nephi 25:5–6 (mission of Elijah)
• 1 Corinthians 15:29; D&C 128:15–18 (work for the dead)
• D&C 138 (redemption of the dead)

The indexing program of the Church has taken off in recent years. Millions of names have been indexed from census records, marriage, military, death and birth records. If you speak more than one language there are records from many countries that need to be indexed. These indexed records help others to find their ancestors. There is a powerful spirit that attends the indexing of names and records. The nice thing about the indexing program is that anyone can do it, whether or not they are members of the Church. The batches are relatively small, so you can do as little or as much as you have time and inclination to do.

Chapter 41

The Postmortal Spirit World

Gospel Principles, (2011), 240–44

We have studied the premortal life early on in this book. When we came to earth it was to prove ourselves to the Lord. The bulk of our proving whether we will be obedient to God's commandments does take place in mortality, but for many, the proving grounds is not mortality, but the postmortal spirit world. If the gospel was not available to them in their time in mortality, they still have to be taught the gospel and either accept it or reject it. There is much to be done in the spirit world. It is a busy place.

Life after Death

• What happens to us after we die?

Heavenly Father prepared a plan for our salvation. As part of this plan, He sent us from His presence to live on earth and receive mortal bodies of flesh and blood. Eventually our mortal bodies will die, and our spirits will go to the spirit world. The spirit world is a place of waiting, working, learning, and, for the righteous, resting from care and sorrow. Our spirits will live there until we are ready for our resurrection. Then our mortal bodies will once more unite with our spirits, and we will receive the degree of glory we have prepared for (see chapter 46 in this book).

Many people have wondered what the spirit world is like. The scriptures and latter-day prophets have given us information about the spirit world.

• What comfort do you receive from your knowledge that there is life after death? How can we use our understanding of the postmortal spirit world to comfort others?

Remember, we are eternal beings, just as God, our Father is an eternal being. We never die in the sense that we stop existing. If we did then we wouldn't be eternal, would we?

Where Is the Postmortal Spirit World?

Latter-day prophets have said that the spirits of those who have died are not far from us. President Ezra Taft Benson said: "Sometimes the veil between this life and the life beyond becomes very thin. Our loved ones who have passed on are not far from us" (in Conference Report, Apr. 1971, 18; or Ensign, June 1971, 33). President Brigham Young taught that the postmortal spirit world is on the earth, around us (see Teachings of Presidents of the Church: Brigham Young [1997], 279).

Planet earth is a very busy place. Satan and his followers were cast out of heaven to earth. Our mortal experience takes place here on earth. The postmortal spirit world is also here on earth. For the universe being such a big place, the Lord appears to be a very efficient user of space. This gives Satan access to both sides of the veil, both mortality and the postmortal spirit world.

What Is the Nature of Our Spirits?

Spirit beings have the same bodily form as mortals except that the spirit body is in perfect form (see Ether 3:16). Spirits carry with them from earth their attitudes of devotion or antagonism toward things of righteousness (see Alma 34:34). They have the same appetites and desires that they had when they lived on earth. All spirits are in adult form. They were adults before their mortal existence, and they are in adult form after death, even if they die as infants or children (see Teachings of Presidents of the Church: Joseph F. Smith [1998], 131–32).

The trouble with thinking that suicide will solve your problems is that what causes the problems in the first place usually follows us into the postmortal world. What makes us who we are doesn't change because we step across the veil. Our desires, our addictions, our loves will all be intact after we leave mortality. But trying to get rid of an addiction that is mental, emotional, and physical when the physical body is absent from the equation is very difficult. It takes longer to repent and change without the body present. This is why we need to do our repenting while we are still here and able to read this commentary. <wink>

• Why is it important to know that our spirits will have the same attitudes in the spirit world that they have now?

What Are the Conditions in the Postmortal Spirit World?

The prophet Alma in the Book of Mormon taught about two divisions or states in the spirit world:

"The spirits of those who are righteous are received into a state of happiness, which is called paradise, a state of rest, a state of peace, where they shall rest from all their troubles and from all care, and sorrow.

"And then shall it come to pass, that the spirits of the wicked, yea, who are evil—for behold, they have no part nor portion of the Spirit of the Lord; for behold, they chose evil works rather than good; therefore the spirit of the devil did enter into them, and take possession of their house—and these shall be cast out into outer darkness; there shall be weeping, and wailing, and gnashing of teeth, and this because of their own iniquity, being led captive by the will of the devil.

"Now this is the state of the souls of the wicked, yea, in darkness, and a state of awful, fearful looking for the fiery indignation of the wrath of God upon them; thus they remain in this state, as well as the righteous in paradise, until the time of their resurrection" (Alma 40:12–14).

The spirits are classified according to the purity of their lives and their obedience to the will of the Lord while on earth. The righteous and the wicked are separated (see 1 Nephi 15:28–30), but the spirits may progress as they learn gospel principles and live in accordance with them. The spirits in paradise can teach the spirits in prison (see D&C 138).

For teachers: To help class members or family members understand the differences between paradise and spirit prison, consider drawing a vertical line in the middle of the board or on a large piece of paper, making two columns. At the top of one column, write State of the Righteous. At the top of the other column, write State of the Wicked. Ask members to describe each state in the spirit world, based on their reading in this section. Summarize their comments in the appropriate columns.

Paradise

According to the prophet Alma, the righteous spirits rest from earthly care and sorrow. Nevertheless, they are occupied in doing the work of the Lord. President Joseph F. Smith saw in a vision that immediately after Jesus Christ was crucified, He visited the righteous in the spirit world. He appointed messengers, gave them power and authority,

For those who have accepted the covenants of the Lord and have been obedient to His commandments, the spirit world is both a rest from their earthly cares and sorrows, a time and place of peace and happiness, and a busy time for there is much work for them to do on that side of the veil.

This classification of the soul takes place upon leaving mortality and entering the spirit world. God makes that mini judgment and assigns us where we need to be. Those who are in paradise spend their time doing missionary work among those who did not accept the gospel in mortality, either because they rejected it in mortality or because they never heard the gospel message while they were still here. Once they have accepted the gospel and conformed to God's commandments they can move out of spirit prison and into paradise. It is all based on faith and obedience.

I strongly encourage you to read the whole of Doctrine and Covenants 138. It is a very powerful vision, and very moving. It is from references elsewhere in the scriptures, but most especially from D&C 138 that we learn that Christ organized his missionary forces during the three days he was in the spirit world. Missionary work has been going on ever since that time, and will continue until the time of the second coming of Christ.

and commissioned them to "carry the light of the gospel to them that were in darkness, even to all the spirits of men" (D&C 138:30).

The Church is organized in the spirit world, and priesthood holders continue their responsibilities there (see D&C 138:30). President Wilford Woodruff taught: "The same Priesthood exists on the other side of the veil. … Every Apostle, every Seventy, every Elder, etc., who has died in the faith as soon as he passes to the other side of the veil, enters into the work of the ministry" (Deseret News, Jan. 25, 1882, 818).

Family relationships are also important. President Jedediah M. Grant, a counselor to Brigham Young, saw the spirit world and described to Heber C. Kimball the organization that exists there: "He said that the people he there saw were organized in family capacities. … He said, 'When I looked at families, there was a deficiency in some, … for I saw families that would not be permitted to come and dwell together, because they had not honored their calling here'" (Deseret News, Dec. 10, 1856, 316–17).

When we talk about becoming a member of the Lord's Church, we are saying that this is his kingdom. This kingdom exists on both sides of the veil, and Christ is the King. The works is moved forward on both sides of the veil by his prophets. The priesthood and its power is no different here than it is there.

It is important to remember that God will force no one to be happy. Happiness is only ultimately achieved through obedience to God's commandments. Some families have children who have wandered and haven't come back yet. This explains why some homes had vacancies. We place our faith in the Lord that He will do all that is possible to help bring these family members back to us some day.

Spirit Prison

The Apostle Peter referred to the postmortal spirit world as a prison, which it is for some (see 1 Peter 3:18–20). In the spirit prison are the spirits of those who have not yet received the gospel of Jesus Christ. These spirits have agency and may be enticed by both good and evil. If they accept the gospel and the ordinances performed for them in the temples, they may leave the spirit prison and dwell in paradise.

Those who have not yet accepted the gospel can still be tempted by Satan and his followers. Over those in paradise Satan holds no power because they don't listen to him. But for those who have not chosen whose side they want to be on, Satan can tempt them and try to prevent them from accepting Christ's atoning sacrifice in their behalf.

Also in the spirit prison are those who rejected the gospel after it was preached to them either on earth or in the spirit prison. These spirits suffer in a condition known as hell. They have removed themselves from the mercy of Jesus Christ, who said, "Behold, I, God, have suffered these things for all, that they might not suffer if they would repent; but if they would not repent they must suffer even as I; which suffering caused myself, even God, the greatest of all, to tremble because of pain, and to bleed at every pore, and to suffer both body and spirit" (D&C 19:16–18). After suffering for their sins, they will be allowed, through the Atonement of Jesus Christ, to inherit the lowest degree of glory, which is the telestial kingdom.

The purpose of hell is not to punish someone for the sake of being punished. If I am presented with the gospel of Christ, which, if accepted, will allow Christ's atonement to pay for my sins and allow me to be forgiven for the laws of God I have broken, then rejecting that atoning sacrifice leaves me fully exposed to the demands of God's eternal laws. Justice requires that payment be made for every law broken. If I won't let Jesus pay for those sins then I have to pay for them myself, to the best of my ability. I can't pay for the full amount required, so after I have suffered all I possibly can, Jesus still let's me out of hell to receive a kingdom of glory. I will not be able to go and live with God again, but I will be assigned to the telestial kingdom, depending on how I behaved in mortality and in my time in the spirit world. Hell is reserved only for those who reject the atonement of Christ. These people insist on paying for their own sins because they did not, for whatever reason, want to submit to Christ's requirements so He could pay for our sins for us.

• How are conditions in the spirit world similar to conditions in this life?

Additional Scriptures

- 1 Peter 4:6 (gospel preached to the dead)
- Moses 7:37–39 (spirit prison prepared for the wicked)
- D&C 76 (revelation about the three kingdoms of glory)
- Luke 16:19–31 (fate of beggar and rich man in the spirit world)

Chapter 42

The Gathering of the House of Israel

Gospel Principles, (2011), 245–50

The House of Israel Are God's Covenant People

• What responsibilities do God's covenant people have to the nations of the world?

Jacob was a great prophet who lived hundreds of years before the time of Christ. Because Jacob was faithful, the Lord gave him the special name of Israel, which means "one who prevails with God" or "let God prevail" (Bible Dictionary, "Israel," 708). Jacob had twelve sons. These sons and their families became known as the twelve tribes of Israel, or Israelites (see Genesis 49:28).

Jacob was a grandson of Abraham. The Lord made an everlasting covenant with Abraham that was renewed with Isaac and with Jacob and his children (see chapter 15 in this book; see also the visual in this chapter, depicting Jacob blessing his sons). God promised that the Israelites would be His covenant people as long as they would obey His commandments (see Deuteronomy 28:9–10). They would be a blessing to all the nations of the world by taking the gospel and the priesthood to them (see Abraham 2:9–11). Thus, they would keep their covenant with the Lord and He would keep His covenant with them.

Today we sometimes joke about a large family by referring to them as a "tribe." In the case of Jacob (Israel) his twelve sons really did have tribes. Each of those families eventually grew to be tens of thousands strong. By the time Moses lead them out of Egypt, after 400 years of captivity, the descendants of Jacob numbered in the millions.

The blessing pronounced on the head of Abraham couldn't be fulfilled in his lifetime. He was promised that his posterity would become as numerous as the sands of the sea and the stars in the heavens. He was told that through his lineage all the nations of the earth would be blessed with the priesthood blessings the Lord bestowed on Abraham.

This demonstrates how clearly the Lord understands the future. As long as the family or house of Israel was righteous they were commanded to stick to themselves and not spread the gospel message. The Lord wanted them to grow strong and be a "pure" people. But when they had grown large as a people and then became wicked the Lord scattered them for their wickedness throughout the world. After many centuries of mixing their blood and lineage with those of the surrounding nations of the earth, God has begun to gather back the descendants of Israel into his Church. Truly now the fulfillment of the promises made to Abraham are coming to pass that all the nations of the world will be blessed with the promises that come with having the priesthood. After so much time has passed, most of the peoples of the earth have the blood of Jacob running in their veins. Even though they don't know it, these people are of the chosen house or family of Israel (Jacob), and are entitled to his inheritance of spiritual blessings. These are the ones who hear the gospel message and it sound familiar to them and they embrace it.

The House of Israel Was Scattered

Again and again prophets of the Lord warned the house of Israel what would happen if they were wicked. Moses prophesied, "And the Lord shall scatter thee among all people, from the one end of the earth even unto the other" (Deuteronomy 28:64).

Despite this warning, the Israelites consistently broke the commandments of God. They fought among themselves and split into two kingdoms: the Northern Kingdom, called the kingdom of Israel, and the Southern Kingdom, called the kingdom of Judah. Ten of the twelve tribes of Israel lived in the Northern Kingdom. During a war they were conquered by their enemies and carried away into captivity. Some of them later escaped into the lands of the north and became lost to the rest of the world.

About 100 years after the capture of the Northern Kingdom, the Southern Kingdom was conquered. The capital city of Jerusalem was destroyed in 586 B.C., and many members of the remaining two tribes of Israel were taken captive. Later, some of the members of these tribes returned and rebuilt Jerusalem. Just before Jerusalem was destroyed, Lehi and his family, who were members of the house of Israel, left the city and settled in the Americas.

After the time of Christ, Jerusalem was again destroyed, this time by Roman soldiers. The Jews were scattered over much of the world. Today Israelites are found in all countries of the world. Many of these people do not know that they are descended from the ancient house of Israel.

• What benefits have come to God's children because His covenant people have been scattered throughout the earth?

The House of Israel Must Be Gathered
• Why does the Lord want His people to be gathered?

• How will the house of Israel be gathered?

The Lord promised that His covenant people would someday be gathered: "I will gather the remnant of my flock out of all countries whither I have driven them" (Jeremiah 23:3).

God gathers His children through missionary work. As people come to a knowledge of Jesus Christ, receiving the ordinances of salvation and keeping the associated covenants, they become "the children of the covenant" (3 Nephi 20:26). He has important reasons for gathering His children. He gathers them so they can learn the teachings of the gospel and prepare themselves to meet the Savior

Even though the northern kingdom had the bulk of the Israelites, it was the descendants of Judah, the Jews, who were known for their fierce fighting spirit. While the northern kingdom was taken captive and lost to history, the couple of tribes in the Southern Kingdom lasted another century before they were finally captured and taken away to Babylon.

In the Book of Mormon we learn that the Lord led portions of Israel away into distant lands from time to time. The only ones for which we have a record is Lehi and his expedition to the Americas.

The scattering of the Jews at Jerusalem by the Romans completed the scattering of Israel. The Jews in particular were driven from country to country for almost two thousand years until they were returned to Jerusalem by the governments of Europe after World War II.

For a reason known only to God, those who have descended from the lineage of Abraham, Isaac, and Jacob are entitled to special blessings from Him because of the righteousness of those three men. God renewed His covenant with both Isaac and Jacob after Abraham died, promising them the same thing He promised to their father. All of this scattering and gathering is in fulfillment of those promises.

This is why we do missionary work. How will someone know of the blessings God has to offer His children if no one tells people about them? With the priesthood comes the gift of the Holy Ghost, who teaches us all things and leads us back home to God, our Father. This is why missionary work is a requirement of all those who embrace the covenants given to us from the Lord.

The kingdom of God that will exist when Jesus returns again is what was restored through Joseph Smith. The missionary work we perform is to gather as many of the Lord's covenant people as we can before his return. When he comes again his kingdom will already be operating and flourishing around the world.

when He comes again. He gathers them so they will build temples and perform sacred ordinances for ancestors who have died without having this opportunity. He gathers them so they can strengthen one another and be unified in the gospel, finding protection from unrighteous influences in the world. He also gathers them so they can prepare themselves to share the gospel with others.

The members of his church will always be in the minority compared with the rest of the world, but we are also spread all over the world. When Christ comes again it will be from these little centers of Saints that the blessings of the Lord will spread across the world during the Millennium.

The power and authority to direct the work of gathering the house of Israel was given to Joseph Smith by the prophet Moses, who appeared in 1836 in the Kirtland Temple (see D&C 110:11). Since that time, each prophet has held the keys for the gathering of the house of Israel, and this gathering has been an important part of the Church's work. The covenant people are now being gathered as they accept the restored gospel and serve the God of Abraham, Isaac, and Jacob (see Deuteronomy 30:1–5).

One of the most important responsibilities of the living prophet is to reach as many of God's children as possible to find those whom God has prepared to hear his gospel. The purpose of the apostles is to testify of the divinity of Jesus Christ, and of his resurrection. It is important that people realize we worship a living God, and one who is actively involved in saving his people.

The Israelites are to be gathered spiritually first and then physically. They are gathered spiritually as they join The Church of Jesus Christ of Latter-day Saints and make and keep sacred covenants. This spiritual gathering began during the time of the Prophet Joseph Smith and continues today all over the world. Converts to the Church are Israelites either by blood or adoption. They belong to the family of Abraham and Jacob (see Abraham 2:9–11; Galatians 3:26–29).

It is important to remember that the Lord accepts anyone into his kingdom who is willing to make covenants with him and keep them. So when someone gets baptized, if they are not a blood descendant of Jacob then they are adopted into the family. The covenant was only made with this one family, so in a very real sense when we say we are all brothers and sisters, we mean it.

President Joseph Fielding Smith said: "There are many nations represented in the … Church. … They have come because the Spirit of the Lord rested upon them; … receiving the spirit of gathering, they left everything for the sake of the gospel" (Doctrines of Salvation, comp. Bruce R. McConkie, 3 vols. [1954–56], 3:256; italics in original).

The physical gathering of Israel means that the covenant people will be "gathered home to the lands of their inheritance, and shall be established in all their lands of promise" (2 Nephi 9:2). The tribes of Ephraim and Manasseh will be gathered in the Americas. The tribe of Judah will return to the city of Jerusalem and the area surrounding it. The ten lost tribes will receive from the tribe of Ephraim their promised blessings (see D&C 133:26–34).

The reason the tribe of Ephraim figures so strongly in the blessings pronounced on the family of Jacob is because Ephraim received as his birthright the rights to carry the priesthood for the family. Most of the church are descendants of Ephraim, though there are other tribe members represented. Ephraim is responsible for missionary work and the spread of the message or gospel of Christ.

When the Church was first established, the Saints were instructed to gather in Ohio, then Missouri, and then the Salt Lake Valley. Today, however, modern prophets have taught that Church members are to build up the kingdom of God in their own lands. Elder Russell M. Nelson said: "The choice to come unto Christ is not a matter of physical location; it is a matter of individual commitment. People can be 'brought to the knowledge of the Lord' [3 Nephi 20:13] without leaving their homelands. True, in the early days of the Church, conversion often meant emigration as

For a time there was a physical gathering of the Saints, to build numbers and guaranty their survival. After they became sufficiently strong, the Saints were told to stay in their home countries and build the kingdom where they were. Coming to Zion now means coming to the Church, wherever you live.

well. But now the gathering takes place in each nation. …
The place of gathering for Brazilian Saints is in Brazil; the
place of gathering for Nigerian Saints is in Nigeria; the
place of gathering for Korean Saints is in Korea; and so
forth. Zion is 'the pure in heart.' [D&C 97:21.] Zion is
wherever righteous Saints are" (in Conference Report, Oct.
2006, 85; or Ensign, Nov. 2006, 81).

The physical gathering of Israel will not be complete until
the Second Coming of the Savior and on into the
Millennium (see Joseph Smith—Matthew 1:37). Then the
Lord's promise will be fulfilled:

"Behold, the days come, saith the Lord, that it shall no
more be said, The Lord liveth, that brought up the children
of Israel out of the land of Egypt;

"But, The Lord liveth, that brought up the children of
Israel from the land of the north, and from all the lands
whither he had driven them: and I will bring them again
into their land that I gave unto their fathers" (Jeremiah
16:14–15).

• In what ways have you been gathered spiritually as one of
the Lord's covenant people?

• In what ways have you participated in the gathering of
others?

The Lord is a patient man. His promises will all be fulfilled,
but his promises to Abraham and his descendants will not
be completed until on into the millennium. The Lord is
faithful and will always fulfill his promises.

Every time we do indexing, temple work, genealogy work,
or family history work we are participating in some way as
part of the gathering process. Missionary work is going on
simultaneously on both sides of the veil for the living and
the dead.

*For teachers: When people share their stories of being
converted to the restored gospel of Jesus Christ, they are
sharing stories about being gathered spiritually. Consider
asking a few people in advance to tell about how they were
converted to the gospel.*

Additional Scriptures
• Genesis 17:1–8 (God's covenant with Abraham)
• Romans 9:4–8; Galatians 3:29 (those who follow Jesus
Christ and His word are the children of the covenant)
• 2 Nephi 30:2; Mosiah 5:10–11 (those who repent, follow
the prophets, and have faith in Jesus Christ become the
Lord's covenant people)
• 2 Kings 17 (Northern Kingdom taken captive)
• 2 Chronicles 36:11–20 (Southern Kingdom taken
captive)
• James 1:1 (twelve tribes scattered abroad)
• 1 Nephi 10:12–13 (Nephite migration was part of the
scattering)
• Jeremiah 3:14–18 (one from a city, two from a family)
• Ezekiel 20:33–36 (Israel will be gathered from all
countries)
• 3 Nephi 20:29–46 (Jews will be gathered to Jerusalem)
• 1 Nephi 15:13–18; 3 Nephi 21:26–29 (gathering starts
with Restoration of the gospel)

- D&C 38:31–33 (the Lord's covenant people will be saved)
- Isaiah 11:11–13 (the Lord will recover His people)
- Revelation 18:4–8 (a voice will proclaim the gathering)
- D&C 133:6–15 (Gentiles to Zion, Jews to Jerusalem)

Chapter 43
Signs of the Second Coming
Gospel Principles, (2011), 251–56

Jesus Christ Will Return to the Earth
• What are some of the signs of the Second Coming?

The Savior told Joseph Smith, "I will reveal myself from heaven with power and great glory … and dwell in righteousness with men on earth a thousand years, and the wicked shall not stand" (D&C 29:11; see also chapters 44 and 45 in this book). Jesus has told us that certain signs and events will warn us when the time of His Second Coming is near.

For teachers: Consider assigning each class member or family member one or two of the signs described in this chapter (in large classes, some signs may be assigned to more than one person). As part of the lesson, give them time on their own to study the information about those signs and think about evidence they have seen that the signs are being fulfilled today. Then have them share their insights with each other.

For thousands of years, followers of Jesus Christ have looked forward to the Second Coming as a time of peace and joy. But before the Savior comes, the people of the earth will experience great trials and calamities. Our Heavenly Father wants us to be prepared for these troubles. He also expects us to be spiritually ready when the Savior comes in His glory. Therefore, He has given us signs, which are events that will tell us when the Savior's Second Coming is near. Throughout the ages God has revealed these signs to His prophets. He has said that all faithful followers of Christ will know what the signs are and will be watching for them (see D&C 45:39). If we are obedient and faithful, we will study the scriptures and know of the signs.

Some of the signs foretelling the Second Coming of Jesus Christ have already been or are now being fulfilled. Others will be fulfilled in the future.

We try to focus on the millennial experience rather than the trials and tribulations that will precede the second coming. To be fully honest with ourselves, it will take a lot of preparation for us to be ready for the calamities what will be coming our way shortly. It will require great faith on the part of each member of the Church, and the ability to follow the living prophet with exactness.

We may not know the hour of the second coming, but if we become familiar with the signs that must come to pass, we can have an idea as to how prepared we need to be. But even with all our preparation his coming will still be considered "like a thief in the night."

Wickedness, War, and Turmoil

Many of the signs are terrifying and dreadful. The prophets have warned that the earth will experience great turmoil, wickedness, war, and suffering. The prophet Daniel said that the time before the Second Coming would be a time of trouble such as the earth has never known (see Daniel 12:1). The Lord said, "The love of men shall wax cold, and iniquity shall abound" (D&C 45:27). "And all things shall be in commotion; and … fear shall come upon all people" (D&C 88:91). We can expect earthquakes, disease,

The earth physically reacts to the amount of wickedness that is upon her face. The more wicked people become the more upheavals and devastation we will see from the planet herself. The Lord has told us that these earthquakes, eruptions, tidal waves, droughts, etc. are all signs of his impending coming.

famines, great storms, lightnings, and thunder (see Matthew 24:7; D&C 88:90). Hailstorms will destroy the crops of the earth (see D&C 29:16).

Jesus told His disciples that war would fill the earth: "Ye shall hear of wars and rumours of wars. ... For nation shall rise against nation, and kingdom against kingdom" (Matthew 24:6–7). The Prophet Joseph Smith said: "Be not discouraged when we tell you of perilous times, for they must shortly come, for the sword, famine, and pestilence are approaching. There shall be great destructions upon the face of this land, for ye need not suppose that one jot or tittle of the prophecies of all the holy prophets shall fail, and there are many that remain to be fulfilled yet" (Teachings of Presidents of the Church: Joseph Smith [2007], 252).

Satan is working hard to divide all people from each other. The Lord knows there is strength in unity. Satan tries to prevent unity by creating chaos and division. This leads to war and hatred. The more successful he becomes, the more wars and rumors of wars we will see.

Many of these signs are being fulfilled. Wickedness is everywhere. Nations are constantly at war. Earthquakes and other calamities are occurring. Many people now suffer from devastating storms, drought, hunger, and diseases. We can be certain that these calamities will become more severe before the Lord comes.

Many of these calamities have not happened yet in the United States, but it will come. We will not be spared the destructions that wickedness brings. Only repentance can avert these things, and the world is not going to repent, though we continue to pray and work to that end.

However, not all the events preceding the Second Coming are dreadful. Many of them bring joy to the world.

The Restoration of the Gospel

The Lord said, "Light shall break forth among them that sit in darkness, and it shall be the fulness of my gospel" (D&C 45:28). Prophets of old foretold the Restoration of the gospel. The Apostle John saw that the gospel would be restored by an angel (see Revelation 14:6–7). In fulfillment of this prophecy, the angel Moroni and other heavenly visitors brought the gospel of Jesus Christ to Joseph Smith.

The Lord keeps things in balance. He will never allow wickedness to completely overwhelm those who want to be righteous. In the last days, though much of the news is unpleasant, there is also much good news. With the restoration of the gospel of Christ the Lord has set up his kingdom on the earth. We have a prophet to lead us and show us how to be prepared for what is coming. The Lord promised us in Malachi that he would never do anything to the people without first telling the prophets so they could prepare the people.

The Coming Forth of the Book of Mormon

The Lord told the Nephites of another sign: the Book of Mormon would come to their descendants (see 3 Nephi 21). In Old Testament times the prophets Isaiah and Ezekiel foresaw the coming of the Book of Mormon (see Isaiah 29:4–18; Ezekiel 37:16–20). These prophecies are now being fulfilled. The Book of Mormon has been brought forth and is being taken to all the world.

The Book of Mormon was written by the ancient prophets in the Americas specifically to help us be prepared for the trials of the last days. The stories they included, the testimonies and doctrines they included, all of it is for us in the latter days. It was a thousand years in the making. What a sign of God's love for us that he would spend a thousand years having a record readied for us to help us be prepared for the hardships of our day.

The Gospel Preached to All the World

Another sign of the last days is that the "gospel of the kingdom shall be preached in all the world for a witness unto all nations" (Matthew 24:14; see also Joseph Smith—Matthew 1:31). All people will hear the fulness of the gospel in their own language (see D&C 90:11). Ever since the Restoration of the Church, missionaries have

Never in the history of the world, since the days of Noah, has the gospel message gone forth to the whole world. This is indeed a special time, and we get to be part of it. We are preaching the gospel in a large portion of the world, but we still have almost half the world to reach. The Lord will perform miracles that will permit the Church to teach the rest of these people the gospel message. In preached the gospel. The missionary effort has increased until now tens of thousands of missionaries preach in many countries of the world in many languages. Before the Second Coming and during the Millennium, the Lord will provide ways to bring the truth to all nations.

The Coming of Elijah

The prophet Malachi prophesied that before the Savior's Second Coming, the prophet Elijah would be sent to the earth. Elijah would restore the sealing powers so families could be sealed together. He would also inspire people to be concerned about their ancestors and descendants. (See Malachi 4:5–6; D&C 2.) The prophet Elijah came to Joseph Smith in April 1836. Since that time, interest in genealogy and family history has grown. We are also able to perform sealing ordinances in the temples for the living and the dead.

Lehi's Descendants Will Become a Great People

The Lord said that when His coming was near, the Lamanites would become a righteous and respected people. He said, "Before the great day of the Lord shall come, … the Lamanites shall blossom as the rose" (D&C 49:24). Great numbers of Lehi's descendants are now receiving the blessings of the gospel.

Building of the New Jerusalem

Near the time of the coming of Jesus Christ, the faithful Saints will build a righteous city, a city of God, called the New Jerusalem. Jesus Christ Himself will rule there. (See 3 Nephi 21:23–25; Moses 7:62–64; Articles of Faith 1:10.) The Lord said the city will be built in the state of Missouri in the United States (see D&C 84:2–3).

These are only a few of the signs that the Lord has given us. The scriptures describe many more.

• What evidence do you see that the signs are being fulfilled?
Knowing the Signs of the Times Can Help Us

• How can we remain calm and at peace even when some of the signs are terrifying and dreadful?

Speaking of His Second Coming, the Lord said, "The hour and the day no man knoweth, neither the angels in heaven" (D&C 49:7). He taught this with the parable of the fig tree.

the meantime we do what we can where we are already permitted to teach and baptize.

The sealing keys given to Joseph Smith by Elijah are what permit us to be married for eternity, and to seal our children to us, and us to our forefathers. This is the power that provides a spiritual welding link through the priesthood from generation to generation from us back to our first parents. It will take to the end of the millennium for us to complete this great task. The world-wide interest in genealogy is directly connected to the coming of the spirit of Elijah.

These prophecies regarding the descendants of Lehi and Ishmael in the Book of Mormon are beginning to come to pass. The people of central and south America are joining the church in great numbers and are coming to the United States in great numbers. The blossoming of these people into greatness is still being awaited, but it will happen.

There is still much that must take place in Missouri before the New Jerusalem can be built, but all in due time.

The Lord tells us in multiple places in the scriptures that if we are prepared we will not fear. Those who have no idea what is going on are the ones who are most fearful. He has tried to help us be courageous by telling us well in advance what will happen so when we see things happening we recognize that God is at work in the events we are seeing. This lets us give praises to the Lord instead of crying out in fear from lack of understanding.

He said that when we see a fig tree putting forth leaves, we can tell that summer will soon come. Likewise, when we see the signs described in the scriptures, we can know that His coming is near. (See Matthew 24:32–33.)

The Lord gives these signs to help us. We can put our lives in order and prepare ourselves and our families for those things yet to come.

We have been warned of calamities and told to prepare for them, but we can also look forward to the coming of the Savior and be glad. The Lord said, "Be not troubled, for, when all these things [the signs] shall come to pass, ye may know that the promises which have been made unto you shall be fulfilled" (D&C 45:35). He said those who are righteous when He comes will not be destroyed "but shall abide the day. And the earth shall be given unto them for an inheritance; … and their children shall grow up without sin. … For the Lord shall be in their midst, and his glory shall be upon them, and he will be their king and their lawgiver" (D&C 45:57–59).

It is important to realize that the prophets warn us and try to prepare us well in advance of when the need arrives so as many as possible are prepared for the trial. Think of the Proclamation on the Family. It was written more than 20 years ago, and it is only now that we are seeing just how important a document it really is. We have been told to store food, have money set aside for emergencies, etc. We have been told to hold family home evenings and to learn to keep the Sabbath day holy. All these things are preparing us for what is to come. When that day arrives it will be too late to prepare. We need to follow the prophets now.

Additional Scriptures
• 1 Corinthians 15:22–28 (the end cometh; death is done away)
• Matthew 16:1–4 (discern signs of the times)
• Matthew 24; D&C 29:14–23; 45:17–57; 88:87–94; Joseph Smith—Matthew 1 (signs of the Second Coming)
• 1 Thessalonians 5:1–6 (watch for the signs and prepare)
• D&C 38:30 (prepare so we might not fear)
• D&C 68:11 (we can know the signs)

Chapter 44

The Second Coming of Jesus Christ

Gospel Principles, (2011), 257–62

Looking forward to the Savior's Second Coming

Forty days after His Resurrection, Jesus and His Apostles were gathered together on the Mount of Olives. The time had come for Jesus to leave the earth. He had completed all the work that He had to do at that time. He was to return to our Heavenly Father until the time of His Second Coming.

After He had instructed His Apostles, Jesus ascended into heaven. While the Apostles looked up into the heavens, two angels stood beside them and said, "Ye men of Galilee, why stand ye gazing up into heaven? this same Jesus, which is taken up from you into heaven, shall so come in like manner as ye have seen him go" (Acts 1:11).

From that time until the present day, the followers of Jesus Christ have looked forward to the Second Coming.

What Will Jesus Do When He Comes Again?

For teachers: Consider assigning each class member or family member one of the five numbered items in this chapter. Ask each person to work individually, studying his or her assigned item, including the scripture passages. Then invite everyone to discuss what they have learned.

When Jesus Christ comes again to the earth, He will do the following things:
1. He will cleanse the earth. When Jesus comes again, He will come in power and great glory. At that time the wicked will be destroyed. All things that are corrupt will be burned, and the earth will be cleansed by fire (see D&C 101:24–25).

2. He will judge His people. When Jesus comes again, He will judge the nations and will divide the righteous from the wicked (see Matthew 25:31–46; see also chapter 46 in this book). John the Revelator wrote about this judgment: "I saw thrones, and they sat upon them, and judgment was given unto them: and I saw the souls of them that were beheaded for the witness of Jesus, and for the word of God, … and they lived and reigned with Christ a thousand years." The wicked he saw "lived not again until the thousand years were finished" (Revelation 20:4–5; see also D&C 88:95–98).

3. He will usher in the Millennium. The Millennium is the thousand-year period when Jesus will reign on the earth.

Jesus leaving to return to his Father didn't mean he abandoned us or that he had nothing to do with us until he decides to return for the second time. While in mortality, Jesus worked every waking hour for the salvation of all those around him. Returning home to our Father he has been working every hour of every day since for the salvation of the entire human race. He has been directing the course of all human affairs from heaven ever since his return home.

For more than four thousand years before his birth Jesus worked to guide us back to God through his prophets. Since his ascension to heaven he has continued to work through his prophets to teach people what they need to do to be saved. We look forward to his second coming because we will once again have his personal presence with us to teach us and lead us, but this time for a thousand years.

The advent of the second coming will change the face of the whole earth. When all corruption is burned away, leaving only those things that are pure and righteous, we will have peace. For a thousand years we will be governed by God Himself, and there will be no war, nor evil in the world. It will be a time of unprecedented peace, prosperity, and righteousness. During this time those who died serving the Lord will be resurrected and will be given leadership roles in governing the nations. This means we will have worthy leaders in every community and country, all loyal to the Lord and His ways.

The righteous will be caught up to meet Jesus at His coming (see D&C 88:96). His coming will begin the millennial reign. (See chapter 45 in this book.)

President Brigham Young said:

"In the Millennium, when the Kingdom of God is established on the earth in power, glory and perfection, and the reign of wickedness that has so long prevailed is subdued, the Saints of God will have the privilege of building their temples, and of entering into them, becoming, as it were, pillars in the temples of God [see Revelation 3:12], and they will officiate for their dead. Then we will see our friends come up, and perhaps some that we have been acquainted with here. … And we will have revelations to know our forefathers clear back to Father Adam and Mother Eve, and we will enter into the temples of God and officiate for them. Then [children] will be sealed to [parents] until the chain is made perfect back to Adam, so that there will be a perfect chain of Priesthood from Adam to the winding-up scene" (Teachings of Presidents of the Church: Brigham Young [1997], 333–34).

4. He will complete the First Resurrection. Those who have obtained the privilege of coming forth in the resurrection of the just will rise from their graves. They will be caught up to meet the Savior as He comes down from heaven. (See D&C 88:97–98.)

After Jesus Christ rose from the dead, other righteous people who had died were also resurrected. They appeared in Jerusalem and also on the American continent. (See Matthew 27:52–53; 3 Nephi 23:9–10.) This was the beginning of the First Resurrection. Some people have been resurrected since then. Those who already have been resurrected and those who will be resurrected at the time of His coming will all inherit the glory of the celestial kingdom (see D&C 76:50–70).

After the resurrection of those who will inherit celestial glory, another group will be resurrected: those who will receive a terrestrial glory. When all these people have been resurrected, the First Resurrection will be completed.

The wicked who are living at the time of the Second Coming of the Lord will be destroyed in the flesh. They, along with the wicked who are already dead, will have to wait until the last resurrection. All of the remaining dead will rise to meet God. They will either inherit the telestial kingdom or be cast into outer darkness with Satan (see D&C 76:32–33, 81–112).

5. He will take His rightful place as King of heaven and earth. When Jesus comes, He will establish His government on the earth. The Church will become part of

The millennium will be a time of great temple work. All the generations of the earth who have not already had their work done for them in mortality will have the opportunity to accept the covenants of baptism and the gift of the Holy Ghost and all temple covenants during this time. The work will not be completed until every person who has ever lived has been given the opportunity to accept the gospel of Christ. No one will be omitted. The world will be covered with temples in every land as this great work gets underway.

The scriptures tell us that the knowledge of the Lord will cover the earth like the waters cover the seas. That is a lot of knowledge. There will be great revelations and we will have resurrected beings visit on a regular basis.

This is the resurrection we hope to be part of. These are the people who will be worthy of a celestial glory. The other kingdoms will be resurrected later.

The terrestrial resurrection will take place throughout the thousand year period of the millennium.

Those who are destroyed at the time of Christ's coming, and those who have been in spirit prison up to that point will go to hell. There they will spend the next thousand years suffering for their sins because they refused to let Christ pay for their sins for them. When they are released from hell at the end of the thousand years they will either go to the telestial kingdom or outer darkness.

When Christ first came it was as a humble baby in a manger. When he comes again it will be as a king and ruler. His Church is part of His kingdom, and it is already covering much of the earth. Until He comes again his that kingdom. He will rule all the people of the earth in peace for 1,000 years.

When Jesus Christ first came to the earth, He did not come in glory. He was born in a lowly stable and laid in a manger of hay. He did not come with great armies as the Jews had expected of their Savior. Instead, He came saying, "Love your enemies, … do good to them that hate you, and pray for them which despitefully use you" (Matthew 5:44). He was rejected and crucified. But He will not be rejected at His Second Coming, "for every ear shall hear it, and every knee shall bow, and every tongue shall confess" that Jesus is the Christ (D&C 88:104). He will be greeted as "Lord of lords, and King of kings" (Revelation 17:14). He will be called "Wonderful, Counsellor, The mighty God, The everlasting Father, The Prince of Peace" (Isaiah 9:6).

• What are your thoughts and feelings as you contemplate the events of the Second Coming?

How Will We Know When the Savior's Coming Is Near?

This question is answered in the lesson previous to this one.

When Jesus Christ was born, very few people knew that the Savior of the world had come. When He comes again, there will be no doubt who He is. No one knows the exact time that the Savior will come again. "Of that day and hour knoweth no man, no, not the angels of heaven, but my Father only" (Matthew 24:36; see also D&C 49:7).

Whereas angels had to let people know that Jesus was born, and where to find him, when he comes again all the nations of the earth will see Him come at the same time. There will be no question as to who He is.

The Lord used a parable to give us an idea of the time of His coming:

"Now learn a parable of the fig tree; When her branch is yet tender, and putteth forth leaves, ye know that summer is near:

"So ye in like manner, when ye shall see these things come to pass, know that it is nigh, even at the doors" (Mark 13:28–29).

The Lord has also given us some signs to let us know when His coming is near. After revealing the signs, He cautioned:

"Watch therefore: for ye know not what hour your Lord doth come. …

"… Be ye also ready: for in such an hour as ye think not the Son of man cometh" (Matthew 24:42, 44).

For more information about how we will know when Jesus's Second Coming is near, see chapter 43 in this book.

church will never be large, but it will be protected by him and his Saints will receive great spiritual power from him to handle the trials and catastrophes of the last days.

How Can We Be Ready When the Savior Comes?

The best way we can prepare for the Savior's coming is to accept the teachings of the gospel and make them part of our lives. We should live each day the best we can, just as Jesus taught when He was on the earth. We can look to the prophet for guidance and follow his counsel. We can live worthy to have the Holy Ghost guide us. Then we will look forward to the Savior's coming with happiness and not with fear. The Lord said: "Fear not, little flock, the kingdom is yours until I come. Behold, I come quickly. Even so. Amen" (D&C 35:27).

• Why should we be concerned about our preparedness rather than the exact timing of the Second Coming?

Additional Scriptures
• John 14:2–3; Matthew 26:64 (Jesus to prepare a place and come again)
• Malachi 3:2–3; 4:1; D&C 64:23–24 (earth to be burned)
• D&C 133:41–51 (wicked to be destroyed)
• Matthew 13:40–43 (the Judgment predicted)
• 1 Corinthians 15:40–42; D&C 76; 88:17–35 (kingdoms of glory)
• D&C 43:29–30; 29:11 (the Savior's coming will usher in the Millennium)
• Articles of Faith 1:10 (Jesus to reign)
• Alma 11:43–44; 40:23 (the Resurrection explained)
• D&C 88:96–98 (the dead to rise)
• Zechariah 14:9; Revelation 11:15; 1 Nephi 22:24–26 (Jesus to reign as King)

The important lesson is not to know when he is coming. The important lesson is to be ready whenever that is. For it doesn't really matter when he comes. All that matters is that our souls are in a condition to be caught up to meet him when he comes. The last place we want to be found is still standing on the ground when those who are worthy of him are caught up to meet him. For those who are still standing on the ground will be burned with fire and sent to hell for a thousand years.

Chapter 45

The Millennium
Gospel Principles, (2011), 263–67

People on the Earth during the Millennium
• Who will be on the earth during the Millennium?

A thousand years of peace, love, and joy will begin on the earth at the Second Coming of Jesus Christ. This thousand-year period is called the Millennium. The scriptures and the prophets help us understand what it will be like to live on the earth during the Millennium.

For teachers: The subject of the Millennium sometimes leads people to speculate about ideas that are not found in the scriptures or the teachings of latter-day prophets. As you guide this lesson, be careful to avoid such speculation.

Because of the destruction of the wicked at the Savior's Second Coming, only righteous people will live on the earth at the beginning of the Millennium. They will be those who have lived virtuous and honest lives. These people will inherit either the terrestrial or celestial kingdom.

Those who are terrestrial in nature will be the good people of the earth, from both inside and outside the church. They won't all be Christians. It will take some longer to accept Christ than others, but eventually they will all accept Him.

During the Millennium, mortals will still live on earth, and they will continue to have children as we do now (see D&C 45:58). Joseph Smith said that immortal beings will frequently visit the earth. These resurrected beings will help with the government and other work. (See Teachings of the Prophet Joseph Smith, sel. Joseph Fielding Smith [1976], 268.)

The earth will receive her paradisiacal glory and all mortals living on earth will be terrestrial in nature. Imagine what a difference it will be to have the earth completely healed of all the damage done to her by the wickedness of mankind. People will no longer die of sickness, disease, or old age.

People will still have their agency, and for a time many will be free to continue with their religions and ideas. Eventually everyone will confess that Jesus Christ is the Savior.

Remember, the intolerance of the past and present will not exist in that future society. We will see each other for the family of God that we are.

During the Millennium, Jesus will "reign personally upon the earth" (Articles of Faith 1:10). Joseph Smith explained that Jesus will "reign over the Saints and come down and instruct" (Teachings of Presidents of the Church: Joseph Smith [2007], 258).

He won't necessarily live on earth, but will spend a lot of time here.

The Work of the Church during the Millennium
• What are the two great works that will be done during the Millennium?

There will be two great works for members of the Church during the Millennium: temple work and missionary work. Temple work involves the ordinances that are necessary for exaltation. These include baptism, the laying on of hands for the gift of the Holy Ghost, and the temple

The Father's work and glory is to bring to pass our eternal life. That means all His children need to be offered the covenants of the celestial kingdom. Whether they accept it or not is up to each person, but the offer has been promised to us all. This is why missionary work, the ordinances—the endowment, temple marriage, and the sealing together of family units.

Many people have died without receiving these ordinances. People on the earth must perform these ordinances for them. This work is now being done in the temples of the Lord. There is too much work to finish before the Millennium begins, so it will be completed during that time. Resurrected beings will help us correct the mistakes we have made in doing research concerning our dead ancestors. They will also help us find the information we need to complete our records. (See Joseph Fielding Smith, Doctrines of Salvation, comp. Bruce R. McConkie, 3 vols. [1954–56], 2:167, 251–52.)

The other great work during the Millennium will be missionary work. The gospel will be taught with great power to all people. Eventually there will be no need to teach others the first principles of the gospel because "they shall all know me, from the least of them unto the greatest of them, saith the Lord" (Jeremiah 31:34).

• How can we prepare now for work in the Millennium?

proclaiming of the gospel, will be the main focus during this thousand year period.

For those who have already experienced mortality, they need someone currently in mortality to do their work for them in the temples. This is why temples will be built all over the planet, and the main work of humanity will be to go to the temples and complete the work for the rest of the children of God so they can either accept or reject the offer of eternal life our Father promised to all of his children.

It will take working closely with heavenly beings to correct the mistakes and receive the records of those who need their work done. There are so many who have lived whose records no longer exist on earth, but the Lord has been keeping track in heaven.

We all need to set our sites on the temple. We need to go then attend regularly so doing temple work becomes second nature to us. We also need to learn to overcome our fear of opening our mouths and saying something about our religion. But in the meantime we can live it well and not be ashamed to admit we belong to the Lord's Church.

Conditions during the Millennium

• In what ways will life during the Millennium be different from life on the earth now?

The Prophet Joseph Smith taught that during the Millennium, "the earth will be renewed and receive its paradisiacal glory" (Articles of Faith 1:10).

Read the accounts of the way the garden of Eden was. That is how the whole earth will be. It will be fruitful and at peace.

Satan Bound

During the Millennium, Satan will be bound. This means he will not have power to tempt those who are living at that time (see D&C 101:28). The "children shall grow up without sin unto salvation" (D&C 45:58). "Because of the righteousness of [the Lord's] people, Satan has no power; wherefore, he cannot be loosed for the space of many years; for he hath no power over the hearts of the people, for they dwell in righteousness, and the Holy One of Israel reigneth" (1 Nephi 22:26).

Satan could be bound now if we would refuse to listen to him. Wickedness is only on the earth because there are those who seek it out and don't turn away from it when it is presented to them. During the millennium we will have completely "sin-free" cities and countries. I'm not saying no one will have need to repent of anything. I'm saying that we won't have murder, crime, cheaters, thieves, etc. The world will be a very safe place to live, and as more and more are filled with the Spirit, the love of God will fill the hearts of all mankind.

Peace on the Earth

Many professions that are needed today will no longer be needed. There will be no need of funeral homes or ammunition factories, for example.

During the Millennium, there will be no war. People will live in peace and harmony together. Things that have been used for war will be turned to useful purposes. "They shall beat their swords into plowshares, and their spears into pruninghooks: nation shall not lift up sword against nation, neither shall they learn war any more" (Isaiah 2:4; see also Isaiah 11:6–7; D&C 101:26).

Righteous Government

President John Taylor taught: "The Lord will be king over all the earth, and all mankind literally under his sovereignty, and every nation under the heavens will have to acknowledge his authority, and bow to his scepter. Those who serve him in righteousness will have communications with God, and with Jesus; will have the ministering of angels, and will know the past, the present, and the future; and other people, who may not yield full obedience to his laws, nor be fully instructed in his covenants, will, nevertheless, have to yield full obedience to his government. For it will be the reign of God upon the earth, and he will enforce his laws, and command that obedience from the nations of the world which is legitimately his right" (Teachings of Presidents of the Church: John Taylor [2001], 225).

Christ's title of King of kings and Lord of lords will be realized during the millennium. Every country will live by the laws He sets. All governments will answer to Him.

No Death

During the Millennium, there will be no death as we know it. When people have lived to an old age, they will not die and be buried. Instead, they will be changed from their mortal condition to an immortal condition in "the twinkling of an eye." (See D&C 63:51; 101:29–31.)

Think how wonderful it will be to be healthy right up to the hour you are changed from mortality to immortality in an instance. There will be no more sorrow of the loss of loved ones at death, for they will still stand before us, but as immortal souls. All the things in this life that give us grief and sorrow will cease to exist.

All Things Revealed

Some truths have not been revealed to us. All things will be revealed during the Millennium. The Lord said He will "reveal all things—things which have passed, and hidden things which no man knew, things of the earth, by which it was made, and the purpose and the end thereof—things most precious, things that are above, and things that are beneath, things that are in the earth, and upon the earth, and in heaven" (D&C 101:32–34).

We will finally know how the earth was made, and will learn the future God intends for this earth. We will learn all about how it works, its systems and operation. We will learn more about the sciences than anyone can currently imagine.

Other Millennial Activities

In many ways, life will be much as it is now, except that everything will be done in righteousness. People will eat and drink and will wear clothing. (See Teachings of Presidents of the Church: Brigham Young [1997], 333.) People will continue to plant and harvest crops and build houses (see Isaiah 65:21).

Some churches paint a picture of the millennium in such a way that everyone thinks all there is to do is picnic all day, every day. There will still be farms to run, businesses to operate, clothing to make, things to sell to those who need them, communications to be had, and governments to be run. The difference is that those things that cause us stress and distress now will be gone. Everyone will be honest in their dealings with each other.

• What are your thoughts and feelings about the conditions that will exist during the Millennium?

One Final Struggle after the Millennium
• What will be the final destiny of the earth?

At the end of the 1,000 years, Satan will be set free for a short time. Some people will turn away from Heavenly Father. Satan will gather his armies, and Michael (Adam) will gather the hosts of heaven. In this great struggle, Satan and his followers will be cast out forever. The earth will be changed into a celestial kingdom. (See D&C 29:22–29; 88:17–20, 110–15.)

When we are told that Satan will be unbound that means that there will be those who will once again listen to his lies and temptations. Those who turn away from God will do so with their eyes wide open in rebellion. They will know what they are doing, just as Satan and his followers did in the premortal life when they rebelled against God.

He will gather as many as he can and wage one last war on God's family. It is only after this last struggle that Satan will finally be sent to outer darkness for eternity, along with all those who followed him.

Additional Scriptures
• Zechariah 14:4–9; 1 Nephi 22:24–25 (Jesus to reign on earth)
• Daniel 7:27 (Saints to be given the kingdom)
• D&C 88:87–110 (conditions during the Millennium)
• Revelation 20:1–3; 1 Nephi 22:26 (Satan to be bound)
• D&C 101:22–31 (enmity to cease; no death; Satan to have no power to tempt)
• Isaiah 11:1–9 (wolf and lamb to dwell together)
• D&C 43:31; Revelation 20:7–10 (Satan loosed for a little season)

Chapter 46

The Final Judgment
Gospel Principles, (2011), 268–74

Judgments of God
• What are some different judgments that come before the Final Judgment? How do all these judgments relate to one another?

For teachers: You do not need to teach everything in each chapter. As you prayerfully prepare to teach, seek the Spirit's guidance to know which portions of the chapter you should cover.

We are often told in the scriptures that the day will come when we will stand before God and be judged. We need to understand how judgment takes place so we can be better prepared for this important event.

The scriptures teach that all of us will be judged according to our works: "And I saw the dead, small and great, stand before God; and the books were opened: and another book was opened, which is the book of life: and the dead were judged out of those things which were written in the books, according to their works" (Revelation 20:12; see also D&C 76:111; 1 Nephi 15:32; Abraham 3:25–28). We will also be judged "according to the desire of [our] hearts" (D&C 137:9; see also Alma 41:3).

Here on earth we are often judged as to our worthiness to receive opportunities within the kingdom of God. When we are baptized we are judged worthy to receive this ordinance. When we are called to serve in the Church or interviewed for a priesthood advancement or a temple recommend, we are judged.

Alma taught that when we die our spirits are assigned to a state of happiness or of misery (see Alma 40:11–15). This is a judgment.

Our Words, Works, and Thoughts Are Used to Judge Us
• Imagine being judged for all your thoughts, words, and actions.

The prophet Alma testified, "Our words will condemn us, yea, all our works will condemn us; … and our thoughts will also condemn us" (Alma 12:14).

Sometimes the desires of our hearts are referred to as the "thoughts and intents" of our hearts. They both refer to what we think and how we feel about things.

The point of this section is that there are mini judgments that take place a various times in our life that let us know if we are on the right track. Each time we go to tithing settlement we declare our worthiness with regards to that law. Each time we go in for a temple recommend we declare our worthiness to enter the Lord's house.

When we first make a covenant with the Lord we are judged worthy to make that covenant before we do it. In the case of baptism, each week we renew that covenant and declare to the Lord that we are worthy. If we eat and drink unworthily the Lord says we are eating and drinking damnation to our souls. This should cause us to think carefully about our individual worthiness to partake of the sacrament each week.

What we think on a regular basis shows where our heart is at. If we entertain evil thoughts and don't seek out clean and uplifting thoughts, it doesn't matter how we behave on the outside because our hearts are evil. So yes, it does matter what we think.

The Lord said: "Every idle word that men shall speak, they shall give account thereof in the day of judgment. For by thy words thou shalt be justified, and by thy words thou shalt be condemned" (Matthew 12:36–37).

Faith in Jesus Christ helps us be prepared for the Final Judgment. Through faithful discipleship to Him and repentance of all our sins, we can be forgiven for our sins and become pure and holy so that we can dwell in the presence of God. As we repent of our sins, giving up every impure thought and act, the Holy Ghost will change our hearts so we no longer have even the desire to sin (see Mosiah 5:2). Then when we are judged, we will be found ready to enter into God's presence.

• Think about what you can do to improve your thoughts, words, and actions.

We Will Be Judged by Records
• From what records will we be judged? Who will judge us?

The Prophet Joseph Smith said that the dead will be judged out of records kept on earth. We will also be judged out of the "book of life," which is kept in heaven (see D&C 128:6–8).

"Every one of you … must stand before 'the judgment-seat of the Holy One of Israel … and then must … be judged according to the holy judgment of God.' (II Nephi 9:15.) And according to the vision of John, 'The books were opened: and another book was opened, which is the book of life: and the dead were judged out of those things which were written in the books, according to their works.' (Rev. 20:12.) The 'books' spoken of refer to the 'records [of your works] which are kept on the earth. … The book of life is the record which is kept in heaven.' (Doc. and Cov. 128:7.)" (Teachings of Presidents of the Church: Harold B. Lee [2000], 226–27).

There is another record that will be used to judge us. The Apostle Paul taught that we ourselves are a record of our life (see Romans 2:15). Stored in our body and mind is a complete history of everything we have done. President John Taylor taught this truth: "[The individual] tells the story himself, and bears witness against himself. … That record that is written by the man himself in the tablets of his own mind, that record that cannot lie will in that day be unfolded before God and angels, and those who shall sit as judges" (Deseret News, Mar. 8, 1865, 179).

The important thing to remember about our thoughts is that we cannot control which thoughts enter our minds, but we have complete control over which thoughts stay in our minds. We will be judged on the thoughts we keep and entertain, not what comes in uninvited.

Notice in this paragraph that it doesn't tell us we need to change our hearts and our desires before dinner time tonight. This is something we need to be working on all the time. It is a gradual conversion and the progress takes years. But it is years of consistent work and effort on our part. That means it has to be something we are aware of and willing to work for. As long as we are willing to put in the work the Holy Ghost will do the rest. Only God can change our hearts, but we have to seek for that blessing.

We will be judged on the opportunities we have been given in this life. Those who have had more opportunities or greater capacities will have more to answer for than those who have less. Remember that where there is no law there is no punishment. If we never had the opportunity to do something in life then we will not be held accountable for not having done something about it. It is only those opportunities we were given we will be held accountable for.

As the prophets have taught, we all stand on neutral ground until we accept or reject the gospel of Christ, once we understand what we are looking at. From then on we can never return to neutral ground.

A counselor once told me that it doesn't matter what we think happened to us in the past, because the body never forgets. That is why little children traumatized by certain events will act out later in life, long after the actual events are behind them. They body is still trying to deal with the events. When we get to the judgment bar of God, every thought we entertained and kept in our head, every action we ever took, every intent we ever had, all of it will be there to be played back for all to see. For those things we have repented of, those things will not condemn us. We will only be condemned for the things we did not repent of.

The Apostle John taught that "the Father judgeth no man, but hath committed all judgment unto the Son" (John 5:22). The Son, in turn, will call upon others to assist in the Judgment. The Twelve who were with Him in His ministry will judge the twelve tribes of Israel (see Matthew 19:28; Luke 22:30). The twelve Nephite disciples will judge the Nephite and Lamanite people (see 1 Nephi 12:9–10; Mormon 3:18–19).

Inheriting a Place in a Kingdom of Glory
• How will our faithfulness during our life on earth influence our life in the eternities?

At the Final Judgment we will inherit a place in the kingdom for which we are prepared. The scriptures teach of three kingdoms of glory—the celestial kingdom, the terrestrial kingdom, and the telestial kingdom (see D&C 88:20–32).

In Doctrine and Covenants 76, the Lord described the ways we can choose to live our mortal lives. He explained that our choices will determine which kingdom we are prepared for. We learn from this revelation that even members of the Church will inherit different kingdoms because they will not be equally faithful and valiant in their obedience to Christ.

The following are the kinds of lives we can choose to live and the kingdoms our choices will obtain for us.

Celestial

"They are they who received the testimony of Jesus, and believed on his name and were baptized, … that by keeping the commandments they might be washed and cleansed from all their sins, and receive the Holy Spirit." These are they who overcome the world by their faith. They are just and true so that the Holy Ghost can seal their blessings upon them. (See D&C 76:51–53.) Those who inherit the highest degree of the celestial kingdom, who become gods, must also have been married for eternity in the temple (see D&C 131:1–4). All who inherit the celestial kingdom will live with Heavenly Father and Jesus Christ forever (see D&C 76:62).

Through the work we do in temples, all people who have lived on the earth can have an equal opportunity to receive the fulness of the gospel and the ordinances of salvation so they can inherit a place in the highest degree of celestial glory.

Terrestrial

These are they who rejected the gospel on earth but afterward received it in the spirit world. These are the honorable people on the earth who were blinded to the gospel of Jesus Christ by the craftiness of men. These are

These are they who made covenants with God and kept them and were faithful to them up to the very end of their lives. We say they "endured" to the end. These are the people who want nothing more than to be found worthy to live with our Father in Heaven and Christ for eternity. These are the people who work hard to keep their family faithful, who fulfill their callings at church, who share the gospel with others, who have learned the Christlike virtues of love, patience, tolerance, forgiveness, etc. These are the people who are led by the Spirit daily, who pray and study their scriptures and seek to be like Christ. Notice I did not say, "who are just like Christ," but are trying to be like Christ.

These people accept the gospel in mortality when it is presented to them. If they do not have it presented to them until the spirit world, then they accept it and live the gospel to the best of their ability there.

There is a reason it makes us sad when someone rejects the gospel in mortality. Even if they accept it later they will not be able to go to the celestial kingdom. The terrestrial kingdom will be the home of all good people who either were not valiant to the covenants they made with the Lord or who never made covenants, but were also they who received the gospel and a testimony of Jesus but then were not valiant. They will be visited by Jesus Christ but not by our Heavenly Father. (See D&C 76:73–79.)

Telestial

These people did not receive the gospel or the testimony of Jesus either on earth or in the spirit world. They will suffer for their own sins in hell until after the Millennium, when they will be resurrected. "These are they who are liars, and sorcerers, and adulterers, and whoremongers, and whosoever loves and makes a lie." These people are as numerous as the stars in heaven and the sand on the seashore. They will be visited by the Holy Ghost but not by the Father or the Son. (See D&C 76:81–88, 103–6, 109.)

Outer Darkness

These are they who had testimonies of Jesus through the Holy Ghost and knew the power of the Lord but allowed Satan to overcome them. They denied the truth and defied the power of the Lord. There is no forgiveness for them, for they denied the Holy Spirit after having received it. They will not have a kingdom of glory. They will live in eternal darkness, torment, and misery with Satan and his angels forever. (See D&C 76:28–35, 44–48.)

• According to Doctrine and Covenants 76:50–53, 62–70, what are the characteristics of a person who overcomes the world by faith and is valiant in the testimony of Jesus?

We Should Prepare Now for Judgment
• What must we do to be ready for the Final Judgment?

In reality, every day is a day of judgment. We speak, think, and act according to celestial, terrestrial, or telestial law. Our faith in Jesus Christ, as shown by our daily actions, determines which kingdom we will inherit.

We have the restored gospel of Jesus Christ in its fulness. The gospel is the law of the celestial kingdom. All the priesthood ordinances necessary for our progression have been revealed. We have entered the waters of baptism and have made a covenant to live Christlike lives. If we are faithful and keep the covenants we have made, the Lord has told us what our judgment will be. He will say unto us, "Come, ye blessed of my Father, inherit the kingdom prepared for you from the foundation of the world" (Matthew 25:34).

Additional Scriptures
• Romans 2:6–9; Revelation 20:12–13 (the Judgment)

honorable and kind and lived the law they were raised with. This includes people of all nationalities and religions.

These are the only ones who go through hell. Once they are released from hell they will go to either the telestial kingdom or to outer darkness. These can be thought of as the worst of the worst. Even the worst of the worst in mortality will receive a kingdom of glory, but in comparison with the other two higher kingdoms it isn't much. But it is still much better than what we have on earth. Premeditated murder is a one way ticket to this kingdom.

Besides Satan and his original followers, only those who knew Christ to be the Christ through the witness of the Holy Ghost then turned on Him, denied Him, and would seek to kill him themselves if they could, fall in this category. For that kind of betrayal there is no forgiveness.

Why is it important to think about the judgment? It is important because we don't know when our time in mortality will end. This life is the time set for us by God to prove what we are made of. This is the place we were sent to demonstrate the desires of our heart. This is the great learning experience that will prove to us where we belong for the rest of eternity. We learn faith here, and get to see what it is like to have a family. This is where we learn to control a mortal body like what our heavenly parents have. If we squander our time here and don't take this seriously, we will have all of eternity to think about our mistake, as we sit in a lesser kingdom of glory.

• Alma 11:41, 45; Mormon 7:6; 9:13–14 (we are judged in a resurrected state)
• 2 Nephi 29:11; 3 Nephi 27:23–26 (books used in the Judgment)
• Alma 41:2–7 (our judgment is determined by our works, the desires of our hearts, repentance, enduring to the end)
• Mormon 3:22 (repent and prepare to stand before the judgment seat)
• Luke 12:47–48; D&C 82:3 (of whom much is given, much is required)
• D&C 88:16–33 (we each receive that for which we are worthy)

Chapter 47

Exaltation

Gospel Principles, (2011), 275–80

The Plan for Our Progression

When we lived with our Heavenly Father, He explained a plan for our progression. We could become like Him, an exalted being. The plan required that we be separated from Him and come to earth. This separation was necessary to prove whether we would obey our Father's commandments even though we were no longer in His presence. The plan provided that when earth life ended, we would be judged and rewarded according to the degree of our faith and obedience.

From the scriptures we learn that there are three kingdoms of glory in heaven. The Apostle Paul mentioned that he knew a man who was "caught up to the third heaven" (2 Corinthians 12:2). Paul named two of the kingdoms in heaven: the celestial and the terrestrial (see 1 Corinthians 15:40–42). The celestial is the highest, and the terrestrial is second. Through latter-day revelation we learn that the third kingdom is the telestial kingdom (see D&C 76:81). We also learn that there are three heavens or degrees within the celestial kingdom (see D&C 131:1).

Exaltation

• What is exaltation?
Exaltation is eternal life, the kind of life God lives. He lives in great glory. He is perfect. He possesses all knowledge and all wisdom. He is the Father of spirit children. He is a creator. We can become like our Heavenly Father. This is exaltation.

If we prove faithful to the Lord, we will live in the highest degree of the celestial kingdom of heaven. We will become exalted, to live with our Heavenly Father in eternal families. Exaltation is the greatest gift that Heavenly Father can give His children (see D&C 14:7).

Blessings of Exaltation

• What are some blessings that will be given to those who are exalted?

Our Heavenly Father is perfect, and He glories in the fact that it is possible for His children to become like Him. His work and glory is "to bring to pass the immortality and eternal life of man" (Moses 1:39).

Our Father's purpose is to bring to pass our immortality and eternal life. What we call the gospel of Christ is actually the plan our Father in Heaven presented to us in heaven before we came to earth. He selected Jesus to be the Savior, the one who would provide us with immortality, and who would pay for our sins committed while here if we would repent and follow the commandments He would give us.

Every step we take along the path back to our heavenly home was planned out and planned for by God before it was ever shown to us. Our Father in Heaven thought of every detail and had an answer for every question. In Job it says we were so happy we all shouted for joy.

We needed to be separated from our parents just like a teenager needs to leave home and learn and grow on their own. We had experiences we needed to have that could not happen at home. It was time for us all to leave and get on with our lives.

Those who were obedient to God and accepted the plan he offered us were guaranteed a kingdom of glory after mortality. Which kingdom we receive will depend on our obedience and behavior while here and in the spirit world after mortality. The kingdom that is most desirable is the celestial kingdom, since that is where God, Christ, and the Holy Ghost live. They are in the highest level of the celestial kingdom.

Eternal life is not the same as life eternal. Life eternal just means to live forever. Eternal is one of the names of God, so eternal life becomes the same as saying "God's life." Eternal life includes all the blessings, joys, responsibilities, and happiness that God enjoys. Those of us who live worthy of this blessing will learn and grow to become like our heavenly parents.

Since exaltation or eternal life includes all that God is and has, there isn't anything better He could give us.

Those who receive exaltation in the celestial kingdom through faith in Jesus Christ will receive special blessings. The Lord has promised, "All things are theirs" (D&C 76:59). These are some of the blessings given to exalted people:

1. They will live eternally in the presence of Heavenly Father and Jesus Christ (see D&C 76:62).
2. They will become gods (see D&C 132:20–23).
3. They will be united eternally with their righteous family members and will be able to have eternal increase.
4. They will receive a fulness of joy.
5. They will have everything that our Heavenly Father and Jesus Christ have—all power, glory, dominion, and knowledge (see D&C 132:19–20). President Joseph Fielding Smith wrote: "The Father has promised through the Son that all that he has shall be given to those who are obedient to His commandments. They shall increase in knowledge, wisdom, and power, going from grace to grace, until the fulness of the perfect day shall burst upon them" (Doctrines of Salvation, comp. Bruce R. McConkie, 3 vols. [1954–56], 2:36; italics in original).

Only gods can have children and populate and create planets. This privilege is reserved for righteous couples who have been sealed in the temple as husband and wife.

Requirements for Exaltation

The time to fulfill the requirements for exaltation is now (see Alma 34:32–34). President Joseph Fielding Smith said, "In order to obtain the exaltation we must accept the gospel and all its covenants; and take upon us the obligations which the Lord has offered; and walk in the light and the understanding of the truth; and 'live by every word that proceedeth forth from the mouth of God'" (Doctrines of Salvation, 2:43).

To be exalted, we first must place our faith in Jesus Christ and then endure in that faith to the end of our lives. Our faith in Him must be such that we repent of our sins and obey His commandments.

Covenants are only required of those who want to go back to live with God. Either of the other two kingdoms of glory require no covenants. Our obedience in the premortal spirit world guaranteed one of those kingdoms. The proof that we really do want to become like God is in our willingness to sacrifice anything to be obedient to the commandments we have received from Christ.

He commands us all to receive certain ordinances:

1. We must be baptized.
2. We must receive the laying on of hands to be confirmed a member of the Church of Jesus Christ and to receive the gift of the Holy Ghost.
3. Brethren must receive the Melchizedek Priesthood and magnify their callings in the priesthood.
4. We must receive the temple endowment.
5. We must be married for eternity, either in this life or in the next.

The Holy Ghost is made available to us through the priesthood we have been blessed to hold. The Holy Ghost is the one who teaches us and guides us and takes us home to our Father. The gift of the Holy Ghost is only available through the confirmation of our membership in God's kingdom through God's priesthood power.

In addition to receiving the required ordinances, the Lord commands all of us to:

1. Love God and our neighbors.
2. Keep the commandments.
3. Repent of our wrongdoings.

The commandments we have received are not about what to do or not to do. The purpose of the commandments is to change us into the kind of people who will feel comfortable living in the presence of God all the time. As we learn to exercise faith in Christ, repent of our sins,

4. Search out our kindred dead and receive the saving ordinances of the gospel for them.

5. Attend our Church meetings as regularly as possible so we can renew our baptismal covenants by partaking of the sacrament.

6. Love our family members and strengthen them in the ways of the Lord.

7. Have family and individual prayers every day.

8. Teach the gospel to others by word and example.

9. Study the scriptures.

10. Listen to and obey the inspired words of the prophets of the Lord.

Finally, each of us needs to receive the Holy Ghost and learn to follow His direction in our individual lives.

• How do ordinances and covenants prepare us for exaltation?

• How does faith in Jesus Christ help us obey the commandments?

• Why must we learn to follow the direction of the Holy Ghost to become exalted?

humbly approach the Lord in prayer, forgive others, and learn to love others and Christ loves us, we are changed by the Holy Ghost. We lose our desire for sinning, and we gain a stronger desire to be with God.

Everything having to do with our Father in Heaven is about us becoming, not about us doing.

The privilege of having the gift of the Holy Ghost is that we have one of the three members of the Godhead by our side all the time, teaching us, bearing witness of truth, whispering peace to our souls, and giving us strength to do what we need to do to get back home. Who else has such a blessing?

After We Have Been Faithful and Endured to the End

• What happens when we have endured to the end in faithful discipleship to Christ?

The Lord has said, "If you keep my commandments and endure to the end you shall have eternal life, which gift is the greatest of all the gifts of God" (D&C 14:7). President Joseph Fielding Smith said, "If we will continue in God; that is, keep his commandments, worship him and live his truth; then the time will come when we shall be bathed in the fulness of truth, which shall grow brighter and brighter until the perfect day" (Doctrines of Salvation, 2:36).

Truth doesn't consist of just facts. Truth is the realization of how things really are, not just how they appear to be. Someone can offer you a baggy with some white powder in it and tell you that it will help you feel good. The truth will tell you that this person is trying to get you addicted to a drug that might be very dangerous for you.

Many in the world claim they are telling us the truth, but it is the scriptures, the prophets, and the Holy Ghost who can reveal the actual truth to our souls. Real truth takes a realization of how a fact affects us and what we need to do about it. It is far more than just a fact. If the world tells me something is a fact, and the prophet of God tells me something else is the fact I should be listening to, I will take the prophet of God, for he is led by the Savior Himself.

When the scriptures say the truth will grow brighter and brighter until the perfect day, it is saying that we will have realization upon realization until we can comprehend the things of God as God understands them.

The Prophet Joseph Smith taught: "When you climb up a ladder, you must begin at the bottom, and ascend step by step, until you arrive at the top; and so it is with the principles of the gospel—you must begin with the first, and go on until you learn all the principles of exaltation. But it will be a great while after you have passed through the veil [died] before you will have learned them. It is not all to be comprehended in this world; it will be a great work to learn our salvation and exaltation even beyond the grave" (Teachings of Presidents of the Church: Joseph Smith [2007], 268).

Joseph Smith taught: "It is the first principle of the Gospel to know for a certainty the Character of God. ... He was once a man like us; ... God himself, the Father of us all, dwelt on an earth, the same as Jesus Christ himself did" (Teachings of the Prophet Joseph Smith, sel. Joseph Fielding Smith [1976], 345–46).

Our Heavenly Father knows our trials, our weaknesses, and our sins. He has compassion and mercy on us. He wants us to succeed even as He did.

Imagine what joy each of us will have when we return to our Heavenly Father if we can say: "Father, I lived according to Thy will. I have been faithful and have kept Thy commandments. I am happy to be home again." Then we will hear Him say, "Well done ... ; thou hast been faithful over a few things, I will make thee ruler over many things: enter thou into the joy of thy lord" (Matthew 25:23).

• Review Matthew 25:23. Think about how you would feel if you heard the Lord say these words to you.

For teachers: When you give class members or family members time to ponder gospel truths, reflect on their lives, or think about their love for Heavenly Father and Jesus Christ, you give them an opportunity to be taught by the Holy Ghost.

Additional Scriptures
• D&C 132:3–4, 16–26, 37 (pertaining to exaltation)
• D&C 131:1–4 (eternal marriage is key to exaltation)
• D&C 76:59–70 (blessings of celestial glory explained)
• D&C 84:20–21 (the power of godliness is manifest through priesthood ordinances)

Exaltation is done with a physical body and a spirit combined. This is a new experience for all of us, as we have never had a physical body before. There are no shortcuts as we learn how to feel and behave, and feel and sense spiritual things while in our bodies. We must learn to use our body for good. It will take a long time for us to learn and grow into our godhood. It cannot happen in this short life.

In order for us to have the faith we need to become like our Father in Heaven we need to have a correct knowledge of His character and nature. This requires the priesthood, the Holy Ghost, and lots of time and practice. But this is how our Father in Heaven learned to be what he is today. He had to come to an earth and learn his lessons as well. From generation to generation the process is the same.

ABOUT THE AUTHOR

Kelly Merrill lives in Rexburg, Idaho. He writes for www.mormonbasics.com and sells doctrinal commentaries and LDS merchandise on the website. Kelly has been writing articles since July, 2013. He has written for LDSLiving.com, LDSBlogs.com, and several other independently-owned web sites. As of this publication he has written almost 700 gospel-centered articles, and published five other books: Premortal Promises, Contributions to the Kingdom, Gospel Studies - Old Testament, and Doctrinal Insights Vol. 1 and Vol. 2.

Made in the USA
Columbia, SC
31 July 2024

39715267R00126